Trollope and Victorian Moral Philosophy

Trollope & Victorian Moral Philosophy

Jane Nardin

OHIO UNIVERSITY PRESS
ATHENS

Ohio University Press, Athens, Ohio 45701

Printed in the United States of America

Ohio University Press books
are printed on acid-free paper

01 00 99 98 97 96 5 4 3 2 1

Library of Congress Cataloging-in-Publication Data
Nardin, Jane, 1944–
Trollope and Victorian moral philosophy / Jane Nardin
p. cm.
Includes index.
ISBN 0-8214-1139-X (alk. paper)
1. Trollope, Anthony, 1815–1882—Ethics.
2. Didactic fiction, English—History and criticism.
3. Moral conditions in literature.
4. Ethics, Modern—19th century.
5. Ethics in literature.
I. Title.
PR5688.E8N37 1995
823′.8—dc20 95-33251
CIP

For Sophia and Rachel
ever the best of friends

Contents

Trollope and Victorian Moral Philosophy

I

Anthony Trollope and Common Morality

EIGHTEENTH- AND NINETEENTH-CENTURY British novelists rely upon the moral concepts they share with their readers to control the responses that their fictions evoke. When Bulstrode disobeys a doctor's orders in hopes that an expedient death will result, for example, readers of *Middlemarch* can be counted upon to reject the casuistry by which he justifies his conduct.[1] And because the tradition of moral judgment to which George Eliot and her fellow novelists appeal is relatively stable and extremely long lived, it still exercises a controlling influence upon twentieth-century readers.

But in spite of the fact that many English novelists appeal to shared moral values, they do not share *all* their moral commitments, either with their readers or with one another. Richardson's ideal gentleman, the courteous and restrained Sir Charles Grandison, is a different sort of good man from Fielding's warm-hearted and impulsive Tom Jones. Austen's Anne Elliot, critical and self-respecting, is a different sort of good woman from Dickens's indiscriminately affectionate, compulsively self-abnegating Esther Summerson.

Different writers emphasize different aspects of their moral heritage. Austen and Richardson value strict conformity to principle, Fielding and Dickens value benevolence. But it is still recognizably the same heritage: a degree of consensus underlies these moral visions. Sir Charles, Tom, Anne, and Esther are all honest, charitable, and careful to respect the autonomy of their fellows.

Because no morality is unambiguous or static, consensus on moral issues can never be complete. Understanding this, many British novelists of the eighteenth and nineteenth centuries problematize their own moral tradition even as they use it to define the dilemmas their characters face. And they find the tensions within that tradition a fruitful source of fictional conflict. Their characters interpret and apply moral concepts in different ways, arguing endlessly with one another about what decency demands, especially where the finer points of conduct are concerned.

These novelists know that moral distinctions are frequently forgotten and that moral commitments are often perverted by practical concerns. Their novels suggest that, when closely examined, England's morality reveals inconsistencies which should be eliminated. They also suggest that in periods of rapid social change, norms of conduct deriving from an earlier era may lose their authority. Novels like *Mansfield Park, Vanity Fair,* and *Our Mutual Friend* examine such periods of moral confusion and readjustment.

The difficulties of moral interpretation and the ambiguities of moral judgment are traditional concerns of the English novel. If morality helps to stabilize theme and character in novels of the eighteenth and nineteenth centuries, it also helps to generate the complexities that make these novels so interesting. Only with Hardy does a delicate balance shift decisively in the direction of a pervasive moral skepticism.

From his first novel to his last, Anthony Trollope both uses and problematizes England's moral tradition in the self-conscious manner that I have just described. But several of his novels reveal a different kind of interest in morality as well, an interest that can be called philosophical. Many of the novels Trollope wrote after 1870 do not merely examine what ordinary people think about moral conduct. They also consider what Victorian philosophers have to say about the nature of morality.

Trollope is by no means the only English novelist whose works reveal an interest in moral philosophy. During the eighteenth and nineteenth centuries, the ordinary man's morality came under the increasingly minute and hostile scrutiny of philosophers who hoped to explain, clarify, systematize, or improve it. As a result, philosophical challenges to commonly accepted moral notions took their place among the thorny moral issues to which novelists turned their attention. *Sense and Sensibility,* for example, considers some implications of the "moral sense" theory developed by the Earl of Shaftesbury and Francis Hutcheson. And it has been argued that *Tom Jones* offers a comprehensive critique of Bishop Joseph Butler's ethical theories, especially the view that virtuous conduct is grounded in rational self-interest.[2] But Trollope's interest in moral philosophy is more persistent and comprehensive than that of many other English novelists. During the last ten years of his career, his novels engage repeatedly with the ethical theories of contemporary philosophers.

As we shall see shortly, Victorian moral philosophers disagree about a variety of important issues and attack one another's views with great polemical zeal. But they tend to share the belief that the ordinary Englishman's morality is a jumble of more or less irrational prejudices inherited from the past, in need of drastic reexamination. And most of them believe that an improved morality founded upon basic truths about human nature can be devised. With impressive sophistication, Trollope's novels consider their criticisms and defend England's moral tradition against them.

The novels do this in two ways. First, the protagonists of such works as *Mr. Scarborough's Family* and *The Fixed Period* advocate one of the innovative moral notions under discussion in mid-Victorian England. As these characters put their theories into practice, the deficiencies of their ethical reasoning are revealed.[3] Second, several novels are premised upon far-fetched plot situations designed to test some aspect of contemporary ethical thought. *Lady Anna,* for example, invalidates the currently fashionable theory of psychological hedonism by presenting its heroine with an exceptionally pure temptation to pleasure, which she resists in the name of such traditional moral values as loyalty and integrity.

Trollope is sympathetic with the Victorian philosophers who yearn to confer on mankind the blessing of an improved morality by which to live. Their motives are undeniably generous. But he sees their enterprise as fundamentally misguided.

COMMON MORALITY

What, exactly, *is* the tradition of moral thought that Trollope defends against its philosophic critics? In order to answer this question, we need a description of both its history and its structure.

The History of Common Morality

According to the philosopher Alan Donagan, moralists in Western Europe and the societies which are its offshoots have not ordinarily used the term "morality" as a synonym for a "system of mores" (or social customs). Rather, Donagan suggests, the word has traditionally referred to a minimal set of standards "by which systems of mores, actual and possible, were to be judged and by which everybody ought to live, no matter what the mores of his neighbors might be."[4] Over the centuries, such a morality evolved in Europe. Its development was assisted by philosophers and theologians who explained and systematized it.

Disturbed by the offensive social customs practiced by their neighbors, the Athenian Stoics wondered if there was any principle, apart from custom itself, by which right and wrong conduct could be distinguished. They concluded that, although the diversity of mores will never be eliminated, human reason can indeed identify a few rules that are binding upon every individual, regardless of nationality, by virtue of his or her nature as a human being. According to Cicero, an essentially Stoic moralist whose ethical thought influenced Trollope deeply, right reason proves that some actions are forbidden by natural law, even if they are not prohibited by the laws or customs of a given community.

Like Stoicism, both Judaism and Christianity distinguish between minimal moral precepts that are binding upon all mankind and detailed customs that are specific to particular communities. According to Maimonides, one part of the Torah applies universally: the seven Noachite precepts, which forbid such actions as adultery and murder. The remainder of the Torah tells Jews—and Jews alone—exactly what they must do to live a *Jewish* life. Similarly, many Christian moralists have argued that the Ten Commandments (or *some* of them) apply to all mankind. Other parts of the Bible tell believers how to live a fully Christian life, but do not apply to mankind at large.

The Stoics thought that reason could establish the universal authority of natural law. And many Jewish and Christian thinkers made similar claims for the Noachite precepts and the Ten Commandments. But one need not accept these claims. For it can be argued that Stoics, Jews, and Christians mistook ethical principles that were generally accepted in the Mediterranean region for universal principles mandated by reason. If this is so, the morality that they jointly developed was really a regional (as opposed to a merely local) ethic, derived from reflection upon *existing* standards of conduct and the rationale that might be offered for them.

Stoics, Jews, and Christians share the view that man is naturally a rational creature, free to choose among alternative courses of action, who has only one life to live. These premises cannot be proven: they can only be assumed. If they *are* assumed, as we shall see shortly, Stoic-Hebrew-Christian morality can be derived from them by a process of loosely inferential reasoning. This is why Stoics, Jews, and Christians have so often claimed that their morality is given in "nature" and "reason." But much that seems undeniably reasonable to thinkers in this tradition would not seem reasonable to those who do not share their view of the human condition. The Hindu belief that people suffer in one incarnation as punishment for their transgressions in earlier incarnations, for example, implies a rejection of such centrally important Western moral concepts as innocence, guilt, and responsibility (Donagan, 33–35).

Whether they were simply systematizing their own moral tradition as it had already evolved, or whether, as many of them thought, they had discovered a demonstrably rational morality, Stoics, Jews, and Christians agreed that a minimal set of moral principles possessing a wider authority could be separated conceptually from the rich and detailed mores of particular communities. The minimal morality that these thinkers helped to define has for many centuries been the core morality of the West. And because this morality has remained relatively stable, it has provided the basis for much effective criticism of local mores.

Though this core morality is often called "Stoic-Hebrew-Christian morality," I am going to follow Donagan in calling it "common morality," because I want to suggest that, long before Trollope's time, it had become the common possession of ordinary people. As children, Victorian men and women learned about common morality in two ways: by means of theoretical instruction in its abstract principles ("Thou shalt not steal") and by means of the countless specific directives concerning conduct which interpret and apply those abstractions ("Give that back. It belongs to your sister."). Because common morality is both a practice and a set of abstractions that describe and guide that practice, one need not achieve complete mastery of its abstractions to fall under its sway. For ordinary Victorians, then, morality was not just a list of precepts defining right and wrong actions, but a deeply habitual disposition of conduct and judgment as well.

Unlike so many moralists in this tradition, Trollope never argues that either reason or revelation can establish the truth of common morality. Quite the contrary: he describes the core morality of his society as a historical product, which owes much to the teachings of Christ, but which is not completely dependent upon, or coextensive with, those teachings. In some of his writings, Trollope implies that common morality's stern prohibitions come from Judaism, while its stress on benevolence is a Christian addition. In an essay on "The Fourth Commandment," Trollope writes that "to be just was the duty of a Jew [in Biblical times],—and the duty of a Jew hardly went beyond justice."[5] Upon such negative commands as those forbidding one to "take from his neighbour unjustly [either] life, [or] property, [or] good name,"[6] Christ superimposed the positive injunction that every man should "love his neighbour as himself" and should demonstrate this love in acts of "charity" and "forbearance."[7] But when Trollope portrays a charitable and forbearing Jewish character, like the banker Ezekiel Breghert in *The Way We Live Now,* he implies that by the nineteenth century *all* the basic principles of this morality have become the common possession of Jews and Christians.[8]

At other times, however, Trollope suggests that in Stoic morality a tacit acknowledgment that one should love one's neighbor predates the explicit enunciation of this principle by Christ. He marvels, in his *Life of Cicero,* at the resemblance between Christian morality and the views expressed in Cicero's *De Officiis* and *De Legibus*: "[Cicero] could love another as himself . . . and he taught such love as a doctrine."[9] Trollope does indeed, as A.O.J. Cockshut claims, intuit in Cicero's writings the presence of "a moral code, which was adumbrated," to some degree at least, "before Christ enunciated it."[10]

This response to Stoic ethics was fairly common at the time. The Victorian philosopher William Whewell remarks, for example, that "it is impossible not to be struck with the higher . . . tone of the [Stoic] moral philosophers, of Seneca, for instance, who . . . Christianizes."[11] Though they did not always distinguish clearly among the contributions that Stoicism, Judaism, and Christianity had made to it, Victorians like Trollope and Whewell sensed how long-lived the core morality of their society was when they read the Bible and the Stoics.

The Structure of Common Morality

Philosophers interested in common morality generally agree that, at its most basic level, it is a morality of restraint. And these philosophers also agree that the precepts of common morality can be inferred from a single central principle, which states that the autonomy and rationality that human beings are assumed to possess must be respected. But philosophers formulate this principle in many different ways. The formulation Donagan prefers is this: "Act always so that you respect every human being, yourself or another, as being a rational creature." That is different (but not totally distinct) from the formulation of the principle as the Golden Rule. It is also different from the scriptural version, "Love thy Neighbor as Thyself"—the version that Trollope prefers and that he thought Cicero had discovered without Christ's aid (Donagan, 65). And it differs from one of the Kantian variants, which commands that human beings never be treated as only the means to an end.

This disagreement over the formulation of its central principle is by no means the only disagreement about what common morality means or entails. Because the inferential reasoning on which it is based is by no means strictly syllogistic, nearly *any* assertion that one might make about this morality can be—and has been—disputed by moralists working within its bounds. And Trollope is well aware of this fact. His novels make it clear that he views morality as a set of interrelated concepts, all of which are subject to debate.

This debate is highly structured, but necessarily endless. Neither the rules of morality, nor their relationship to each other, nor their applications, can ever be authoritatively established. Trollope would have agreed with the twentieth-century political philosopher Michael Walzer that morality "is something we have to argue about. The argument implies common possession, but common possession does not imply agreement."[12]

As Mr. Arabin puts it in *Barchester Towers,* the "antipathies and enmities" that characterize moral and theological disputes are unavoidable, but they are beneficent as well.[13] "What is all our work [as clergymen] but fighting, and hard fighting, if it be well done?" Arabin asks (*BT,* 400). What may appear to bystanders as pointless "wars about trifles" between participants in the same moral tradition must continue if that tradition is neither to ossify nor to disintegrate (*BT,* 401). Arabin denies that such disputes discredit the tradition within which they arise.

Although common morality has always been a subject of debate, so that any description of it must be disputable, I am now going to give such a description, emphasizing the precepts and principles of the tradition that I think are most important to Trollope.[14] I hope to prove that they *are* important to Trollope by illustrating them with examples from his writing.

Common morality provides three kinds of principles to guide moral judgment. The first set defines the moral status of actions, which may be permissible, forbidden, or obligatory. The second set tells us how to judge the responsibility of men and women for the acts they perform: they may be guilty or innocent. And finally, common morality suggests some notions about motivation that are helpful in evaluating moral character. (Common morality also includes a precept for ordering its commands, should they happen to conflict: the so-called "Pauline principle" that one may not do evil so that good shall come of it. A Latin variant of this precept, *ruat caelum, fiat justitia,* "let justice be done though the heavens fall," is frequently cited by Trollope's narrators and characters.)

Common morality defines many kinds of conduct as permissible, a smaller number as forbidden, and a few as obligatory. And because it permits more activities than it forbids or prescribes, common morality is frequently unable to identify the right course of action when a choice must be made. The guidance it offers is circumscribed in two important ways.

First, most situations in which a morally significant choice must be made offer more than one morally permissible option. Suppose that a woman, deeply in debt, considers several courses of action: murdering her creditor, stealing money to repay the debt, earning it, or asking a rich relative to give it to her. Common morality forbids the woman to choose murder or theft, but it permits her to select either of the remaining possibilities.

Second, many situations in which a choice must be made raise no issues with which common morality is concerned. Common morality cannot help settle such mundane problems as whether to take the bus or the train to work, whether to build a cottage or a bungalow, and so forth. And because common morality is a minimal morality, not a system of mores prescribing a way of life in all its richness and detail, it refuses to meddle with many of the choices that *are* ethically significant to a given community. A Catholic may be required to attend church, but the imperatives that require this are those of Catholicism, not of common morality.

In many situations, in fact, none of the available choices involves the violation of a moral prohibition. And in such situations *all* courses of action are permissible, as far as common morality is concerned. When Phineas Finn must decide, in *Phineas Redux,* if he should resign a secure job in order to run for Parliament, he concludes that morality leaves him free to please himself. "He had no one belonging to him. . . . He could ruin no one but himself. Where could there be a man in all the world who had a more perfect right to play a trick with his own prospects?" he asks himself.[15] He may take this dangerous "leap in the dark," if he wishes, since doing so will harm no one to whom he owes protection (*PR,* 11). But it would be equally allowable for him to retain his sinecure.

Because common morality is premised upon the notion that every human being is a rational agent, it must by its very nature leave great scope for freedom of choice. But common morality does place strict limits upon the ways in which people can pursue their individually chosen ends. Its precepts attempt to prohibit every action that violates its central principle of respect, though moralists often disagree about which actions fall under this ban.

On the ground that one must respect one's own humanity, as well as that of others, it has usually been considered impermissible to take one's own life (though the exceptions to this prohibition have been a matter for heated debate). When Phineas Finn, in the scene discussed above, considers suicide, "the bare bodkin," as a resource in case of failure, he quickly remembers that "against these modes of riddance there is a canon set" (*PR,* 9).

For the same reason, one may not knowingly impair one's health, though this prohibition has not generally been thought to exclude the choice of risky occupations and pastimes or the use of intoxicants. Certainly it does not exclude these things in the judgment of the accident-prone foxhunters and hard-drinking squires who populate the pages of Trollope's novels. In his *Travelling Sketches,* Trollope argues that those who wish to ban mountain climbing because it is dangerous should not be so "chary of human life."[16]

On the ground that people must respect the autonomy of their fellows, it has been judged impermissible for one person to use force against another. More specifically, no one may kill or injure another person. It is allowable, however, to use force in order to defend the innocent from the unjust force or violence of others. For this reason, the principles limiting the use of force are not generally thought to forbid warfare in a just cause or the apprehension and punishment of criminals.

But those whose rationality is clearly deficient, such as children and madmen, may be subject to force, even where defense of the innocent is not the issue. Do women fall into the category of the imperfectly rational, whose choices may justly be constrained by legal penalties or physical punishments? This is an important question in a number of Trollope's later novels, especially *He Knew He Was Right* and *Is He Popenjoy?*.

Stealing is also forbidden, whether it is done violently or furtively. This prohibition looms large in Trollope's fiction. Moral purists like Josiah Crawley in *The Last Chronicle of Barset* and Priscilla Stanbury in *He Knew He Was Right* would rather endure semi-starvation than touch anything that does not belong to them, while immoralists like Lizzie Eustace in *The Eustace Diamonds* blithely plead poverty as an excuse for their failure to distinguish strictly between "meum" and "tuum."

Another set of precepts defines what is due to the honor and reputation of others. It is not allowable to disparage others or to treat them impolitely. These two prohibitions are especially important to the "gentle, courteous" Mr. Harding, the moral center of the Barsetshire novels, who makes it a "practice [never] to say much evil of anyone" (*BT*, 264). Even valid information that is discreditable to others should be concealed, unless divulging it is necessary to prevent a wrong. Thus several characters in *Orley Farm* feel justified in hiding their knowledge that Lady Mason is guilty of forgery, *after* she has agreed to restore the property she acquired by her fraud.

There is no moral obligation to share one's thoughts with others, but if one does choose to do so, the respect one owes one's auditors as rational beings demands that an accurate account be given. Therefore, no one, in conditions of free communication between responsible persons, may express an opinion he does not hold—even for a good end. But what counts as free communication? And who counts as a responsible person? Most moralists agree that the truth need not be told to anyone who clearly intends to misuse it. Acting on this principle, Harry Annesley, in *Mr. Scarborough's Family*, lies about a midnight brawl in which he took part. He believes that if he reveals anything at all about the incident, his questioner will try to harm him by spreading a slanted version of his story—and under such circumstances, he feels no obligation to tell the truth.

Common morality forbids one to break a freely made promise to do something which is in itself morally allowable, though this rule has given rise to a long (and often contested) list of exceptions. The complexities of promise ethics, indeed, have generated an extensive casuistical literature. In such Trollopian works as *Lady Anna* and *The Eustace Diamonds,* the question of when a promise of marriage can blamelessly be broken is considered in some detail.

In addition to defining permissible and impermissible actions, common morality also describes a few kinds of conduct that are obligatory. It is obligatory that every human being adopt a plan of life according to which, by morally acceptable actions, his or her mental and physical powers may be developed. Above all else, the pathetic wastrel Felix Carbury, in *The Way We Live Now,* is guilty of failing to obey this positive injunction. His villainy is so halfhearted and inefficient that he inflicts little harm on others, but his aimless self-indulgence ruins his own life completely.[17]

Corollary to this self-regarding duty is a duty to others. Every human being must promote the well-being of others by morally acceptable actions, insofar as it can be done without disproportionate inconvenience. This injunction does not demand great feats of benevolence—a fact which helps to explain Trollope's tolerant attitude toward characters like Squire Dale in *The Small House at Allington,* whose charitable impulses struggle against other temperamental proclivities. When the irritable, grudging Dale gives his two nieces so parsimonious a present of silk "that the due manufacture of two dresses out of the material [was] found to be beyond the art of woman," Trollope grants him some moral credit for giving them anything at all.[18]

It should be noted that, although common morality prohibits particular actions such as theft and murder, the two positive injunctions just discussed do not demand the performance of specific actions. They can be fulfilled in many ways.[19] The Pauline principle forbids the violation of specific moral commands, even in cases of extremity. But only where the violation of a specific moral command is at issue does common morality exclude considerations of expediency from the process of moral decision making.

In common morality, the precepts defining allowable, prohibited, and obligatory actions, which I have just described, are supplemented by a *second* class of rules for judging the responsibility of the moral agents who perform those actions. It would be easy to judge the responsibility of moral agents if all actions that flowed from "good" motives were right, while all actions that flowed from "bad" motives were wrong. And it would be equally easy if all wrong actions were blameable and all right actions blameless. But according to common morality, the moral permissibility of actions is not determined by the motives that prompt them. Nor does common morality always judge people who act wrongly as culpable, or those who act rightly as innocent. Here are some of the exceptions.

Prohibited actions performed in ignorance can sometimes be excused, but the ignorance must not result from a perverse refusal to learn the truth. One can perform a wrong action because one is ignorant of the factual circumstances surrounding it (as Mr. Peacocke in *Dr. Wortle's School* does when he marries on the erroneous supposition that his bride's former husband has died). Factual ignorance of this sort is culpable only if it springs from negligence in investigating the situation.

And if a person acts wrongly because he is ignorant of the moral principles that prohibit certain actions, his ignorance must also be genuine, if he is to be held blameless. In his *Life of Cicero,* Trollope struggles with the question of what counts as perverse moral ignorance. Can people who live in a degenerate society plead ignorance of the principles with which their community has lost touch to justify their misconduct? The answer depends on how thoroughly out of touch with the moral principles in question the society is. Trollope cannot exonerate the average man of Cicero's era for failing to obey rules of conduct that had gone out of fashion, because those rules still influenced the behavior of his most decent contemporaries. "In the time of Cicero," Trollope writes, "greed, feeding itself on usury, rapine and dishonesty, was so fully the recognized condition of life that its indulgence entailed no disgrace. But Cicero . . . perceived the baseness of the stain."[20] The ordinary Roman was at fault for failing to perceive it as well.

People are responsible for their intentions. Common morality holds that it is impermissible to do what it is impermissible to intend. One is culpable in other words, if one performs a right action with the intention of performing a wrong one. In *Phineas Redux,* the conservative prime minister Mr. Daubeny sponsors a bill to disestablish the Anglican church. Though many of his contemporaries think that disestablishment is a just measure, Daubeny himself does not. His only motive in introducing this bill, which he believes to be evil in its tendency, is to embarrass his liberal opponents. Even staunch supporters of disestablishment must acknowledge Daubeny's culpability in *intending* to enact a pernicious law.

It is also impermissible to intend what it is impermissible to do. A bad intention is not rendered innocent because it miscarries. When George

Vavasor shoots at John Grey in *Can You Forgive Her?,* we don't exonerate him because he happens to miss.[21]

In addition to rules for judging the moral status of particular actions and the guilt or innocence of those who perform them, common morality suggests some considerations people should keep in mind when judging the moral character of others. The good and bad motives, the virtues and vices, that constitute character are, of course, generally revealed in action. But judging a person's moral character as a whole is a different enterprise from that of judging his or her actions. There are two reasons why this is so.

The first reason is that men and women who lack opportunities and resources may be unable to do what they truly want to do. Many of the women in Trollope's novels—ambitious, intelligent, conscientious women like Lady Laura Kennedy and Lady Mabel Grex—are destroyed because society offers them no way to realize their aspirations in action. The moral character of powerless individuals cannot be judged solely in terms of their moral achievements.

A second reason why judging character differs from judging actions is to be found in the diversity of moral standards. The principles of common morality raise complex issues of definition and application. Each conscientious person in Trollope's novels interprets them differently. And each has his or her own idiosyncratic moral commitments, which often go far beyond what common morality requires. The loving Mrs. Dale in *The Small House at Allington,* for example, thinks it her duty to "bury herself in order that her daughters might live well above ground" (*SH,* 20), though common morality does not demand such extreme self-sacrifice. The actions which each person's moral commitments engender must be judged contextually, in relation to the aims and values of the actor. For these two reasons, moralists in our tradition often argue that one's motives in acting are more important than the acts themselves in evaluating moral character.[22]

In judging character, as well as in prescribing rules for action, common morality enjoins respect for human rationality and autonomy. It does not encourage people to pry too closely into the principles or behavior of their fellows. That is why the old-fashioned moralist Dr. Grantly, in *Barchester Towers,* is "not troubled with a propensity to be curious" about the conduct of his parishioners (*BT,* 231).[23] Although his own moral standards are very firm and consistent, Trollope rarely censures the idiosyncratic, even bizarre, patterns of moral commitment that many of his characters exhibit. The respect for moral autonomy that common morality enjoins may explain this aspect of his ethical outlook.

MORALITY AND MORES

There is a complex relationship between the precepts of common morality, which define minimal standards of conduct, and the laws and customs of particular communities. Since human beings develop most freely in an ordered society whose rules they understand and can rely upon, the respect that people owe one another mandates obedience to the laws of the community in which they live. But if a law commands the violation of a moral precept, then it *must* be disobeyed. Morality, in other words, claims precedence over law, where the two conflict.[24]

The relationship between common morality and mores is analogous to that between morality and law. One should honor the expectations created by the customs of one's society, as well as those created by its laws. However, this obligation has rather narrow limits. Many customs are too trivial to create expectations whose disappointment would be truly injurious (morality does not forbid you to eat your peas with a knife). Further, customs are always changing, and unstable customs do not create expectations that must be honored. The most important point, however, is that customs, like laws, must be ignored if they command what is morally impermissible.

Where laws and customs are egregiously immoral, no one may follow their dictates. Where they are only *arguably* immoral, the proper course of action is much less clear. But in either case, the precepts of common morality provide the basis for a critique of law and custom. When a law or custom is in tension with a principle of common morality, it should be reformed—even if it is not so clearly immoral as to justify men and women in ignoring it *before* it has been altered. The principles of common morality that have proved most valuable for criticizing law and custom are those that define impermissible actions.

Some people have been bothered by the stress that common morality places on prohibitions. The many "thou shalt nots" of this morality seem vastly to outweigh its sparse and anemic positive injunctions. Critics claim that a coldhearted man, who cares nothing about the happiness of others, could easily obey every precept of common morality. Those who take this line are not being entirely fair to common morality, but they do have a point. The virtues that this morality demands most imperatively are the negative virtues of self-control and rectitude; it does not require great benevolence.

Many Victorians criticized common morality from this perspective. They longed for a consensus about the ends of action that would heal their divided society by uniting all men in the pursuit of a single moral goal. But Trollope did not share these dreams. When he describes himself, in *An Autobiography,* as "an advanced, but still a conservative Liberal," Trollope reveals both a desire for reform and a belief that consensus on goals can never be achieved.[25] Because society cannot agree about the ends it should pursue, the prohibitions of common morality, which constrain its members to respect one another as they seek to realize their different goals, offer the only generally acceptable standard by which its laws and mores can be evaluated. This is the first reason why moral prohibitions are central to the evaluative process.

A second reason why they offer a useful standard for criticizing mores is to be found in their specificity. The rules that prohibit particular actions provide a fairly clear standard against which laws and customs can be measured. Thus nineteenth-century abolitionists argue powerfully that slavery must be eliminated because it violates the prohibition against using force to constrain fully rational human beings.

The injunctions to "develop one's powers" and "promote the good of others" also provide a standard against which the moral acceptability of laws and customs can be measured. But because these injunctions are vague, their role is less important than that of common morality's specific, exceptionless prohibitions. It is easy to show that slavery violates the prohibition against constraining force. But it would be harder to show that a given custom makes it impossible for some group of people to "develop their powers" in any fashion whatever. Its negativity is thus common morality's greatest strength as an agent for reform.

But does Trollope himself think of moral prohibitions as stable, meaningful, widely authoritative, and specific directives against which shifting social customs should be measured? The answer is yes: Trollope both grasps and accepts the distinction, so crucial to common morality, between the mores of particular communities and the minimal moral principles that possess a more extensive authority. Discussing American courtship customs, for example, he remarks that "these practices are right or wrong, not in accordance with a fixed rule of morality prevailing over all the earth—such a rule, for instance, as that which orders men not to steal—but right or wrong according to the usages of the country in which they are practiced."[26]

Although the task of interpreting a moral tradition is never easy, the prohibitions of common morality do have an undeniable *center* of meaning in Trollope's novels. In the Prague of *Nina Balatka,* the France of *La Vendee,* the Ireland of *Castle Richmond,* the Australia of *Harry Heathcote of Gangoil,* and the twentieth-century world of *The Fixed Period,* no less than in Barsetshire and London, there are things that no decent man will do. And they are generally the same things, though these novels certainly document the great variability of local custom.

At the same time, Trollope acknowledges that the fixed rules of morality that prevail "over the earth" do not, in fact, prevail over all the *peoples* of the earth. They are European rules and prevail only where Western civilization dominates. Trollope claims, in an essay on "Kafir Land," that the "black man" in Africa has not yet learned "to love his neighbour as himself" from his contact with the British. In other words, the central principle of common morality is alien to the indigenous ethical system.[27] (Nor, Trollope implies cynically, will the black man learn this principle while the British continue to treat him in a manner that flagrantly violates it.) Trollope notes that the natives do not disapprove of violence if it falls short of murder. Further, their custom of punishing offenses with fines is incompatible with Western views of moral responsibility, for "if the delinquent cannot pay, his family has to pay for him."[28] Trollope would have rejected a contemporary writer's sweeping claim that "the moral character of good and evil is a real, universal, and eternal distinction, existing through all worlds and forever."[29]

Ironically, a widely shared understanding of common morality's central prohibitions is sometimes revealed by the very Trollopian characters who deny that such an understanding exists. In *Phineas Finn,* for example, Mr. Monk tells Phineas that "there are general laws current in the world as to morality. 'Thou shalt not steal' for instance. . . . But the first man you meet in the street will have ideas about theft so different from yours, that, if you knew them as you know your own, you would say that his law and yours were not even founded on the same principle. It is compatible with this man's honesty to cheat you in a matter of horseflesh, with that man's in a traffic of railway shares."[30]

Although Monk denies that common morality's prohibition against theft is meaningful in Victorian Britain, he tacitly appeals to a concept of honesty which he (rightly) assumes that he and Phineas do share. Monk's remarks clearly imply that no truly honest Englishman would cheat in matters of horseflesh or securities, even if local mores tolerate such conduct. Seeking interpretive certainty, depressed by the phenomenon of moral disagreement, Monk ignores the considerable interpretive consensus that actually exists.

In the moral world of Trollope's novels, the prohibitions of common morality are central, both in evaluating mores and in evaluating the conduct of individuals. As evidence of their primacy in the judgment of character, consider the case of Septimus Harding. Mr. Harding, the moral heart of the Barsetshire novels, exemplifies the virtues of restraint. He refuses to take anything that does not belong to him in justice, even if it is his by law. He never judges harshly, or lies, or gossips, and he is invariably tactful in his dealings with others. He is motivated at all times by an "intense desire" to know that he is "wronging no man" (Warden, 78).

But Mr. Harding's desire to do good is far less intense than his desire to avoid doing wrong. Even his "warmest admirers cannot say that Mr. Harding was ever an industrious man" (Warden, 8). It's true that he raises the daily stipend of the Bedesmen in Hiram's Hospital by twopence—but this pallid act of charity is the only one he ever performs. Mr. Harding's devotion to the rules defining what a man must *not* do, his sensitivity to the feelings of those around him, and his horror of committing a trespass, make him a moral exemplar. It doesn't matter that he is not especially benevolent, that he lacks "active" virtues. Readers love Mr. Harding because he is "guided by the precepts that he has striven to teach:" the prohibitions of common morality (*BT,* 746).[31]

Common morality does not require heroic displays of generosity or self-suppression. And so it is not surprising that Trollope, a novelist who celebrates the natural human desire for "the good things" of life, should espouse and defend it. His most admirable characters—Mr. Harding, Plantagenet Palliser, and Madame Max Goesler—are all, in their different styles, scrupulous, rather than benevolent, and conscientious, but not self-abnegating.[32] In a discussion of contemporary popular novels of moral exhortation, Trollope writes that no morality ought to demand "such . . . renunciation . . . as to ordinary men and women is manifestly impossible."[33]

We do not find characters like Dickens's Joe Gargery, who lives for others and demands no reward whatever, in the novels of Anthony Trollope. Nor do we find characters like Eliot's Dorothea Brooke, who accedes to the obviously illegitimate demands of her husband, because she cannot bear to hurt him. By elevating selflessness above adherence to principle, Dickens and Eliot "improve upon" common morality in a manner that is quite typical of the Victorian age, as we shall see in the following chapter. But Trollope was not inclined to follow in their footsteps.[34]

2

Common Morality and Victorian Ethics

THE PREMISE of my study is that an understanding of Victorian moral philosophy illuminates Trollope's later novels. In this chapter, I will draw upon the work of several philosophers for their formulations of the most important issues at stake in contemporary ethical debates, issues to which I shall return in succeeding chapters. Some of these thinkers possessed impressive philosophical talents; others, less talented, were nonetheless influential in their own time. Collectively, they defined the moral controversies which interested Trollope.

THE VICTORIAN MORAL PHILOSOPHERS

Intellectual historians often group these philosophers into three schools: utilitarians, intuitionists, and idealists. I wish to begin by describing these schools in order to clarify the areas of disagreement between them. But in succeeding sections of this chapter, I shall argue that despite their differences, the three schools share certain assumptions and aims, which place them at odds with the tradition of common morality.

THE UTILITARIANS

During the Victorian era, a number of philosophers tried to improve upon the innovative theory of morality which they had inherited from Jeremy Bentham. Their work spans the entire period. J.S. Mill discussed ethics in *A System of Logic,* which came out in 1843; Alexander Bain published *Moral Science* two decades later; and Henry Sidgwick, whose *Methods of Ethics* appeared in 1874, continued to revise it until his death in 1900.

Bentham argues that it can be established, on the basis of empirical evidence, that men desire one thing and one thing only: pleasure. Since pleasure is the sole object of desire, it is not possible for human conduct to aim at any other goal. Inductive reasoning thus establishes the "greatest happiness of the greatest number" as the correct end of moral conduct.

Mill, Bain, and Sidgwick all endorse Bentham's greatest happiness principle. But they differ about the relationship between happiness and pleasure, and between various kinds of pleasure. None of them can quite accept Bentham's dictum that all pleasures are equal, that pushpin is as good as poetry, if people find them equally enjoyable.

Nor do any of these thinkers accept the view—dubbed "act utilitarianism" in the mid-twentieth century—that routine moral choices should be based upon a *direct* calculation of their consequences. For they realize that highly complex calculations are involved in deciding which of several acts will yield the most felicific result. And they are disturbed that such an approach appears to sanction moral enormities whenever their expediency can be demonstrated.

So Mill, Bain, and Sidgwick move towards the position that later came to be called "rule utilitarianism": the view that we need moral rules embodying judgments about the consequences of various kinds of action to guide us, at least in routine situations. For rule utilitarians, the greatest happiness principle is more valuable in evaluating the adequacy of moral rules, than in judging the rightness of actions. When utilitarian analysis suggests that the consequences of a rule are not felicific, it should be altered. But rule utilitarians need not be hostile to common morality; Sidgwick, Mill, and Bain all try to demonstrate the felicific value of many (if not all) of the moral rules that common sense intuitively favors, within an overarching utilitarian scheme.

According to Herbert Spencer—whose *Data of Ethics* appeared in 1879 and who might be called an "evolutionary utilitarian"—no organism can survive unless it finds pleasure in self-preservative activities. For organisms voluntarily engage only in activities that they enjoy. As human evolution progresses, Spencer argues, what individuals find pleasant and what has survival value for them will coincide ever more closely. And this process will gradually remove any necessity for moral effort, as men come to desire only what is good for them.

Contrary to Spencer, Leslie Stephen argues in *The Science of Ethics* (1882) that it is the race—not the individual—which responds to evolutionary pressures. Races that develop cohesive social customs triumph over competing races in the struggle for existence. But the cohesive culture "which makes a race survive may not always be a source of advantage to every individual" of that race.[1] Some customs which benefit the race may harm the individual who follows them: it is to such customs that we give the name morality.

The Intuitionists

The intuitionist school was neither as long-lived, nor as intellectually unified, as the utilitarian school. The most prominent intuitionist, William Whewell, published *The Elements of Morality* in 1845. Many commentators also classify John Grote, whose *Examination of the Utilitarian Philosophy* and *A Treatise on the Moral Ideals* were published in 1870 and 1876, and F.D. Maurice as intuitionists. Jerome Schneewind argues in his book on Victorian ethics that Whewell, Grote, and Maurice have two things in common: "They are all defending a spiritual and religious . . . outlook" and "they are all strongly opposed to philosophical empiricism" (the view that knowledge is derived inductively from evidence provided by the senses).[2]

Whewell, Grote, and Maurice are devout Anglicans. Each hopes to defend his own conception of morality by placing it upon an intellectually defensible basis. In fact, the intuitionists fervently believe in the power of reason, although they deny that empirical observation is the primary source of moral knowledge. As Schneewind puts it, they wish "to find some unifying ground in human rationality behind the many intuitions of moral truth which, they would have agreed, we all have."[3] Where many earlier moralists argued that moral intuitions must be accepted simply because we *sense* their validity, Whewell and Grote hope to *prove* their validity through philosophical introspection. Such introspection, they suggest, can yield valid insights into human nature and human needs—and upon these insights a valid morality can be grounded.

Maurice, however, relies upon feeling, rather than upon moral rules arrived at through introspection, as the basis for an intellectually defensible morality. He argues that it is impossible for people to devise completely reliable moral rules, but easy for them to understand their own motives. An assessment of the feelings motivating each available choice, then, offers a rational guide to conduct: one should always choose the course of action that benevolent feeling motivates. The only important intuitionist who had no ties to Cambridge, James Martineau, follows Maurice in rejecting rule-based ethics in favor of a motive-based theory of moral obligation.

The Idealists

T.H. Green, whose *Prolegomena to Ethics* was published posthumously in 1882, and F.H. Bradley, whose *Ethical Studies* came out in 1876, are the most prominent ethical idealists of the mid-Victorian period. Idealism can be thought of as the intellectual successor to intuitionism, for Green and Bradley share both the intuitionists' religious commitments and their distaste for empirical, inductive approaches to ethics.

Green and Bradley ground their moral theories upon a complicated, anti-empiricist metaphysics. Thus Green argues that a sensation cannot be the "primary datum" of experience, as the empiricists claim, because "a sensation can only form an object of experience" if an intelligent subject realizes that what it is experiencing *is* a sensation.[4] In other words, consciousness must exist *before* sensations can be experienced.

Consciousness is the active principle that creates patterns in the natural world. But if the natural world were merely the product of chance, it would not be regular and predictable—for patterns, as we know from introspection, are products of consciousness. Green therefore concludes that the patterns consciousness creates provide a stable, predictable "map" of the natural world, because nature is itself the patterned product of a universal mind or spirit.

Green's metaphysics supports an ethical theory whereby this "universal spirit" gradually realizes itself through the moral efforts of man. Since all moral progress has been guided by the self-realizing universal spirit, men must study the direction that past progress has taken in order to identify those future moral changes that accord with the spirit's plan. The spirit is manifested in existing morality, but it constantly seeks fuller realization.

Although John Henry Newman is primarily a theologian, he devotes much attention to moral issues. His views are close to those of the idealists, whose hostility to empiricism he shares. In *A Grammar of Assent* (1879), Newman claims that syllogistic reasoning which proceeds from inductively established premises cannot resolve the practical problems of human conduct. Instead, such matters must be attacked by a process of loosely inferential reasoning, which, because it is grounded in *personal* experience, proceeds from different premises and takes a different course in each individual. This kind of reasoning, which Newman calls the Illative Sense, can only be learned by participating in human activities. But although morality, like other practical matters, baffles "our powers of analysis, and cannot be brought under logical rule,"[5] "from probabilities" provided by the Illative Sense, the moralist can "construct legitimate proof, sufficient for certitude" in adjudicating questions of conduct.[6]

FOUR ISSUES IN VICTORIAN MORAL PHILOSOPHY

Many Victorian philosophers hope to improve upon the inherited moral norms of their society. They suggest various ways in which this might be done, but generally find one another's proposals unacceptable. Adherents of common morality like Trollope could learn from their trenchant criticisms of one another, while rejecting the innovations proposed by each school. Let us see how this process played itself out in four ethical controversies.

Interpretation versus Foundationalism

Before one can begin to *do* moral philosophy, one must answer some questions about its nature. One such question concerns the relationship of moral philosophy to the moral practices of particular societies. Should moral philosophers concern themselves with the moral tradition that actually exists in their society, even if they cannot defend that tradition in any ultimate sense? "Interpretive" moral philosophers answer this question affirmatively. Taking an existing morality as the subject matter of their study, they attempt to describe, apply, and systematize its principles.

Interpretive moralists argue that existing moralities must be taken seriously—whether or not they can be justified by reason—because their authority rests upon their acceptance, rather than upon the validity of the arguments that are offered to support them. Their own morality is authoritative for the members of a given community, because it is only by virtue of its existence that they exist as moral beings.[7] Moral practices tend to be resilient because they define what counts as moral for those whose minds they have helped to form. When interpretive moral philosophers argue for change, they argue from inside a given moral tradition, pointing out its inconsistencies, pursuing the unrealized possibilities that its logic seems to intimate, and demanding that its principles be respected in practice.

But moral philosophers need not confine themselves to the interpretation or application of existing moralities. They can also attempt to ground an existing morality in some absolute, such as reason, nature, logic, or science. They can debunk existing moralities. And they can attempt to determine what morality ideally ought to be (without regard to what it actually *is* in any given society).

During the seventeenth and eighteenth centuries, many European moralists were forced to acknowledge, as Jerome Schneewind puts it, "that religion could no longer provide a commonly acceptable account of the ways in which we should live."[8] Innovative approaches to moral philosophy gained currency. By the nineteenth century, English moral philosophers *routinely* reject the interpretation of existing morality as their "given" task. They hope instead to identify principles of action that everyone *must* accept—and to find a way of *proving* that they must be accepted. The basic impulse of some Victorian philosophers is destructive. Others are conservative and hope that their unfettered investigations will establish the authority of a moral system that resembles ordinary morality. But even the most religious of the thinkers with whom this study is concerned hope to free morality from its dependence upon revelation and to place it, in an age of declining faith, upon less shaky ground.

And they are unwilling to accept common morality as authoritative simply because it enjoys widespread acceptance. Most of the Victorian moral philosophers agree with Mill that, if we can say nothing more of a morality than that "it exists because it exists,"[9] there is no real reason for anyone to follow its dictates. With the confident rationalism that Schneewind finds characteristic of the era, Victorian philosophers scrutinize their moral tradition, hoping to find a way to defend it—or some other morality of their own devising—from the charge that it is arbitrary.[10] Each one wishes to place the morality he favors on a firm philosophical foundation, so that its authority cannot be shaken. As Mill puts it, for morality to "be made a matter of reason . . . is essential to the very idea of moral philosophy" (Mill, *Essays,* 171). What we would today call "foundationalism" becomes the dominant mode of moral philosophy.

The Victorian moral philosophers hope to ground morality in empirical science, introspective reasoning, logic, or metaphysics. Evolutionary utilitarians like Spencer and Stephen assert that their moral theories are derived directly from basic principles of evolutionary science. But other thinkers make more complicated claims concerning the relationship between science and a rationally defensible morality.

According to William Whewell, whose moral theory is grounded in introspection, recent advances in the philosophy of science have made the construction of a scientific ethical system feasible for the first time in history. Whewell's moral theory is premised upon an analogy between morality and the physical sciences. He thinks that human beings can sense the truth of fundamental moral claims, just as they can sense that the first principles of sciences like mechanics are valid.

But Whewell argues that the earliest practitioners of a science intuit its basic truths with less precision than their successors achieve. Scientific pioneers "search at the same time for true propositions and for precise definitions. Each of these elements depends upon the other. . . . The proposition that the planets are directed by a central force, became more and more certain, as the conception of a central force became more and more clear."[11] And so it is with the axioms of morals: we know them intuitively, but empirical study helps to clarify them.

J. S. Mill takes a different position concerning the role that science should play in the construction of a demonstrably rational morality. In *A System of Logic,* Mill asserts that morality is not a science, but an art. He argues that every art proposes an end and tells its practitioners what they must do to achieve that end. The end of painting is the production of beautiful pictures; the rules of perspective, balance, and color tell artists how to produce them. "Whatever speaks in rules, or precepts, not in assertions respecting matters of fact, is art," Mill claims (Mill, *Essays,* 121). But "the reasons" upon which the rules of any art are based "can be no other than the theorems of the . . . science" related to its subject matter (Mill, *Essays,* 122). The sciences that correspond to the art of ethics are the nascent disciplines of psychology, economics, and sociology for which the Victorians had such great expectations.

Although morality depends upon science for the "theorems" through which its end is realized, morality *itself,* like any art, must define its own "end." But Mill is not willing to accept a goal that is "taken for granted without analysis or questioning" as the end of morality (Mill, *Essays,* 129). And so he calls science in for another consultation. A "complete doctrine of Teleology" is needed, so that the ends of moral conduct can be identified in a scientific manner, Mill announces (Mill, *Essays,* 128).

He is unperturbed by the inconsistency of this claim with his earlier assertion that science can play no role in determining the ends of art. Without describing the teleological science through whose aid the goal of ethics is to be defined, Mill states flatly that "the promotion of happiness is the ultimate principle of Teleology" and hence must be the "end" which the art of ethics aims to promote (Mill, *Essays,* 130).

In later works, of course, Mill does try to "prove" the proposition that universal happiness is the proper end of moral conduct. But in this early book, he employs a strategy that testifies to the prestige science enjoyed in the mid-nineteenth century. Unwilling to accept the implications of the sharp distinction between art and science which he himself has drawn, Mill simply hoists a scientific fig leaf—"the ultimate principle of Teleology"—behind which he can conceal the naked arbitrariness of the greatest happiness principle. John Grote rightly accuses utilitarians like Mill of trying "to lay claim to the scientific prestige" attaching to the inductive method, despite the fact that their systems, by their own admission, are not founded upon empirically established premises.[12]

In his *Methods of Ethics,* Sidgwick accepts Mill's claim that social science can tell us what man is like, but cannot answer the central question of ethics: what ought man to become?[13] But unlike Mill, Sidgwick acknowledges frankly that if this point is valid, an empirically based ethical system becomes an impossibility. He therefore begins his search for moral foundations by asking himself if the desirability of any end of human conduct can be established by purely logical reasoning.

After a rigorous examination of many possibilities, Sidgwick concludes that two ends—"the greatest happiness of the greatest number" and "the agent's own good on the whole"—can indeed be so established. From the point of view of the universe as a whole, the good of all sentient beings is reasonably to be desired; from the agent's perspective, his own overall good is what he reasonably ought to want. Sidgwick plans to use these premises as the basis for an improved morality, but he admits that the two principles may sometimes mandate different courses of action.

Even those Victorian philosophers who do not believe that science and abstract logic have any relevance to ethics are eager to establish morality upon an unshakable foundation: a metaphysical foundation. Green, for example, denies that ethics can be based upon science. He argues that because the mind gives order to nature, its operations cannot be described as a part of that order (as the effects of natural causes operating according to natural laws). Therefore, scientific generalizations can be made about the natural world, but not about man's thought processes.

Green appears to be headed in the direction of subjectivism. If it is not possible to generalize about human thought or behavior, what follows? One might expect Green to conclude that moral convictions are a purely personal matter. But, as it turns out, he prefers to leap the chasm separating skepticism from certainty than to remain teetering on the brink of an epistemological abyss. Green escapes from subjectivism with the help of the universal spirit, which offers the moral guidance that cannot be found in scientific generalizations. "The self-conditioning and self-distinguishing mind" of the universal spirit reproduces itself in man in "the apprehension of a world . . . which *should be,*" Green writes (Green, 101). To make this imagined world a reality is the goal of moral action. Green's skepticism about science and logic becomes the stepping stone to a moral certainty grounded in metaphysics.

Victorian philosophers of all persuasions, then, share the view that reason can place morality on a firm foundation (though they disagree about what that foundation ought to be). But their attacks upon common morality do not always turn out as expected. A critically minded foundationalist in search of an improved moral system may well conclude his investigations with the discovery that reason mandates a morality resembling that of his own society. And in fact this is the place where many Victorian foundationalists ultimately come to rest. Their bark usually proves worse than their bite. Thus, after Jeremy Bentham "discovered" that man is a pleasure-seeking animal and deduced some startling moral precepts from this premise, his followers, as Michael Walzer puts it, felt impelled to "fiddle with the felicific calculus" until it yielded results closer to the precepts of common morality.[14] This rather comical process reached its apogee when Mill announced in his essay *Utilitarianism* that Bentham's greatest happiness principle—whose implications once seemed so alarming—is really nothing more than the lamblike "golden rule of Jesus of Nazareth" disguised as a calculating, utilitarian wolf.[15]

As I noted above, it is difficult to attack the existing morality of any community from an external standpoint, because that morality defines what counts as moral for the community's members. This line of reasoning may explain why Victorian foundationalists often recant their boldest claims, relapsing into familiar modes of ethical thought. For if one ventures outside an existing moral tradition in an attempt to provide morality with a firm foundation, the conclusions one reaches may be true to the demands of science, logic, or metaphysics, yet violate the imperatives of morality as it is ordinarily understood. If they do, those imperatives are likely to reassert themselves.

Trollope is skeptical about rationalist, foundationalist approaches to moral philosophy for precisely this reason. Unlike most Victorian moral philosophy, his novels suggest that interpretive debate *within* the conceptual field of the existing tradition is the closest thing to moral agreement that can be achieved.[16] Trollope's writing repeatedly stresses "the inefficacy of human reason to effect human happiness."[17]

The Precision of Moral Guidance

How can right and wrong actions be differentiated from one another? Common morality's answer to this question is clear, but most Victorian moral philosophers find it unsatisfactory because the guidance it offers is neither precise nor comprehensive. According to common morality, actions are wrong if they violate a moral rule, whatever their consequences may happen to be. Sometimes the relation of an action to a rule is obvious, but more often it is disputable. Worse still, common morality is unable to identify a single "right" course in many situations of significant moral choice: its rules often permit several alternative actions to be chosen. Victorian philosophers search for a system that can offer more reliable guidance.

Common morality is a deontological morality: one that judges actions in terms of their relationship to authoritative moral principles. Act utilitarianism, on the other hand, is a consequentialist morality: one that judges actions by their consequences. Early utilitarians hoped that this approach would increase the *precision* of moral decision making: by calculating the quantity of pleasure to be produced by alternative courses of action, one could find the right action in every situation of moral choice. The many morally significant situations in which, according to common morality, more than one allowable choice exists would disappear. But it soon became apparent that, in practice, such calculations are difficult. Simple versions of act utilitarianism had no supporters among the major Victorian moral philosophers, as I noted above.

Mill and Bain both contend that the rules of morality encode the accumulated wisdom of mankind concerning the felicific effects of various actions and should, for that reason, be generally obeyed. But if one argues that the rules of common morality are sacrosanct, one is no longer a utilitarian in any meaningful sense. For the essence of both act and rule utilitarianism is their use of the greatest happiness principle to "correct" traditional ways of discriminating between right actions and wrong ones. If utilitarianism cannot provide guidance that is more precise than the guidance offered by common morality, what good is it? When Bain writes in *Moral Science* that certain conventional rules, which "may be styled 'Eternal and Immutable'" because they are so undeniably felicific, cannot be criticized, he compromises his utilitarianism very deeply.[18]

Ironically, the evolutionary utilitarians emerge as extreme ethical conservatives. Spencer and Stephen agree that, because they are adaptive, moralities vary with the conditions in which a given group of people finds itself at a given time.[19] Moralities, Stephen claims, cannot be altered by fiat—as earlier utilitarians had hoped—because "the variation . . . must correspond to a process of evolution, not to what could be called arbitrary modification."[20] Though they start from the utilitarian premises that men seek pleasure and that morality should promote the advantage of all, Spencer and Stephen ultimately deny utilitarianism's reformist pretensions, for both conclude that individuals cannot do better than to obey the moral precepts current in their own societies.

One alternative to reinstating ordinary morality—as Bain, Spencer, and Stephen all do—is to argue that its rules need be obeyed only under routine circumstances. Sidgwick suggests that moral rules *should* be violated when it is highly expedient to do so, or when the agent is so unusual that following them will not produce felicific consequences in his particular case. At such times, either the agent's own interest or the greatest happiness principle ought to guide conduct. Thus, although Sidgwick acknowledges the difficulties of the act utilitarian position, he hopes to retain the advantages it seems to offer by writing an act utilitarian "escape clause" into an essentially rule utilitarian scheme.

F.H. Bradley, however, argues that such attempts to combine act and rule utilitarianism cannot succeed. According to Bradley, rule utilitarianism with an act utilitarian escape clause is not a coherent position, logically distinct from act utilitarianism. Utilitarians of Sidgwick's sort, Bradley writes in *Ethical Studies,* tell us that it is generally better to follow "the [ordinary] rules for living, the moral 'Nautical Almanack,'" than to calculate the consequences of each action, because we "will certainly in this way get the most pleasure." But "the course laid down in the Almanack as a law may, in peculiar cases, lead to pain instead of pleasure; and here [we] must disregard the Almanack."[21]

Bradley points out that where rules have only this kind of provisional authority, there are no real rules. Faced with a choice, one must always decide whether it is more felicific to follow the rules or to do something else. Thus rule utilitarianism collapses into act utilitarianism, the theory whose difficulties led to its invention in the first place.

In spite of this logical problem, however, a number of Victorian philosophers find rule utilitarianism with an act utilitarian escape clause an attractive position. For unlike common morality, this morality enables one to identify the right course of action in every situation of significant moral choice. Where following the rules leads to undesirable consequences, or where they do not offer definitive guidance, a careful calculation of consequences can provide an acceptable, precise recommendation.

Intuitionists, as well as utilitarians, hope to find a better way to determine the moral status of actions than that offered by common morality. Where the utilitarians strive for increased *precision* in moral decision making, F.D. Maurice also wishes to *simplify* the process. After all, common morality employs two complex sets of principles for making moral judgments—principles for judging the moral status of actions themselves and principles for judging the guilt or innocence of the agents who perform those actions—yet is often unable to identify the "right" course of action.[22] Maurice thinks he has found a way of reducing these two sets of principles to one. Motive—a concept which, in common morality, is useful primarily in judging moral character—is the criterion by which Maurice hopes to reduce judgments of actions and judgments of responsibility to a single scale. And he believes that his new principle can generate a precise recommendation in every morally significant situation.

Associating a morality of restrictive rules with the sophistries of wily Roman Catholic clerics, Maurice argues that "Rules of the Conscience . . . are unfavourable to goodness and earnestness."[23] "The very lowest kind of human sympathy," Maurice asserts, is a better guide to conduct than any conceivable set of moral precepts (Maurice, 113). If people are motivated by love, they will act well. And so Maurice makes the presence of such motivation the ground for judging both the moral status of actions and the responsibility of agents. Disposition is all. The right moral choice is the choice that love motivates—and agents are never culpable if their acts are motivated by love.

But Maurice's version of what came, in the mid-twentieth century, to be called situation ethics offers no guidance in moral decision making, beyond the vague command to love and do what you will. Maurice's theory aims to improve upon common morality by offering a method that can clearly identify the right course of action in every situation of significant moral choice. But Maurice's critics could retort that, although Maurice's method can indeed identify the "right" choice, the reasoning by which it does so is extremely murky.

And what was Trollope's reaction to these efforts to offer more precise moral guidance than that provided by common morality? The depth of his skepticism concerning the utilitarian approach is revealed in *The Fixed Period* and *The American Senator,* while his negative reaction to motive-based ethical schemes is recorded in *Mr. Scarborough's Family*.

The Scope of Moral Guidance

Victorian philosophers chafe against the limitations that common morality places upon moral judgment. It is not merely that these philosophers, as I have just suggested, hope to find a precise solution to every *moral* difficulty. They also reject the view that people often face choices which raise no morally significant issues. In *The Methods of Ethics,* Sidgwick says that he premised the book upon "the simple assumption (which seems to be made implicitly in all ethical reasoning) that there is something *under any given circumstances* which it is right . . . to do, and that this may be known" (*Methods,* vii; my italics). But this "simple assumption" concerning ethics does not in fact underlie common morality (Sidgwick's parenthetical generalization notwithstanding). Common morality allows people to pursue many goals, provided they observe its constraints and its positive injunctions in doing so. As we have seen, there are many choices about which it has nothing to say.

Most of his contemporaries, however, do share Sidgwick's "simple assumption" that morality should provide a comprehensive guide to action. Intuitionists, idealists, and utilitarians all agree that *every* choice, however trivial, is essentially a moral choice. Whewell, for example, argues that morality aims to develop the capacities that bind together "man and man by the tie of their common humanity."[24] Since it is always possible to become more humane than one already is, even the most mundane choices must be thought of in moral terms: everything a person does contributes to the development of character. "We should place an insurmountable impediment in the way of the Moral Culture of men," Whewell argues, "if we taught them to classify actions as Good, Bad, and Allowable. For they might be led to fill their lives with Allowable actions, to the neglect of those which are Good" (*Elements,* I:306). Whewell's moral scheme does not recognize situations which raise no moral issues: in Whewell's opinion, the best possible action can always be identified and it is always obligatory.

John Grote initially appears to disagree with Whewell on this issue. "In so far as it definitely directs and forbids," Grote argues, "the business of morality lies in a few rules which are themselves simple, though the application of them may sometimes be complicated and difficult. With regard to the larger portion of life, its business is not to prescribe." But Grote does expect morality to *guide* in those situations where it cannot *prescribe*. Morality, he writes, should always be ready "to inspire and animate," although "the definite form which action inspired by it takes must depend very much on individual circumstances and character."[25] So for Grote all decisions are still moral decisions, though he differs from Whewell in allowing for some variation in the way people make them.

Like Sidgwick, Whewell, and Grote, the idealists find the concept of a morally insignificant situation both disturbing and distasteful. Green stresses the fact that every action takes on a moral character according to the feelings that motivate it. "We cannot say with *complete* truth of any action which has been done, that it has been what it ought to have been" unless it expresses a will "of which the dominant interest is in conduct contributory to the perfection of mankind," he remarks sternly (Green, 359). No action which fails this demanding test is morally acceptable—even if it's as trivial as choosing toast for breakfast.

Why are Victorian moral philosophers so eager to expand the scope of moral guidance? Their fear of social instability offers one obvious answer to this question. In an era of corrosive religious doubt and rapid social change, argues the Victorian journalist Frances Power Cobbe, nothing is more necessary than "a sound morality whose fetters no alchemy can dissolve."[26] And Cobbe was by no means the only thinker who longed for a morality that could stabilize every aspect of human behavior. When Green turns the question of how "a normally healthy man should select his food and drink" into an urgent moral issue, we catch the authentic note of Victorian earnestness—the mirror image of Victorian doubt.[27] We hear the same note in James Martineau's grudging admission that "even recreation is not without its place in life," provided we reserve it for those rare moments when no higher motive solicits us.[28] After God became "inconceivable" to many of their countrymen, Victorian philosophers hoped that a "peremptory and absolute" conception of duty could step into the breach left by His departure.[29]

But two philosophical considerations are relevant here as well. First, when science, reason, and metaphysics are asked to provide foundational moral principles, they tend, by their very nature, to generate comprehensive theories. Science aims to subsume all of nature under law; reason seeks propositions that are true for all men, at all times; metaphysics hopes to reveal the deepest, most immutable levels of reality. These approaches, in other words, tend to assume that objective truth exists and can be found. When one thinks about ethics in the foundationalist terms popular during the Victorian era, one may well decide, as Sidgwick does, that there is always something which it is right to do and that this can be known.

Second, each of the philosophers with whom this study is concerned identifies an end for moral conduct—whether it be happiness, the realization of human potentiality, evolutionary adaptation, or obedience to the universal spirit. And this helps to explain their tendency to moralize every aspect of human behavior. For once the proper end of morality has been identified, you can refer even the smallest details of conduct to that end. All decisions become moral decisions.

But to Trollope, as to any supporter of common morality, this tendency in Victorian ethics would have seemed excessive, if not downright offensive. For common morality prescribes no end that anyone must pursue. Its principles are constraints upon the pursuit of those ends that moral agents themselves choose to seek.

Morality, Mores, and Duty in Victorian Ethics

As I noted in Chapter 1, common morality is a minimal morality, not a system of mores specifying a way of life in all its richness and detail. Because Victorian philosophers wish to moralize every decision, they must blur common morality's sharp distinction between customs, which need not always be obeyed, and moral principles, which must. But their endeavor to rethink the relationship between mores and morals raises some serious problems.

The term "duty" is no less important to Victorian novelists than it is to Victorian moral philosophers. For Trollope, one's duty comprises *both* one's obligations under common morality *and* the obligations under custom that one *personally* acknowledges. Similarly placed individuals can therefore define their duty in quite different ways. In *Phineas Redux,* a party boss tells Phineas that he is by no means as "good a man" as a certain politician who, adhering to professional custom, supports his party on every issue—which Phineas refuses to do. To this accusation, Phineas replies, "I say nothing about that. He has his ideas of duty, and I have mine,"[30] thus acknowledging that reasonably "good" men do differ in their views of duty. But Phineas would never say, of a rapist or murderer, "He may be as good a man as I. He has his ideas of morality and I have mine."

For the Victorian intuitionists and idealists, however, custom plays a much more central role in defining the individual's duty. Whewell argues that, because morality aims to develop man's human capacities, some portion of it "must be universal and unchangeable," like human nature itself (*Elements,* I:76). But the eternal truths of morality that Whewell identifies are highly abstract. They consist simply of the acknowledgement that personal safety, property, contract, family, and government are basic human needs and must be provided for in *some* manner.

Whewell's abstract moral truths can only be translated into a set of specific directives in terms of the laws and customs of an actual society. And because laws and customs are so much more central to Whewell's moral scheme than his bloodless, abstract moral universals, he believes that they must be obeyed until they have been altered, even when they appear to be unjust. Thus Whewell argues firmly (in opposition to most Victorian moralists) that pre-Civil War American abolitionists have a moral obligation to obey the fugitive slave law.

Not only must laws and customs be observed, they must not be criticized. Whewell argues that morality is a matter of internal disposition. "Moral precepts," he writes, "express Rules of . . . Will and Intention, of the Desires and Affections. Thus the Law is, *Do Not Steal*; the Moral Precept is, *Do Not Covet*" (*Elements,* I:159). According to Whewell's concept of duty, then, a good man should build the mores of his community, through which moral principles are actualized, into his habitual patterns of thought. Since these mores claim absolute dominion over his will and intention, he may not dissent from them. If he decides, for example, that the local distribution of property is unjust, he is, in a sense, coveting the property of others. Thus Whewell's good man is not free to withdraw his loyalty from a law or custom and advocate its reform. According to Whewell, as Mill rightly argues, "the early Christians, the religious reformers, the founders of all free governments, . . . and all enemies of the rights of slaveowners, must be classed among the wicked," because they criticize law or custom in the name of a higher morality (Mill, *Essays,* 255).

Similar difficulties plague other intuitionists, like Maurice, and idealists like Bradley, who also stress the role of mores in defining the individual's duty. Both these philosophers argue that duty cannot be deduced from moral abstractions, but arises from the specific social relations into which we are born. As Maurice puts it, everyone inhabits a social order whose relations "abide whether we are faithful to them or neglect them . . . [hence] the Conscience in each of us affirms 'I am in this order, I ought to act consistently with it, let my fancies say what they please'" (Maurice, 57). The chapter of Bradley's *Ethical Studies* entitled "My Station and Its Duties" argues in nearly identical language that we don't need philosophy to tell us what our moral responsibilities are. We need only look around us and see what other people expect us to do.

Of course, Maurice and Bradley know that problems arise when one defines "doing one's duty" as synonymous with "obeying all the laws and customs of one's community." Bradley admits that if "the community in which [a man] is a member [is] in a confused or rotten condition," he cannot simply accept his role in it (Bradley, 203). But if an individual learns about morality by playing his prescribed social role, as both Maurice and Bradley contend, from what other source can he obtain the "universal" moral concepts in terms of which his society's moral condition may be judged?

Bradley suggests that we should study all the moralities that have ever existed, in order to abstract the concept of excellence they share. He argues that "by the teaching, tradition, and imagination of our own and other countries and times, we receive a content which we . . . finally detach from all as . . . an ideal type of human perfection" (Bradley, 221). But only faith in God or the universal spirit can assure us that common moral ideals really *do* underlie the many systems of mores which mankind has developed. Without such faith we have no assurance that comparative ethics will yield anything more than a chaos of competing visions.

In the meanwhile, utilitarians like Sidgwick and Mill have their own troubles, as they try to evaluate the moral acceptability of local customs by means of the greatest happiness principle. Having decided that existing mores embody the accumulated judgments of mankind concerning the effects of various behaviors, they grant both custom and morality provisional authority. But I noted above that this authority is *only* provisional. As Sidgwick puts it, "it is the unavoidable duty of a systematic Utilitarianism to make a thorough revision of [customary] rules" to see if more felicific ones can be devised (*Methods,* 467).

But Sidgwick suggests that the duty of revision is difficult as well as unavoidable. Not only are there "uncertainties involved in hedonistic comparison generally," but more importantly, we cannot specify the nature of the human being for whom this maximally felicific code of conduct is to be devised. Because "humanity is not something that exhibits the same properties always and everywhere. . . . it seems *prima facie* absurd to lay down a set of ideal Utilitarian rules for mankind generally" (*Methods,* 467–8). And if we "contract the scope of investigation, and only endeavour to ascertain the rules appropriate to men as we know them, in our own age and country," we will be "immediately met with a dilemma: the men whom we know are beings who accept . . . a certain moral code: if we take them as they are in this respect, we can hardly at the same time conceive them as beings for whom a code is yet to be constructed *de novo*: if, on the other hand, we take an actual man . . . and abstract his morality, what remains is an entity so purely hypothetical, that it is not clear what practical purpose can be served by constructing a system of moral rules for the community of such beings" (*Methods,* 468). By Sidgwick's own account, then, it is difficult to base a thorough revision of custom upon hedonistic calculation, because the consequences of actions depend upon existing customs and the moral feelings they generate. In most situations, Sidgwick concludes reluctantly, utilitarian arguments can only convince men to alter the details of existing customs.

When utilitarians do criticize the details of existing customs, the "uncertainties involved in hedonistic comparison," which Sidgwick acknowledges with his usual honesty, become immediately apparent. In *The Methods of Ethics,* for example, Sidgwick calculates the consequences of the sexual double standard accepted by many Victorians. He suggests that "the existence of a certain limited amount" of illicit sexual intercourse, "(with a special class of women, carefully separated, as at present, from the rest of society) is scarcely a real evil, and may even be a positive gain in respect of general happiness; for continence is perhaps somewhat dangerous to health, and in any case involves a loss of pleasure" (*Methods,* 451). Sidgwick ultimately does decide that the cruel stigmatization of prostitutes, which is necessary "to prevent the contagion of unchastity from spreading" to respectable women, renders the arrangement he describes "on the whole infelicific" (*Methods,* 452), in spite of its many advantages. But the calculations by which he reaches his conclusion are wildly impressionistic and could easily be disputed. Intuitionists and idealists often point out that consequentialist calculations about the felicific value of social practices are more subjective than they seem.

The separation between common morality's invariant (but minimal) principles and the changeable (but detailed) mores of particular communities enables disputes concerning defective mores to be conducted in a more satisfactory manner. Where customs and laws are inexpedient or morally undesirable, but do not require the violation of moral prohibitions, one can argue for their reform on either prudential or moral grounds. Much of the discussion of political and social reform that occurs within the conceptual field of common morality is of this sort. Such discussions tend to be almost as diffuse as reformist discussions carried out under utilitarian auspices—but not quite. The long-lived principles of the tradition give them *some* structure. And where a custom or law seems to require the violation of moral prohibitions, the resulting dispute will be far more orderly than a dispute about its hedonic consequences could possibly be.

When Victorian philosophers rethink the relationship between mores and morals, in an attempt to bring all human conduct firmly under the direction of duty, then, an adherent of common morality might well conclude that they create more difficulties than they solve. Either they interdict reform by identifying mores with morality or they substitute less-structured methods of moral analysis than those provided by common morality. And this result seemed unfortunate to Trollope. *Lady Anna* and *Cousin Henry* point out the dangers of equating duty with custom, while *The Fixed Period* suggests that calculations concerning the felicific effects of custom and law cannot achieve the impartiality with which utilitarians often credit them.

TROLLOPE AND VICTORIAN MORAL PHILOSOPHY

There is no reason to think that Trollope was a close student of the ethical debates just described. But there is every reason to think that he knew of them, for they were an important part of the intellectual life of the time. Both logically and practically, these controversies were linked with other disputes in which Trollope took an interest, such as the factional struggles within the Anglican church and the debates about Benthamite reform of laws and institutions.

Since Victorian England was a small country, Trollope knew—or knew people who knew—many of her moral philosophers. He met Mill, Bain, and Spencer socially, though he didn't hit it off particularly well with the former. He was friendly with Frances Power Cobbe, who wrote on ethical subjects from a Kantian perspective, and he modelled Miss Todd, a character who appears in *The Bertrams* and *Miss Mackenzie,* upon her. John Newman, who functions as an offstage character in *Barchester Towers,* admired Trollope's novels. He corresponded briefly with Trollope and he illustrates a moral point in *A Grammar of Assent* with an incident from *Orley Farm*. Leslie Stephen contributed three articles to *St. Paul's Magazine* while Trollope was its editor.[31] Trollope's friends George Eliot and G.H. Lewes were interested in many philosophical subjects, including ethics. They, in turn, were friends of Herbert Spencer (and it was at their house that Trollope encountered him).

But his personal connections with philosophers would not have been Trollope's only source of knowledge about the ethical debates of his day. The moral philosophy of the mid-Victorian period reached a wide audience of educated people. Whewell's *Elements of Morality* went through many editions, as did Mill's *System of Logic* and Sidgwick's *Methods of Ethics*. Mill's *Utilitarianism* was published in a periodical with a general readership, *Fraser's Magazine,* in 1861, and many other essays on moral philosophy came out in *Fraser's* as well (including some by Frances Cobbe). Such essays also appeared in popular magazines like *The Fortnightly* (founded by a group of men that included Trollope himself), *Macmillan's,* and *The Contemporary Review*. A typical issue of *The Fortnightly* that appeared on 15 January 1866 included an essay by Lewes on the philosophy of Comte, an essay by Trollope on the moral authority of the fourth commandment, an essay by Bain discussing free will from a physiological perspective, and an episode of *The Belton Estate!* In fact, the first truly academic journal of philosophy, *Mind,* did not begin publication until 1876. Nor did *Mind* in its early years have nearly the influence that it later achieved.[32] Moral philosophy continued to be published in popular magazines, even after *Mind* began to compete with them for manuscripts.

The founding of *Mind* was, not coincidentally, associated with the emergence of philosophy as an academic discipline. For until the 1870s, moral philosophy was usually written by men with other professional concerns, as Jerome Schneewind remarks: Mill was an official of the East India Company, Whewell a polymath whose interests were primarily scientific, Newman a cleric. But Sidgwick, Bain, and Green were among the first specimens of a new breed, the professional philosopher.[33] The transformation of moral philosophy into an academic discipline, however, was by no means complete at the time of Trollope's death. Spencer, "the last man to write philosophy which both excited public interest and received serious attention from the academics," did not publish his final book on ethics until 1893.[34]

Even the most professional of the philosophers considered in this study were men of letters as well as academics. Their works were widely read, reviewed, and discussed. In his *Prolegomena to Ethics,* Green remarks in passing that theories of ethical hedonism are "the babble of the drawing-room" in Victorian England, a testimony to the interest that educated Englishmen and women took in the controversies of contemporary moral philosophy (Green, 418). Several prominent moral philosophers of the mid-Victorian period were also influential as university teachers, training England's ruling class.

R.J. Collingwood remarks that during the 1860s and 1870s, Green, who died in 1882, sent "into public life a stream of ex-pupils who carried with them the conviction that philosophy . . . was an important thing, and that their vocation was to put it into practice. . . . Through this effect on the minds of its pupils, the philosophy of Green's school might be found, from about 1880–1901, penetrating and fertilizing every part of the national life."[35] It is probably because Green was such a prominent figure that Mrs. Humphry Ward used him as the model for the modern churchman, Mr. Grey, who appears in her popular novel, *Robert Elsmere*.

In succeeding chapters, I will look at the ways that Trollope's later novels use the moral theories discussed in this chapter as structuring devices. It is quite possible that Trollope read only a few of the philosophical works upon which I draw. It is conceivable (though not likely) that he never read a single one of them. But he was certainly familiar with the ideas that they propound and with the debates to which they contribute. This we can infer from evidence offered by the novels themselves, as well as from the fact that those debates were so prominent a part of the intellectual scene.

The furor aroused by the publication of Mill's *Utilitarianism* may in part explain why Trollope grew more interested in moral philosophy during the late 1860s and the 1870s. When Mill published this essay in 1861, his aim was to rehabilitate utilitarianism by suggesting that it resembles ordinary morality more closely than most people suspect. Mill hopes that, shorn of its most frightening implications, utilitarianism will conquer intuitionism once and for all. In his essay, Mill tries to combat the view that utilitarianism is a "pig philosophy," which offers no better ideal for mankind than a lifelong wallow in sensual delights, by introducing a distinction between higher and lower pleasures. He also attempts to show that virtue is part of the happiness that utilitarianism seeks to promote, and that there is no incompatibility between the greatest happiness principle and the Golden Rule. These changes alter Benthamite utilitarianism, which makes *quantity* of pleasure the sole criterion of moral judgment, beyond recognition.

Indeed, Mill's whitewash of utilitarianism appeared so disingenuous that a number of contemporary philosophers decided to attack it in some detail. Sidgwick, Grote, Green, and Bradley all have a field day with Mill's essay in books published between 1870 and 1882. But although it failed to convince philosophers that "moralized" utilitarianism is a logically tenable position, *Utilitarianism* succeeded with the public. While writing the essay in 1861, Mill rightly claimed that intuitionism was the dominant school of British ethics. But Bradley was equally correct when he noted that utilitarianism was replacing it as the dominant approach—with ordinary people, at any rate—by the early 1870s. This shift was largely the work of Mill's essay.

Another development that helps explain Trollope's growing interest in moral philosophy during the 1870s is to be found in his increasing involvement with Latin literature. As he prepared to write the biography of Cicero that was published in 1881, Trollope reread Cicero's ethical writings several times. *Cousin Henry,* in particular, suggests that he was struck by the contrast between the clear account of practical Stoic ethics (so similar to common morality) that Cicero offers in *De Officiis* and some of the murkier moral theories currently under discussion.

T.H.S. Escott suggests that Trollope's friendship with Eliot and Lewes, which dated from about 1865, is responsible for the intellectually ambitious quality that distinguishes his novels of the 1870s and 1880s.[36] Close contact with Eliot's stringent and typically mid-Victorian moral views may well have provoked Trollope to assert his own position with increased vehemence. Critical studies of Trollope's fiction often, and rightly, contrast his tolerant, descriptive approach to ethics, with Eliot's demanding morality.[37]

Trollope, no consequentialist, would have watched the growing influence of Mill's *Utilitarianism* with dismay. But he would not have been impressed by the philosophical alternatives suggested between the late 1860s and his death in 1882: Grote's rationalized intuitionism, Sidgwick's qualified utilitarianism, Maurice's morality of good-feeling, Spencer's and Stephen's evolutionary ethics, or Green's and Bradley's idealism, with its elevated talk of the universal spirit. Trollope may have focused upon moral issues in several of the novels he wrote during the 1870s and 1880s because he disliked the way contemporary philosophers had formulated them. Succeeding chapters will try to demonstrate that these novels have a mission: to defend common morality against the well-meaning efforts of Victorian philosophers to improve upon it.

3

Morality and Social Advantage in *The Eustace Diamonds*

Some Victorian writers suggest that the landed gentleman of their era still observes the high standards of veracity that have traditionally distinguished his class. He inherits the independence that allowed his forebears to speak their minds without fear of consequences, because his income and rank, like theirs, are secure. The same writers claim that men who earn their livelihood find it more difficult to be honest. For, according to a line of argument dating back at least as far as Cicero, commerce fosters sharp dealing in small practitioners and deception on a grand scale in its moguls. The self-aggrandizing standards of conduct that characterize the professions are also in tension with the demands of honesty. Lawyers distort, physicians obfuscate, and clerics conceal their doubts.

For these reasons, many Victorians feared that the decline of England's simple, agrarian economy threatened veracity, as a distinctively English virtue. Because commerce was so often thought inimical to honesty, the diffuse fear that social change could shred the moral fabric became specific where this virtue was concerned. And as time passed, a growing number of authors suggested that even the gentry were beginning to succumb to the prevailing climate of greed and deceit.

It is therefore not surprising that Victorian moral philosophers should wish to prove that their startling new theories, so far from contributing to the decline of honesty, would re-establish its importance. But it *is* surprising that thinkers in *both* the intuitionist and the utilitarian schools take a utilitarian tack in explaining why honesty occupies a central position among the virtues. They argue that without trust, the predictability needed in social life cannot be achieved—and an intolerable level of social disorder results.

In *The Elements of Morality,* Whewell claims that the existence of language as a distinctively human attribute implies an obligation to speak the truth. "That a Lie is a violation of the general understanding of mankind, is the reason why the Rule, *Lie Not,* is universally accepted by mankind as an absolute Rule," Whewell writes (*Elements,* I:222). This classically intuitionist argument deduces a moral principle from an aspect of human nature: in this case, from man's nature as a user of language. But Whewell goes on to develop this idea along utilitarian lines.

In "Whewell on Moral Philosophy," a scathing critique of *The Elements of Morality,* Mill argues that Whewell often "supports his [supposedly self-evident moral] propositions by utilitarian reasons" (Mill, *Essays,* 261). Whewell's discussion of veracity, Mill suggests, demonstrates this tendency with special clarity. Whewell's claim that we must tell the truth because "lying and deceit . . . make all actions implying mutual dependence, that is, all social action and social life, impossible," does indeed offer a consequentialist justification for a supposedly a priori ethical principle (Mill, *Essays,* 261).

Because he believes that honesty is vital to social order, Whewell advocates an exceptionally strict standard of veracity. A man kidnapped by bandits, who has been released after promising to pay a ransom, is morally obligated to pay the sum so extorted: "Not as what is due to robbers, but as . . . an act of reverence to truth" (*Elements,* I:276). Whewell fears to sanction even the minimal dishonesty involved in breaking a promise given under duress, lest such sanction lower the general standard of veracity. Echoing Whewell, John Grote remarks that "our consideration of the vast usefulness and absolute necessity of truthfulness to society is well calculated to enlarge . . . our notion of the duty of it."[1]

And if intuitionists like Whewell and Grote are anxious about the consequences of declining honesty, it is natural that utilitarians should share their concern. In *Utilitarianism,* Mill joins Whewell in arguing that unvarying veracity is necessary to the preservation of order: Every "deviation from truth does that much towards weakening the trustworthiness of human assertion, which is . . . the principal support of all present social well-being." From these premises, Mill infers "that the violation, for a present advantage, of a rule of such transcendent expediency, is not expedient" (Mill, *Essays,* 294–5).

Mill knows that he must combat the general impression that utilitarian morality—an "economic" ethic which balances gains in pleasure against losses in pain—sanctions expedient lies. By demonstrating that utilitarianism values honesty, he hopes to convince his readers that its acceptance does not threaten this endangered virtue. But his use of the oxymoron "transcendent expediency" reveals a flaw in his argument. One cannot justify an exceptionless, "transcendent" moral principle on expediential grounds. For one can always imagine circumstances in which the consequences of violating the rule will be worse than those of obeying it—even when the effects of setting an unfortunate precedent are taken into account.

Some utilitarians therefore reject Mill's claim that truth-telling is "transcendently expedient." For Sidgwick, it is expedient, but not transcendently so. The rules mandating veracity can sometimes be violated for utilitarian reasons. Like Mill, however, Sidgwick does not wish to be accused of lowering the general standard of truthfulness. So he too appeals to the social importance of honesty, arguing that the "danger of unveracity . . . constitutes a strong . . . utilitarian ground for speaking the truth" (*Methods,* 319).

In his early novels, Trollope often equates gentility with honesty. Works like *The Three Clerks* and *Orley Farm* suggest that most men of gentle birth and nurture can be relied upon to tell the truth, even if they are employed in trade or the professions. During the 1870s and 1880s, however, Trollope's novels begin to suggest that commercial values have infected the entire society. The gentlemen who remain honest are increasingly isolated and seem almost irrelevant to the world they inhabit.[2] Like many of his contemporaries, then, Trollope fears that the standard of honesty in Victorian England may be declining at an alarming rate.

But *The Eustace Diamonds* (1873) takes issue with Trollope's contemporaries on one important point: the view that this development is alarming because truthfulness is vital to the preservation of social order. By examining the phenomenon of declining veracity in particular, Trollope can test a general proposition of utilitarian ethics: that the authority of a moral precept depends upon the social benefits which obedience to it secures. Of course Trollope thinks that people should be truthful, but here, as elsewhere, he denies that morality can be defended by appeals to its social utility.

The principles of common morality offer guidance to individuals, showing them how to respect the autonomy of others. But common morality does not pretend to identify the principles of conduct that are most advantageous, "all things considered," for society as a whole. And Trollope is well aware of this. Hence it is not surprising that other questions about honesty seem more significant to him than the issue of its social utility. What happens to the honest person in a dishonest world? What happens to the concept of honesty itself? These are the questions—and the dangers—upon which Trollope focuses in *The Eustace Diamonds*.

The Eustace Diamonds depicts an upper-class milieu that appears to take truthfulness seriously. But appearances are deceiving. Among the fashionable Londoners who people the book, dishonesty is the unmentionable sin. When one character accuses another of lying, she receives a stern reproof: "No lady should use such a word to a gentleman."[3] As the narrator puts it, "the one offence which a gentleman is supposed never to commit is that of speaking an untruth. The offence may be one committed oftener than any other by gentlemen—as also by all other people; but, nevertheless, it is regarded by the usages of society as being the one thing which a gentleman never does" (*Eustace*, 299).

Although veracity is no longer required among the gentry, its putative possession is still vital to the social preeminence that the gentry claims. One may not say—even truthfully—that gentlemen can be liars, lest one diminish the respect in which gentlemen are held. No one seems to care that this distortion may well diminish respect for truth. Euphemisms for the unmentionable word "lie" proliferate and become a running joke: untruth, fib, incorrect version, story. These sickly euphemisms reveal how dishonest this world really is.

More routinely than in Trollope's early works, professionals in *The Eustace Diamonds* lie to succeed. When the parliamentary opposition attacks a government policy, the narrator notes that, had any other policy been chosen, "the attack would have been as venomous, and . . . would have come from the same quarter" (*Eustace*, 99). When scandal touches one of its members, the Liberal party closes ranks behind him. Its "esprit de corps, which is the glorious characteristic of English statesmen," as the narrator sarcastically remarks, is utterly unaffected by the merits of the issue (*Eustace*, 531). Barristers bamboozle juries by enveloping their cases "in increased mystery" (*Eustace*, 155). The novel makes it clear that independent politicians and straightforward barristers have a poor chance of success.

The novel's aristocrats and landed gentry are no better than its professionals. In its avid search for sensation, the haut monde embraces a style of gossip that borders upon defamation: "Everybody on a sudden adopts an idea that some particular man is over head and ears in debt . . . or that some ill-fated woman is cruelly ill-used by her husband . . . whereas the man doesn't owe a shilling, [and] the woman never hears a harsh word from her lord" (*Eustace*, 188).[4] This society is cavalier about promises, even promises of marriage. "There used to be a sort of feeling that if a man behaved badly something would be done to him; but that's all over now," says a peer's daughter, with a certain perverse satisfaction (*Eustace,* 581).

One searches *The Eustace Diamonds* in vain for the sort of truly honest gentleman who turns up regularly in Trollope's early novels. Only a degenerate version of the type appears: Lord Fawn, a man "most anxious to do right so that he might not be accused of being in the wrong—and at the same time gifted with but little of that insight into things which teaches men to know what is right and what is wrong" (*Eustace,* 538).[5] Fawn's conscience cannot direct him, so he falls back on public opinion as a guide. But public opinion is morally so unreliable that the vacillations which result are grimly comic.

Though so many Victorian philosophers argue that honesty is indispensable to social order, *The Eustace Diamonds* suggests that dishonesty can be nearly as predictable as veracity itself. If men can no longer be counted on to honor promises of marriage, it doesn't really matter, because "the girls,—they all know that it is so" and adjust their conduct accordingly. Indeed, keeping and breaking such promises "comes to the same thing in the long run. The men have to marry, and what one girl loses another girl gets" (*Eustace,* 581). The men, for their part, are forewarned to expect deception, in the form of "buckram, whalebone, paint," and insincere professions of feeling, from marriageable girls—and forewarned is forearmed (*Eustace,* 89).

Nor is anyone in the novel really taken in by parliamentary or legal rhetoric. Malicious rumors receive only so much credence as is necessary to make them entertaining. Pretenses to culture are ruthlessly scrutinized. If you quote poetry to parade your learning, "it is expedient to select [a passage] in the middle, or at the end." If you take a quotation from the beginning, no one will "give you credit for [having read] a page beyond that from which your passage comes" (*Eustace,* 233). In *The Eustace Diamonds,* James Kincaid remarks, "nobody suspends disbelief and the dupers hardly expect to dupe."[6]

Those who fail to make the adjustments common sense demands in such a world have only themselves to blame. "He had known that she was a liar, and what else could he have expected but lies?" says the narrator of one such individual (*Eustace,* 686). The confusion people suffer when fooled by predictable lies is, by implication, easily avoidable. In fact, this dishonest society rubs along quite smoothly. Social order is not threatened.

The Eustace Diamonds, then, dismisses the view that truthfulness is needed for the expediential reasons cited by Victorian moral philosophers. The novel suggests a different reason why generalized dishonesty is undesirable: such a social condition maims the individual, particularly the powerless individual. The principles of common morality offer guidance to individuals, but their guidance can most easily be followed in a supportive social environment. Honesty is hard to practice in a society of liars—and in such a society, the survival of veracity is by no means assured.[7]

The Eustace Diamonds is a long novel with three fully developed plots, each concerning a marriageable woman. The heroines' names, Lizzie, Lucy, and Lucinda, sound so similar as to suggest that the girls represent aspects of the same predicament. In fact, their stories do offer variations on a single theme: the fate of female honesty in a mendacious society.

The beautiful protagonist, Lizzie Eustace, is the daughter of an admiral who left her a penniless orphan at nineteen. After luring Sir Florian Eustace into marriage, Lizzie quickly becomes a widow with a large jointure. She also has a diamond necklace, which she falsely claims that her husband gave her and which his family hopes to recover. The necklace is under Lizzie's pillow when the box where she usually keeps it is stolen. On oath, she states that the diamonds were in the stolen box. Later, the necklace really is stolen and the thieves reveal Lizzie's perjury. Lizzie obtains immunity from prosecution, but her reputation is in tatters when the novel ends.

Trollope called his heroine an "aristocratic Becky Sharp," and the parallel is apt. Like Thackeray's Becky, Lizzie reflects the society which produced her—with some very unflattering distortions.[8] Becky is the embodiment of nineteenth-century materialism and snobbery. Lizzie reveals the effects of two social phenomena which promote female dishonesty: women's exclusion from education and their commodification on the marriage market.

In *Vanity Fair,* Thackeray makes fun of the way middle-class youngsters are educated. But he doesn't suggest that the education girls receive is worse than that to which boys are subjected: it's just dreadful in a different way. Hence it is not surprising that Becky seems to know as much as her male victims do—about money, class, and the law. Until her "exposure" midway though the novel, Becky is an efficient manipulator who moves from success to success.

But Trollope is more interested than Thackeray in the role ignorance plays in making women what they are. Lizzie knows almost nothing about law—and not much more about custom.[9] She is not sure if she is committing a crime in retaining the necklace, nor does she comprehend the terms of her own marriage settlement. Indeed, though Lizzie commits perjury, "she hardly knew what perjury was. It sounded like forgery and burglary" (*Eustace,* 511). No wonder that Lizzie is a much less effective manipulator than Becky.

Lizzie achieves only one real success—and it is clear that she is lucky to achieve it. Sir Florian, as the narrator remarks, "must have been dull of intellect, slow of discernment, blear-eyed in his ways about the town" to have been taken in by so lame a deceiver (*Eustace,* 44). Lizzie understands how to tempt men, and she knows how to finagle a loan—beyond that, she can't lie her way out of a paper bag. But Lizzie's ignorance is no different from that of other Victorian ladies. Excluded from professional training and experience outside the home, these women were taught many things in a systematically superficial manner, to ensure that they would not be better informed than their husbands. And this ignorance places Lizzie at a disadvantage in dealing with the worldly men who surround her, as she herself is painfully aware.

The Eustace family lawyer is not above using his legal expertise to bamboozle her. When she meets him with deception, Lizzie believes that she is merely shortening the odds against her—and one can see her point. But her ignorance is so dire that she is never sure what, exactly, she needs to distort or conceal. This explains why her lies are frequently misdirected.

Lizzie thinks, quite correctly, that if she tells the truth, those who understand the world better than she does may use her admissions against her. She feels safe only when she is keeping something back and so she starts to lie automatically, even when there is no obvious reason to do so: "To lie readily and cleverly . . . was, according to the lessons which she had learned, a necessity in woman" (*Eustace,* 762). As time passes, Lizzie's dishonesty becomes increasingly purposeless. She can gain nothing by lying about the first robbery—and yet she does.

Lizzie is also a product of the commodification to which all the novel's women are subjected. To sell her beauty is Lizzie's only chance for success. But in order to sell it, she must pretend that she is giving it away. According to Victorian norms of femininity, a lady must love the man she marries. She may not hesitate between two men "without the loss of that aroma which should be the apple of a young woman's eye," as a character with a poor feel for metaphor puts it (*Eustace,* 506). In a world which trades in women, women must profess only the most personal motives. This society is a school for actresses, like Lizzie.

But no less than her lying, Lizzie's role playing gradually becomes an end in itself. To entrap a husband, she has to suppress her personality so thoroughly that she loses all authentic sense of self. "The guiding motive of her conduct" becomes nothing more than "the desire to make things seem to be other than they were. To be always acting a part . . . was to be everything" (*Eustace,* 212). "Unclean harpy" though she is, Lizzie never forfeits the reader's sympathy, for this compulsive deceiver harms no one but herself.

Through Lizzie's characterization, Trollope implies that it is difficult for the powerless and dependent to be truthful in a world that does not encourage veracity. *The Eustace Diamonds* underscores this point by paralleling Lizzie's experiences to those of its other two heroines. The novel's second impoverished beauty, Lucinda Roanoke, has only a few months in which to find a husband, for her tiny fortune will soon run out. But unlike Lizzie, Lucinda, "who loved the truth," feels a savage antipathy to the predatory life of the marriage market and will not play the role that the situation demands (*Eustace,* 381).

Consequently, Lucinda finds herself with only one suitor, the odious Sir Griffin Tewett, when her money is gone. Although she accepts him, she cannot control the repulsion he evokes.[10] "Of all the people in the world I hate Sir Griffin Tewett the worst," she cries passionately, "[though] I shall have to lie to him" (*Eustace,* 413). But Lucinda is no more able to lie than to play a role. Her sanity snaps and she ends up in a madhouse. In this society, the love of truth can destroy those who possess it.

Lucy Morris, the romantic heroine of *The Eustace Diamonds,* is not beautiful. This (heavily disguised) bit of good fortune enables her to escape the pressure to sell herself in marriage—a pressure which destroys Lizzie and Lucinda as moral beings. Lucy has no choice but to become a governess. "Too fond of the truth to tell lies of herself even to herself" (*Eustace,* 98), Lucy wants to be valued for what she is. For a while, she succeeds in this endeavor. She is hired by Lady Fawn, who appreciates her talents, and she triumphs when the clever barrister Frank Greystock proposes to her. At this point, it looks as if honesty has indeed been the best policy for Lucy. But Lucy's honesty enjoys only a short-lived triumph. The remainder of the novel shows that Lucy is by no means immune from the contagion of the dishonesty pervading her world.

Though Lucy lives in a moral backwater at Fawn Court, Frank (whose Christian name comes to seem inappropriate indeed as the story progresses) does not. He is, in fact, as typical a product of this society as Lizzie herself, though there is less excuse for his failure to eschew its vices. The barrister described earlier in this chapter, who seeks to envelop his cases in increased mystery . . . is Frank. The member of parliament described earlier in this chapter, who is ready to attack the opposing party, whatever the merits of the policy at issue . . . is also Frank. Frank doesn't pay his debts. He admires large scale fraud and asserts that there is an "almost contemptible littleness about honesty" (*Eustace,* 521). Nor, though he loves Lucy, does Frank value female integrity: "He had never declared to himself that deceit or hypocrisy in a woman was especially abominable. . . . [He] would say that some amount of affectation was necessary to a woman's character" (*Eustace,* 151).

No sooner does Frank propose to Lucy than he fears that he would be foolish to marry a woman who has "neither money nor beauty . . . nothing to give . . . beyond her mind and her heart" (*Eustace,* 586). He neglects Lucy cruelly, while flattering himself that he is exhibiting "a truth seldom found in this degenerate age," because he has not *yet* jilted her (*Eustace,* 254). Like the novel's other genteel deceivers, he expects credit for honesty. "Do not use such a word as that to me," he says huffily, when justly accused of lying (*Eustace,* 326).

Though Frank is quite deceitful, he is not a completely bad fellow (as the narrator repeatedly asserts). But even if he has some redeeming features, there is an irony implicit in honest Lucy's loving such a dishonest man.[11] Although the Fawns appreciate Lucy, her life with them is not completely satisfactory and she faces a threatening future. Status and wealth—and not love alone—are the romantic heroine's rewards. If Lucy is to obtain them, she must marry a successful man. But a successful man is likely to share the values of his society. Hence there is a certain symbolic fitness to honest Lucy's choosing dishonest Frank. Lucy's choice between veracity and success is just as dichotomous—if not quite as obvious—as the choices that face Lizzie and Lucinda.

Frank ceases to communicate with Lucy for several months. During those months, his respectable family quietly encourages him to jilt her. It is true that Frank proves himself "nobler than his friends" by deciding to marry Lucy in the end, for they feel no compunction in advising him to break his promise (*Eustace,* 726). But though Frank returns to Lucy, he remains the flawed man he has always been, "noble" only in a limited, comparative sense.

Lucy is in no position to let herself admit this. For if she were to acknowledge that Frank's behavior has revealed a serious flaw in his character, how could she promise at the altar to obey him? But if she does not marry him, she must remain a governess. The best option Lucy has is simply to forget what Frank has done to her. And so, with startling inconsistency, she tells herself that "there was no sin to be forgiven. Everything was, and had been, just as it ought to be" (*Eustace,* 744). When Frank returns to her, Lucy actually kisses his hand—the very hand which had previously landed so many solid blows "on the strong shield of her faith," battering it "out of all form and service" (*Eustace,* 569).

But that's how it has to be. In a dishonest world, honest people must compromise in order to achieve the "happy" ending of social acceptance. And so this story—a romantic comedy in form only—ends on an ironic note, as Lucy, "triumphing, with mingled love and happiness," tells the Fawns that Frank's family has forgiven her for not being rich or beautiful, and has accepted her as his bride (*Eustace,* 745).[12] Lucy never lies, but she has begun to fool herself. The Lizzie-Lucy-Lucinda equation thus turns out to be closer than it initially seemed.

The instinctive honesty of Lucinda and Lucy does not survive intact, because virtues need a supportive environment in order to flourish. If public standards of honesty are low, well-intentioned, but stupid, people like Lord Fawn cannot look to them for guidance. Nor can the powerless retain their honesty unimpaired if it wins little response from those who control their fate. The perversion of virtue—not social disorder—is the penalty exacted by a low general standard of morality.

And a low standard of general veracity may ultimately threaten the survival of honesty as a moral concept, even though the principles of common morality are difficult to eliminate from ordinary thought and speech. The treatment of promise ethics in *The Eustace Diamonds* suggests that the concept of honesty still retains its force in this dishonest world. But it is not clear how long such a state of affairs can continue.

A promise is a statement about one's *intentions*—a binding declaration which is nonetheless subject to certain unstated conditions. Promises can be broken, without dishonesty, in several circumstances. Many principles of common morality concerning the fine points of promise ethics come up in *The Eustace Diamonds* when its characters discuss its three marriage engagements—though their analyses are not always offered in good faith.

Early in the novel, Lizzie engages herself to Lord Fawn, who tries to renege when he learns that she has seized the Eustace diamonds under suspicious circumstances. Promises are generally thought to be contingent on certain suppositions, which are assumed by both the promiser and the promisee. If these suppositions prove false, the promise is not binding. Appealing to this principle, Fawn suggests that his engagement was made on the supposition that a marriage to Lizzie would not disgrace him. Since he did not know about the scandal of the necklace when he proposed, he should now be released. Lizzie retorts that she is merely keeping property that she believes to be her own. Since Fawn must have known that she would keep her own property, there was no false supposition—and the promise must be performed.

Promises are not generally thought to be binding when the promisee releases the promiser from his obligation. Because Lucy agrees, she does *not* offer to release Frank from their engagement when she realizes that he wishes to escape. She knows that Frank does not deserve such easy absolution from the guilt he has incurred. Most interpreters of common morality think that it is wrong to perform an immoral promise: on this premise Lucinda grounds her decision to break her vow to marry a man she hates. And the principle that promises which cannot possibly be kept are null and void is the basis on which Frank's family advises him to jilt Lucy after he learns how poor they will be: "All his friends told Frank Greystock that he would be ruined were he to marry Lucy Morris" (*Eustace,* 725).

In *The Eustace Diamonds,* honest and dishonest characters alike discuss promise ethics in conventional terms. Common morality controls the way they formulate ethical issues, though they inhabit a society which tolerates great misconduct. Even Lizzie, ignorant of so many things, is not morally ignorant: "Of what was wrong and what was right she had a distinct notion" (*Eustace,* 93). And if common morality survives among the novel's characters as a set of concepts, the narrator's remarks on the art of the novel reveal his belief that it also survives in the thought of his readers.

Many Victorian readers shared Frances Cobbe's view that "it is not competent to art . . . to describe society as nothing better than a mass meeting of knaves and fools."[13] According to the narrator of *The Eustace Diamonds,* such readers expect novelists to create idealized heroes and heroines. They can no more stomach an honest representation of people whose antecedents resemble their own, than the novel's genteel characters can stand to hear a genteel liar called by his proper name. Although Victorian authors often indulge readers with the idealizations they demand, the narrator of *The Eustace Diamonds* refuses to participate in this practice of "untrue portraiture" (*Eustace,* 355). Like real people, his characters are "often cross and foolish, and sometimes treacherous and false" (*Eustace,* 357). The narrator's remarks on fiction implicate contemporary readers and writers in the dishonesty that *his* novel describes, while his own practices resist this corruption.

But the very fact that the narrator offers "honest" characterizations suggests that an appeal to honesty *can* succeed. He expects *The Eustace Diamonds* to be read, though he addresses it to an audience which usually prefers flattering fictions to depressing truths.[14] Hope for the future, then, can be found in the integrity of the moral tradition.

The moral tradition may not survive permanently, however. For in Trollope's view, theory tends to follow practice, not the other way round.

In his travel book, *South Africa,* Trollope writes that the "teaching of religion has never brought large numbers of Natives to live in European habits, but . . . European habits will bring about religion."[15] And in *The Fixed Period,* as we shall see in Chapter 9, a philosopher's theoretical attack on common morality is easily deflected by its established authority, as a practice, over the conduct of ordinary people.

The situation in *The Eustace Diamonds* is the opposite of that in *The Fixed Period*. Common morality here has lost much of its authority over conduct, though it still influences the way in which people think about moral issues. This is an inherently unstable situation, because no moral system can be taught solely as a set of abstract concepts divorced from action. Children come to understand common morality primarily through the specific directives about conduct that they receive from adults and from the example those adults set them. Theoretical instruction plays a less significant role. To some degree, then, both the authority *and* the comprehensibility of common morality depend on its consistent observance in practice. Erosion of that observance could compromise its survival, though such a process would take a long time.[16] Unlike many of his contemporaries, Trollope is not worried about the social consequences of declining veracity. But he *is* worried about the moral consequences that might ensue if the actual standard of conduct in English society should fall below a certain level. And this may account for the gloomy tone of *The Eustace Diamonds*.

4

Morality and Individual Advantage in *Phineas Redux*

EIGHTEENTH- AND NINETEENTH-CENTURY utilitarians often suggest that only after wise customs and laws, backed by judicious punishments, have brought the interest of the individual into harmony with that of society as whole, will people in general act morally—or *should* they. In *The Methods of Ethics,* Sidgwick wonders if society has yet reached a condition in which obedience to morality is clearly the best policy for everyone to follow. Is "our present . . . life" in modern Europe really so ordered that "by observing the moral rules that prescribe certain modes of behaviour towards others we shall always tend to secure the greatest balance of happiness to ourselves?" Sidgwick asks (*Methods,* 162–3). His answer to this question is a qualified "no." For although Sidgwick thinks that "conduct commonly recognised as virtuous is *generally* coincident with that which enlightened self-love would dictate," he is also sure that these two paths sometimes diverge (*Methods,* 173).

And when they diverge, Sidgwick does not believe that individuals ought to reject self-interested conduct in favor of "conduct commonly recognised as virtuous." *The Methods of Ethics,* as we saw in Chapter 2, argues that from any agent's perspective, his own "good on the whole" is the *sole* aim that reason can justify. For the basic principle of *utilitarian* ethics—that right actions promote the greatest happiness of the greatest number—is rational from the perspective of the universe, but not from that of any given individual, while the time-honored principles "commonly recognised as virtuous" have no ultimate foundation in reason.

In *Phineas Redux* (1873), Trollope asks a similar question about the relationship between duty and advantage in the modern world. And he offers an answer that has much in common with Sidgwick's.[1] But there are two differences in their analyses: Trollope does not believe that moral confusion need be a serious problem for conscientious men and women; Sidgwick does. And unlike Sidgwick, Trollope rejects the notion that people need not act morally when good conduct proves disadvantageous. In *The Eustace Diamonds,* Trollope denies that the authority of morality can be validated by an appeal to its desirable social consequences—in *Phineas Redux* that its authority can be invalidated by an appeal to its undesirable individual consequences. Taken in conjunction with one another, the two novels demonstrate that, for Trollope, morality is a self-sustaining, autonomous social practice.

Trollope agrees with Sidgwick that moral agents are often punished for doing what morality commands. But here, as always, Trollope draws a sharp distinction between common morality, custom, and law as practices which may dictate different courses of action. When such conflicts occur, Trollope is certain that morality takes precedence over law, which in turn takes precedence over custom. Sidgwick, however, merges these three practices into an all-encompassing system of ethical directives which he calls "the received notions of Duty" (*Methods,* 163).

Sidgwick knows that "the systems of rules" which constitute the received notions of duty "may be mutually conflicting," but he has no way of resolving their demands (*Methods,* 164). He therefore concludes that conflicting moral pressures can create insoluble conceptual difficulties. For Trollope, however, such conceptual problems are rarely serious. Trollope's morally sophisticated characters thus escape one kind of suffering experienced by Sidgwick's conscientious men and women: the painful inability to discover where their duty lies.

In discussing the reasons why moral agents are sometimes punished for doing their duty, Sidgwick follows Bentham in referring to the rewards "consequent on conformity to moral rules" and the punishments "consequent on their violation, as the 'sanctions' of these rules" (*Methods,* 164). Such sanctions are either "external" or "internal." "The former class will include both 'Legal Sanctions,' or penalties inflicted by . . . the sovereign; and 'Social Sanctions,'" which are either the advantages that may be "expected from the approval and goodwill of our fellow-men generally . . . or the annoyance and losses that are to be feared from their distrust" (*Methods,* 164). The "internal" sanctions are either the reactions of conscience, or "some effect on the mental constitution of the agent produced by the maintenance of virtuous . . . habits" (*Methods,* 164).

Sidgwick thinks that this typology of sanctions explains why virtuous conduct and personal advantage diverge when "the received notions of duty" are internally inconsistent. If an individual's own moral code differs from that of his community, for example, he cannot avoid punishment. "External" sanctions threaten him if he violates generally accepted moral norms, "internal" sanctions if he ignores the voice of conscience.

Sidgwick argues that sanctions often conflict when "the Positive Morality of any community undergoes development, and is thus subject to changes which affect the consciences of the few before they are accepted by the many; so that the rules at any time sustained by the strongest social sanctions may not only fall short of, but even clash with, the intuitions of those members of the community who have most moral insight" (*Methods,* 164). In Sidgwick's view, an individual's morality is most likely to diverge from that of his community as the result of moral progress: positive morality is in the process of improvement and this can cause problems for advanced thinkers. Such improvement occurs, of course, when rational consequentialism replaces the chaotic moral tradition Sidgwick calls "the received notions of duty."

But Trollope does not view the replacement of common morality by consequentialism as a progressive development. Trollope and Sidgwick agree that an inherited morality and utilitarianism are both influential in Victorian England. And they agree that creeping consequentialism is to a certain extent characteristic of the era. But unlike Sidgwick, Trollope deplores this trend. For Trollope, moral progress occurs when society applies the *stable* rules of common morality more comprehensively through the medium of improved customs and laws—*not* when it tosses them aside in favor of consequentialist calculation.

In Trollope's novels, then, the decent man's morality is likely to diverge from the "positive morality of the community" because he clings to a deontological approach which some of his fellows no longer respect. Not surprisingly, the Sidgwickian "conflict of sanctions" that Phineas Finn experiences in the early sections of *Phineas Redux* comes about in just this way. As Phineas attempts to re-establish himself in London, he gets into trouble because his code of conduct differs from the communal code, which has indeed drifted towards consequentialism.

When *Phineas Redux* opens, its hero is a moral man whose moral commitments have never been seriously tested. It is true that at the conclusion of *Phineas Finn,* Phineas resisted the temptation to jilt his fiancee when a rich woman offered him her hand—and that he resigned a valuable government office on an issue of conscience. But Phineas was rewarded for his decency with a lovely wife and a sinecure which his political friends gave him as a consolation prize. His scrupulous conduct won him far more than the cold comfort of a clear conscience—Sidgwick's "internal sanction" of good behavior.

In *Phineas Redux,* the hero's moral commitment is again tested in affairs of love and politics. But here the tests are serious indeed. Phineas feels bound to befriend Lady Laura Kennedy, who rejected him in order to marry a wealthy man, because she still loves him, because he once loved her, and because she has aided his career. But her demands, her whining, and her desire for a renewal of his love make the relationship intensely painful to him. Eventually the history of Laura's marriage gets into the newspapers. Since Laura's love for Phineas was indeed the reason why her marriage disintegrated, it's easy for the unscrupulous editor Quintus Slide to tell the tale in a way that bears heavily on Phineas. And the continuing involvement in Laura's affairs that Phineas's loyalty necessitates provides Slide with additional evidence to pervert.

Slide doesn't have a very active conscience, but such conscience as he does possess is thoroughly consequentialist. He believes that public morality improves when fearless editors expose the degeneracy of the "Upper Ten"—even though, in the process, privacy is violated and facts are distorted for effect.[2] The article in which he accuses Phineas of sexual misconduct is "full of falsehood and malice. . . . But Mr. Slide . . . had been led by practice to believe that the use of such weapons by one in his position was . . . beneficial to the public."[3] (Sidgwick, as I noted in Chapter 3, also believes that "beneficent" lies can sometimes be justified.)

Slide's calumnies obtain some credence, and Phineas finds that his reputation has indeed been harmed. But he can defend himself only by publicizing facts about Laura which are sure to be construed in a manner that will injure *her* as unfairly as Phineas himself has already been injured. This course of action, as we saw in Chapter 1, is forbidden by the rules of common morality that define what is due to the honor and reputation of others. Phineas has no choice but to suffer in silence.

Slide's dishonesty is symptomatic: the world of *Phineas Redux* is losing its firm grip on the rules of common morality that Phineas respects so scrupulously. Some people agree with Slide that newspapers may retail scandal in order to deter misconduct and thus promote "purity of morals" (*Redux,* I:194). And those to whom this sort of self-serving consequentialism has become acceptable do not find Slide's conduct reprehensible or admire Phineas's restraint. Phineas has no choice but to "bear his undeserved punishment like a man" (*Redux,* I:283). Though they differ sharply in their judgments of consequentialism, Sidgwick and Trollope agree that individuals must suffer "social sanctions" when their moral commitments differ from those of their society.[4]

Phineas's attempts to obtain political office reveal a second tension between acting rightly and attaining happiness, one that Sidgwick also discusses. Sidgwick argues that the social sanctions punishing immoral behavior are often ineffective because the "turbid and fluctuating streams of social opinion upon which the good or ill repute of individuals mainly depends" contain "conflicting and divergent elements" which lead to divergent moral judgments (*Methods,* 168). Small but unified groups, such as "religious sects and parties . . . trades and professions," develop moralities that conflict "to a certain extent with the opinion of the general public" (*Methods,* 168–9).

According to Sidgwick the "most striking part of this divergence" between "professional" moralities and the communal code consists "in the approval or excusal of practices disapproved by the current morality: as (*e.g.*) licence among soldiers, bribery among politicians . . . unveracity of various degrees among priests or advocates" (*Methods,* 169). When the code of a professional group commands conduct that violates accepted morality, the professional finds himself in a quandary. "For a man who, under these circumstances, conforms to the stricter rule, if he does not actually meet with contempt and aversion from those of his calling, is at least liable to be called eccentric and fantastic" (*Methods,* 169). But if he chooses to follow the professional code, the public will censure him, perhaps severely.

When professional ethics permit conduct which the public disapproves, then, professionals cannot escape "social sanctions." And because such individuals have no way of resolving the conflicting demands of these two codes, they cannot be sure which code they *ought* to obey when public morality conflicts with group morality. Sidgwick argues that they are sure to suffer the "internal" sanction—pangs of conscience—whatever they decide to do.

As a Liberal politician, Phineas learns how painful the conflict between "group morality" and "public morality" can be, but he has little difficulty prioritizing their demands. On his return to England, Phineas realizes that he can win election to Parliament only by advocating the disestablishment of the Church of England. Phineas wins a seat and the voters express such enthusiastic support for disestablishment that the Conservatives decide to advocate the measure—simply as a means of staying in power. The Liberals decide to oppose the Conservatives' bill, a bill that they ought in principle to approve.

Phineas ultimately decides to break his electioneering pledges and support his party. The argument on which he bases this expedient decision is not disingenuous, though it is certainly flimsy. His promise to vote for disestablishment was limited by the tacit condition that the details of the measure would be arranged by trustworthy politicians. Since the Conservatives secretly oppose disestablishment, they cannot be trusted to arrange its details. But it takes some time before Phineas can bring himself to break faith with the voters on the basis of this fragile argument, for the integrity of his own promises is important to him. And his hesitation costs him dearly. The party's leaders decide that Phineas is an unpredictable politician—"eccentric and fantastic," as Sidgwick puts it—not to be trusted with a government appointment.

Honesty does matter more to Phineas than party loyalty—and his breach of professional "ethics" is judged harshly by the party's moral arbiters. One colleague tells Phineas that "a man so burthened with scruples as to be unable to [support his party without any hesitation on any issue] should keep himself aloof from public life" (*Redux,* I:177). For the reasons cited by Sidgwick, Phineas is punished when he reveals dissatisfaction with the lax ethical code of the British politician.

According to Sidgwick, the "professional moralities" that tolerate misconduct are neither more nor less authoritative than the public's moral code—each "system of rules" is one of the "fluctuating streams of social opinion" that together constitute "the received notions of duty." For Trollope, however, these professional "moralities" have no moral authority; they are simply defective customs which must be brought into compliance with the principles of common morality. Phineas suffers when he hesitates to follow their dictates, but no confusion is involved. Unlike Sidgwick, Trollope does not think that such problems result from the incoherence of England's moral inheritance.

In Sidgwick's view, the "systems of rules" that constitute the "received notions of duty" are inherently confusing and confused. He therefore sees morality in Victorian England as a matter of individual choice: each person negotiates an idiosyncratic code of conduct, by choosing among the varied resources of the moral tradition. Under such circumstances, shared moral commitments are at a minimum and no conscientious person can count on the approval of other conscientious people. This is one reason why Sidgwick believes the "social sanction" to be so unreliable.

But Trollope's view of common morality as a stable, structured ethic implies that anyone who honors it can expect many like-minded people to understand and to appreciate the nature of his commitment—even in a society, like that of *Phineas Redux,* where it has lost some of its influence. Cicero says in *De Officiis* that "of all fellowships . . . none is more important, and none stronger, than when good men of similar conduct are bound by familiarity. . . . Nothing is . . . more tightly binding than similarity in conduct that is good."[5] And Trollope agrees. In *Phineas Redux,* Phineas finds that the bonds linking him to his most morally aware friends are indeed exceptional when he is falsely accused of murder (of which more will soon be said). He is deeply moved by "the marvellous love" that a half dozen men and women, who affirm his innocence, shower on him during the murder trial (*Redux,* II:220).[6]

To this extent, the social sanction of good conduct functions much more reliably in Trollope's moral universe than in Sidgwick's. But it is important not to exaggerate the value of this "reward." During Phineas's murder trial, most people believe that he is both disreputable and guilty—and he knows it. The trust of his friends cannot counterbalance this terrible punishment. Though the good man in Trollope's novels can count on a consolation that is denied to the inhabitants of Sidgwick's moral world, this consolation does not tip the balance of advantage in favor of scrupulous behavior.

If the first half of *Phineas Redux* focuses on the social sanctions of moral conduct, its second half is more closely concerned with the relationship between legal sanctions and moral choices. When one can be punished legally for adhering to morality, duty and happiness may diverge dramatically. Like Sidgwick, *Phineas Redux* does indeed suggest that "Law and Positive Morality" are often "at variance."

As systematic consequentialism replaces a chaotic moral tradition, Sidgwick argues, "there may easily be laws [in force] commanding conduct that is considered immoral by some . . . enlightened fraction of the community." For any member of that "fraction," the internal sanction will "operate against the legal [sanction]" (*Methods,* 164). The process of legal change described in the Palliser novels also can create problems for the conscientious individual.

When Phineas runs for Parliament, a law has just been passed forbidding the practice of bribery in parliamentary elections. Trollope views this legislation as an admirable attempt to the apply time-honored principles of common morality forbidding dishonesty to an area where they have not previously operated. Law and morality come into conflict in *Phineas Redux* because this desirable reform proves premature. Though common morality claims precedence over law and custom, each of these three separate practices possesses its own sphere of influence. When they conflict, the results may be unpredictable.

The members of Parliament who passed the antibribery law in response to a powerful moral argument, supported by powerful public pressure, are not enthusiastic about the reform they've enacted. Phineas, however, approves of the new law and determines to run a clean campaign. His opponent, Mr. Browborough, a comic exemplar of the professional ethics of the British politician, votes with his party on every issue and is perfectly willing to purchase his seat. So when the election proves close, Browborough simply offers "£2 10s. a vote" (*Redux,* I:38) and emerges as the winner. Phineas petitions to have the result of the election reversed.

The hearing on Phineas's petition goes smoothly. Phineas proves "that [many] votes were void by reason of gross bribery" and Browborough loses the seat after enduring "two or three very uncomfortable days," during which his dishonesty is exposed. So far the legal sanction for misconduct does fall, as it should, on the guilty Mr. Browborough, while the innocent Phineas is "triumphant" (*Redux,* I:117). Indeed, virtue is so triumphant here, that we can expect an ironic reversal to follow.

Shortly afterwards, Browborough is prosecuted for bribery in the criminal courts. And at the prospect of this new trial, parliamentary sympathy swings in his direction. The antibribery law notwithstanding, the House feels no real need for an electoral purity which few of its members practice. "The idea of putting old Browborough into prison for conduct which habit had made second nature to a large proportion of the House was distressing to Members of Parliament generally," the narrator wryly remarks (*Redux,* II:29). Browborough is acquitted, though "his safety [lies only] in the indifference of his prosecutors—certainly not in his innocence" (*Redux,* II:30).

A law designed to extend the scope of common morality cannot easily be enforced when the customs of the group it affects are at variance with its commands. How can you enforce the new law if most of the members of the profession to which it applies will not obey it and if, in refusing to obey it, they are merely honoring professional mores that "habit has made second nature" to them? No wonder Browborough becomes "quite a hero" for suffering the injustice which the bribery trial is supposed to have done him (*Redux,* II:30–31). In a ridiculous miscarriage of sanctions, he is acclaimed for disregarding both common morality *and* law in favor of custom.[7] But this miscarriage occurs only because the society depicted in *Phineas Redux,* like Sidgwick and other Victorian moral philosophers, does not understand as clearly as it should that morality and law take precedence over custom. (The novel's readers can of course rest assured that this situation is temporary: morality and law *will* eventually succeed in eliminating the custom of electoral bribery).

Sidgwick offers a second reason why the legal sanction cannot be counted upon to punish immoral conduct: "in the most orderly societies . . . the administration of law and justice is never in so perfect a state as to render *secret* crimes always acts of folly, on the score of the legal penalties attached to them" (*Methods,* 165–6). *Phineas Redux* examines two secret crimes, both committed by a Polish con man who calls himself Rev. Joseph Emilius. For one of these crimes, bigamy, Emilius is punished, but he is never convicted of the other, the murder of Phineas's political rival, Mr. Bonteen.

For that crime, Phineas himself is nearly convicted on flimsy circumstantial evidence. The novel's policemen and lawyers are remarkably inefficient and smug: among them, they almost bring the innocent Phineas to the gallows. Phineas is saved only because his friend Madame Max Goesler manages, a few hours before the case goes to the jury, to produce evidence exonerating him. But her success is a fluke. In fact, nothing in the British legal system *itself* guarantees that an innocent man cannot be executed or that a murderer cannot escape, as Emilius ultimately does. The legal sanctions of secret crime are every bit as unreliable as Sidgwick suggests.

Phineas Finn observes the rules of common morality as he struggles with one moral difficulty after another. But because common morality is no longer authoritative for certain of his fellows, his conduct sometimes evokes the "social sanctions" of disapproval and hostility. As Phineas smarts under undeserved censure, his conversation acquires a disagreeable, embittered flavor, revealing how "sore and unhappy" he is (*Redux,* II:35). When "legal sanctions" are added and Phineas nearly dies for a crime he didn't commit, he concludes that "I do not care for my life in a country where such injustice can be done" (*Redux,* II:220). Phineas's experiences, then, certainly support Sidgwick's claim that "the satisfaction that attends the performance of duty" is not "always sufficiently intense to turn the balance of prospective happiness in favour of morality" (*Methods,* 170). But even in the depths of despair, Phineas never considers relaxing his moral commitments in the future or regrets having honored them in the past.

In *Phineas Redux,* neither Parliament nor the legal system turns out to be a marvel of hereditary wisdom. The lofty purposes of these institutions are in tension with the mundane realities of their existence as the sum of the professional mores which compose them. For this reason, the novel's upbeat conclusion does not imply that good people will necessarily obtain their just deserts. Phineas is rehabilitated after his acquittal, but his happiness results from good luck, not from a reliable system of sanctions. It does not neutralize the work's bleak moral vision. The novel closes, not with a celebration, but with a traumatized man's retreat from the world, as Phineas refuses the government office for which he once longed.[8]

Trollope further clarifies the relationship between duty and reward by contrasting Phineas's conduct with that of Lady Laura Kennedy, whose attempts to live a moral life are less successful than his. By marrying Robert Kennedy while in love with Phineas, Laura commits a wrong that cannot be righted. After the marriage, she finds herself in a kind of moral dilemma that will be discussed in detail in Chapter 8: the perplexity that results when a misdeed makes further misconduct inevitable. If Laura pretends to love Kennedy, she will be guilty of dishonesty, and if she leaves him, she will violate her marriage vows. Common morality directs people who find themselves in such situations to choose the lesser evil, since *some* moral principle must be violated whatever they decide to do.

In this case, it seems clear that Laura ought to confine the evil consequences of her own mistake, as far as possible, to herself. She should stay with Kennedy, whatever the cost to her own feelings. For if she seeks relief by leaving her husband, she will bring suffering and scandal upon him, upon Phineas, and upon her own family. Her closest female friend tells Laura that "if a . . . married woman" be oppressed by a guilty love, "she should lay it down at the bottom of her heart, out of sight, never mentioning it, even to herself" (*Redux,* II:99).

Laura disagrees. She leaves Kennedy, arguing that "it can't be right that a woman should pretend to love a man whom she loathes" (*Redux,* I:172). But Laura's argument is disingenuous. Confronted with a choice between two wrongs, Laura simply takes the course that is least unpleasant for herself. She claims that her motive is an unwillingness to violate common morality's prohibition against lying. Yet she is quite willing to violate the rule that forbids one to break a freely given promise.[9] Laura is by no means the conscientious deontologist that she pretends to be, or that Phineas really is.

Like Phineas, Laura is willing to encounter social sanctions if she must and feels victimized by social sanctions gone awry. Laura even sounds a bit like Phineas when she complains that "people are so hard, and cold, and stiff, and cruel, that one can never do what one feels, oneself, to be right" (*Redux,* II:254). But here the similarities between Laura and Phineas end: when Laura falls afoul of the "positive morality" of her friends, it is because *she* has lost touch with common morality, not because they have. Though not consequentialist in form, her moral reasoning is just as self-serving as Quintus Slide's.

Though Laura's friends pity her deeply, they don't admire her conduct. There are good reasons why Laura loses the one social reward which truly decent men and women in the novels of Anthony Trollope almost invariably receive: the recognition of their own decency by like-minded individuals. And her desolation helps the reader to appreciate the value of this reward. It does not outweigh other sanctions, yet it is very important.

Phineas has an impressive grasp of common morality and a sincere desire to do his duty. Though Laura's moral sophistication proves much less impressive, she is misguided rather than comfortably immoral. A complete typology of the connections between attitudes toward duty and the attainment of happiness also must include the person who feels absolutely no allegiance to morality. For this reason, Sidgwick concludes his discussion by considering the possibility that "Rational Egoists" might, in general, do better in life than conscientious men, while in *Phineas Redux,* Trollope invents his own Rational Egoist as a foil to the virtuous Phineas.

Sidgwick's Rational Egoist strives only to maximize his own advantage. As his name implies, the Rational Egoist is not an out-of-control pleasure-seeker: he restrains "each of his passions and impulses . . . within such limits that its indulgence should not involve the sacrifice of some greater gratification" (*Methods,* 172). But, as Sidgwick points out, it is rational for the Rational Egoist to factor the moral sentiments of his community into his egoistic calculations, because these sentiments are "powerfully supported by the sympathy of others, and [by] their expressions of praise and blame." Even if such social sanctions function imperfectly, it would make no sense to ignore them (*Methods,* 173).

The Rational Egoist, then, will act morally whenever he thinks it prudent to do so. What separates Sidgwick's Rational Egoist from his Just Man is the value for good conduct in and of itself: the Rational Egoist does not care about virtue as virtue. He is committed to a selfish principle for judging the rightness or wrongness of actions. If the Rational Egoist behaves immorally while pursuing his own advantage, he will not suffer the internal sanction that punishes adherents of morality in the same situation. Sidgwick concludes that in proportion as the social and legal sanctions miscarry, Rational Egoists will be happier than men who try to follow the confusing, inconsistent rules "prescribed by Duty and Virtue" (*Methods,* 175).

Phineas Redux also uses the contrast between a Rational Egoist and a Just Man to further its examination of the relationship between duty and advantage. The novel's Rational Egoist, Mr. Maule, like its Just Man,

Phineas Finn, is a suitor for the hand of Madame Goesler. The aging, widowed Mr. Maule is able to enjoy himself as a man about town on a limited income, because he completely disregards his responsibilities as a landowner and a father. He seeks his own gratification and nothing else, but he seeks it with extreme care: "No one knew better than Mr. Maule that the continual bloom of lasting summer which he affected requires great accuracy in living. Late hours, nocturnal cigars, and midnight drinkings, pleasurable though they may be . . . are fatal at once to the husbanded candle-ends of age. But such as his days were, every minute of them was precious to him. . . . He had so shuffled off his duties that he had now rarely anything to do that was positively disagreeable" (*Redux,* I:186).

Mr. Maule is indifferent to moral issues and so, like Sidgwick's Rational Egoist, he suffers no pangs of conscience. He also is indifferent to other people's judgments—provided that they don't stop asking him to dinner. And in the somewhat decadent world of *Phineas Redux,* he is easily able to avoid such a serious social sanction as that. Even his twenty-year liaison with a married woman leaves him socially unimpaired. He conducts the affair with his usual discretion and discretion is all this society insists on where sex is concerned. It's true that he fails to marry Madame Goesler, but neither does he let his failure upset him: "Mr. Maule . . . never allowed any aspiration to proceed to such length as to be inconvenient to his feelings should it not be gratified" (*Redux,* I:217). Mr. Maule is the same contented man when the novel closes that he was at its outset: nothing happens to dismay or change him.[10] If the contrast between Phineas and Laura proves the value of the moral recognition that good men receive, the contrast with Mr. Maule shows how little the true immoralist need lose.

To Bradley's ironic query, "Why should I be moral?," Sidgwick answers that one should "be moral" because sanctions really do reward good conduct most of the time (Bradley: 58). And he quickly adds that there is no clear obligation to "be moral," in the old-fashioned sense, in any situation where good conduct is likely to be punished. *Phineas Redux* reaches a different conclusion. Though Trollope shares Sidgwick's belief that the rewards of good conduct do not always outweigh its disadvantages, the best of his characters still feel obliged to adhere to common morality. Like Bradley, the novel argues that often "a man is moral because he likes being moral," even though he does *not* like the consequences (Bradley: 62). By suggesting that its authority over individuals does not depend upon considerations of personal advantage, *Phineas Redux* deflects a serious utilitarian challenge to common morality.

5

Moral Interpretation in *Lady Anna*

THE CLAIM that people *should* pursue their own advantage is sometimes based upon a theory of human motivation which holds that they *cannot* in fact do anything else: this theory is called psychological hedonism. According to the psychological hedonist, all human action is motivated by the desire for pleasure—not necessarily sensual pleasure, of course, but pleasure of some sort. To the objection that many people choose to do the "right thing" at the cost of great personal suffering, the psychological hedonist replies that such individuals are compensated for their sacrifices by the pleasures of a clear conscience or social approval. To an adherent of this theory, Trollope's portrait of Phineas Finn, a man who endeavors to behave well even when the balance of sanctions clearly favors the relaxation of his moral standards, would not be wholly credible.

As a theory of human motivation, psychological hedonism won some acceptance in Victorian Britain. Its merits were asserted by many able utilitarian thinkers, who argued that "pleasure, and freedom from pain, are the only things desirable" for any human being (Mill, *Essays,* 278). And its congruity with ordinary experience also helped to make psychological hedonism acceptable, according to one of the theory's critics, T.H. Green. Men in general, Green suggests, are aware that they feel pleasure when they obtain what they desire. They are therefore disposed to agree when told that this pleasure is what they must have desired in the first place. So intuitively plausible are hedonistic theories, Green claims, that many people whose own moral conduct is actually quite principled "may now be heard arguing" moral issues from a hedonistic perspective, asking "whether this occupation or that, this or that habit of action . . . conveys the greater amount of pleasure and is therefore the more to be approved" (Green, 418).

But despite its many advocates and its apparent congruence with ordinary experience, psychological hedonism remained a controversial theory in Victorian England. It was rejected by the many adherents of common morality who believed that they could resist the promptings of desire if duty demanded it, as well as by intuitionist and idealist moral philosophers. Bradley and Green both attack it vehemently, arguing that, although pleasure accompanies the fruition of desire, this pleasure is not itself the object of desire.

According to Green, one cannot receive pleasure from realizing any state of affairs unless one *already* desires its realization. The awareness of a desire precedes the belief that achieving the desire will generate pleasure. Unless a man *wants* to climb Mount Everest, he would not think of climbing it as a source of pleasure. Although he will derive pleasure from his achievement, we can't say that his motive in undertaking the grueling climb is to get this pleasure, because he gets this pleasure only *if* he is motivated to climb.

Neither Green nor Bradley would deny that pleasures are sometimes sought directly, as when a man eats a cream puff although he is not hungry. But in general, both philosophers hold, that sort of conduct is the exception, not the rule. As Bradley puts it, "happiness, for the ordinary man, neither means a pleasure nor a number of pleasures" (Bradley, 96).

If one rejects psychological hedonism, one must come up with a different theory about what moral agents want and how they ought to act in order to satisfy their desires. Bradley and Green both argue that, in Bradley's words, people seek "the realization of [a] concrete ideal of life" (Bradley, 96). They attempt, in action, to realize an integrated vision of the self: a self that achieves a sense of permanence by linking its own satisfaction with the good of all humanity, and ultimately with the will of the universal spirit. Therefore, Bradley argues, "the self-evolution of ourselves and of humanity [is] the end" of moral conduct (Bradley, 125). But Bradley understands that self-evolution is a vague concept. From what source is it to derive its content?

As we saw in Chapter 2, Bradley holds that the path to self-evolution is defined by the mores of the community. A man "is what he is because he is a born and educated social being, and a member of an individual social organism" (Bradley, 166). He can realize himself as a part of humanity only by participating in the society to which he belongs. Thus the moral man finds a satisfying sense of self in his "station and its duties." He "is one of a people, he was born in a family, he lives in a certain society, in a certain state. What he has to do depends on what his place is, what his function is, and all that comes from his station in the organism" (Bradley, 173).

Bradley acknowledges that in a corrupt or confused community, the moral man must think critically about the mores that define his role. But he does not believe that this situation often arises. In Bradley's view, "my station and its duties" is an adequate guide for most of the people most of the time. "What is moral in any particular case is seldom doubtful. Society pronounces beforehand," Bradley remarks, and for most of us, unquestioning obedience to these commandments is sufficient (Bradley, 198). "If you could be as good as your world," Bradley admonishes the reader who aspires toward an elevated moral standard, "you would be better than most likely you are . . . to wish to be better than the world is to be already on the threshold of immorality" (Bradley, 199).[1]

Like the theories of so many Victorian philosophers, Bradley's moral theory does not discriminate clearly between moral principles (whose dictates must be honored) and mores (whose moral acceptability can never be taken for granted). But Bradley's acknowledgement that mores are *occasionally* so corrupt or confused that the moral man must reject their guidance reveals his inability to dispense with this distinction altogether. For without some such distinction, he can account neither for moral criticism nor for moral progress.

Trollope's 1874 novel, *Lady Anna,* is constructed like those strange hypothetical cases against which philosophers are fond of measuring their theories.[2] Through its farfetched plot, the novel tests contemporary assertions concerning the aims and desires of moral agents: neither the assertion that men and women seek pleasure, nor the assertion that they seek moral self-realization, proves to be an accurate generalization about *all* humanity. Some of the novel's characters seek pleasure; some seek to realize an ideal of life that is not moral at all; and others seek to realize themselves as moral beings. Like common morality, then, *Lady Anna* denies that all humanity shares (or ever will share) a single aim. And it finds the notion that pleasure could be that aim particularly absurd. But it also refutes, with some vehemence, the view that moral self-realization can be achieved by passively following the mores of the community.

Trollope places his heroine, Lady Anna Lovel, in a situation that achieves philosophic significance at the expense of social plausibility. After resisting an exceptionally pure hedonic temptation, Anna finds that "my station and its duties" is also a problematic guide to conduct. She must decide for herself where self-realization can be found and what morality requires her to do. Bradley suggests that most societies offer their citizens such satisfactory guidance that they need make few interpretive efforts for themselves. But *Lady Anna* argues that no society is so perfect that one can simply accept one's place in it. Although Trollope always gives great weight to the community's role as a source of values, he never equates duty with adherence to custom. *Lady Anna* implies that, without active interpretation, there can be no true moral agency.

When *Lady Anna* opens, during the 1810s, Earl Lovel, a rake in the time-honored eighteenth-century style, is devoted to seduction—a "sport" at which he has "acquired great skill."[3] After failing to conquer her by his preferred method, the earl marries Josephine Murray. Shortly afterwards, he tells his wife that their marriage is bigamous and abandons her. *His* conduct certainly appears to validate the premises of psychological hedonism. But few of the novel's other characters resemble him in this particular.

Josephine gives birth to a daughter, Anna. Penniless, she struggles to prove the legality of her marriage. To establish herself and her daughter as members of the aristocracy is the ideal of life that Josephine seeks to realize at great cost to her own comfort. But there is nothing especially moral about this ideal. During her years as an outcast, Josephine's only friend is a radical tailor, Thomas Thwaite, who spends his life savings on her legal fees, motivated by a (moral) desire to punish the earl. His son Daniel is Anna's only friend.

Well, you can see where this is going. Anna and Daniel are engaged when her father dies. His title descends to a young cousin, but Anna will inherit his wealth, unless the young earl can prove that the old earl had a living wife when he married Josephine Murray. It looks as though this will not be easy to do. So the young earl's lawyer suggests that he acknowledge Anna as the heiress, marry her, and share the wealth. It seems like a good idea both to Lord Lovel and to Anna's mother.

Lord Lovel, handsome, charming, honorable, "and every inch a gentleman" (*Anna,* I:61), woos Anna, who is taken to visit at his uncle's country rectory. The contrast between Daniel Thwaite and Lord Lovel could hardly be more striking. Daniel is "swarthy, hardhanded, black-bearded,—with . . . an innate coarseness about his mouth which betokened roughness as well as strength" (*Anna,* I:112). On several occasions he is described as "reeking" with the sweat of manual labor (*Anna,* I:200).[4] He lacks style, to put it mildly. Lord Lovel, on the other hand, seems to Anna "soft . . . tender, so pleasant,—so loving. . . . beautiful, noble,—almost divine" (*Anna,* I:125). When she catches "the sweetness of his breath" (*Anna,* I:126), she nearly swoons.

The contrast between the genteel life at the Lovels' rectory and Anna's rough upbringing with the Thwaites is equally extreme. At the rectory "the niceness, the ease, the grace of the people around [Anna], won upon her day by day, and hour by hour. . . . She seemed to live among roses and perfumes. There was no stern hardness in the life, as there had of necessity been in that which she had ever lived with her mother" (*Anna,* I:158–9).

Perfume in place of stench, ease in lieu of stern necessity, flattery instead of isolation: this is what Lord Lovel's proposal offers to Anna. Sensual joys, social approval, and the happiness of delighting her mother await Anna if she accepts—an alluring mix of what Mill called lower (animalistic) and higher (social) pleasures. Daniel promises Anna no pleasures to compare with these, and the exaggeratedly sensuous imagery with which Trollope describes Lord Lovel's beauty and sweetness underscores this point. By the time Trollope is through with him, Lord Lovel appears to be a sort of hot fudge sundae in human form.

Anna herself is aware that "it would be pleasant to be a Countess, and to go among great people" and she knows that Lord Lovel is an extremely "pleasant" chap (*Anna,* II:186). In fact, the word "pleasant" is repeated dozens of times as the narrator discusses Anna's reaction to the Lovels. So pure, so seductive, is this call to pleasure that Anna nearly yields.

As the narrator later remarks, "the softness of the new Elysium" at the rectory "had well nigh unnerved" Anna, who "had just not fallen into the pot of treacle" (*Anna,* II:149). But this image of cloying, deadly sweetness implies that too much pleasure can prove sickening indeed. By accepting Lord Lovel, Anna will gain a life of pleasure, but lose her identity as a moral being. "When I thought of it alone—I hated myself," she remarks perceptively (*Anna,* II:187).

So Anna does resist, though she knows that she will be punished for resisting—by her mother, by the Lovels, and by society at large. And Trollope presents her decision as a rejection of pleasure in favor of moral self-realization. Indeed, it seems that he has chosen every one of the details that define her unusual situation in an attempt to exclude all ambiguity concerning this point. But Anna's flight from pleasure should not surprise anyone who has read much Trollope.

Trollope's novels do indeed celebrate the natural human desire for such goods as wealth, love, and meaningful work—and they also depict a number of genuine hedonists, like Anna's father, whose selfishness is appalling. But it is nonetheless true that his characters are far more likely to reject pleasure than to seek it in a crassly hedonistic manner. Unlucky men like Josiah Crawley treasure their grievances against society, traumatized women like Lily Dale are unable to pursue happiness, members of Parliament devote their lives to advocating legislative reforms which have no chance of success, and people are addicted to amusements they don't enjoy.

"The man who hunts and doesn't like it," the subject of one of Trollope's sketches, remains devoted to the sport, though he routinely falls from his horse and spends hours chasing the beast through cold, muddy fields, enduring indescribable "misery."[5] Trollope would not have accepted Mill's assertion that "desiring a thing and finding it pleasant . . . are phenomena entirely inseparable" as an accurate account of human motivation (*Utilitarianism,* 237).

But, as Green remarks, psychological hedonism is an attractive theory, which seems to be confirmed by common sense—and this may explain why many readers have resisted *Lady Anna*'s vigorous attempts to discredit it. A few of the novel's critics actually offer hedonistic readings of the attack on psychological hedonism that it develops through Anna's characterization. J. Hillis Miller, for example, argues that Anna's "strong sexual attraction" to Daniel Thwaite—rather than the moral reasons that she herself offers—motivates her rejection of Lord Lovel.

As Miller observes, Daniel certainly is stiffer and more masculine than the boyish earl. But for all that, Anna clearly finds Lord Lovel only too attractive. She feels "a heavenly sweetness between them" (*Anna,* I:161) when Lord Lovel caresses her, tells herself sternly that "there must never be another kiss" (*Anna,* I:162), and resolves that "if it was possible, she would cease even to dream of him" (*Anna,* I:213). A woman sexually obsessed with another man would hardly need to make these resolutions. Yet it is Miller's view that, by remaining true to Daniel, Anna is seeking pleasure after all, the sexual pleasure of a union with the man who really excites her. A latter-day Benthamite, Miller "unmasks" Anna as a closet hedonist, despite all the evidence to the contrary that Trollope has carefully provided.[6]

Like Miller, Anna's friends and family are psychological hedonists. They simply assume that an introduction to the pleasures of aristocratic life will persuade Anna to marry Lord Lovel. But when Anna's conduct disproves their theory, when they come to realize that her strongest motive is the desire to achieve moral self-realization, her friends try to convince her that it is her duty to jilt Daniel. The hedonic seductions which fill the novel's first quarter are replaced by reiterated commands that Anna heed the guidance offered by the moral theory that Bradley calls "my station and its duties."

An impressive array of authority figures—Anna's mother, the lawyers on both sides of the case, and many friends—tell Anna that as an aristocrat she ought to marry within her own order. In a typical episode, an older woman discourses on "the sacred duty which Lady Anna's rank imposed upon her to support her order." This friend tells Anna that "God Almighty has chosen that there should be different ranks to carry out His purposes, and we have His word to tell us that we should all do our duties in that state of life to which it has pleased Him to call us" (*Anna,* II:83). Again and again Anna hears that she will destroy herself morally if she disregards the duties of her station. Unlike Bradley himself, Anna's friends refuse to admit that such a prescription might be problematic in any way.

But Anna rejects this advice in order to remain true to Daniel. She is unable to accept the crass version of "my station and its duties" articulated by her pastors and masters as a satisfactory guide to conduct, because her "station" as an aristocrat does not offer her the morally integrated sense of self she seeks. For Anna's childhood position as a penniless girl of uncertain parentage was very different from the station that her friends now want her to occupy—and the two stations imply different duties.

Anna's rise in status is, of course, unusually dramatic and abrupt. But social mobility of a less startling sort was very common in nineteenth-century England. Though unusual in their details, Anna's experiences are typical of the period in their general outlines. This is suggested by the fact that, as the novel closes, the aristocracy is preparing to absorb not merely the well-born Anna, but the plebeian, radical Daniel as well. The Lovels celebrate Daniel's marriage at their home, and men of fashion begin to talk about proposing him for membership in a London club! Even so extreme a social transition as this can easily be accommodated.[7]

In such a society, the many people who undergo changes in status must negotiate between the obligations of the past and the imperatives of the present. The theory that one's station in life is a given and that the duties pertaining to it are obvious does not offer them adequate guidance. These men and women must define their own duties for themselves—case by case. Bradley's view that "my station and its duties" is a generally reliable guide to morality harks back to a simpler, more stable era (and Bradley is indeed far more conservative, both socially and politically, than Trollope).

Anna herself is never convinced that her newly acquired position as a titled heiress must, in an unambiguous sense, be her station in the world—or that her only duties must be those of her new position. Before her status changed so radically, she made commitments with implications for the future. For many years, Anna says, she "was a poor girl . . . sometimes almost without shoes to my feet, often ragged, solitary. . . . Then there came one lad, who played with me. . . . He was good to me, when all others were bad" (*Anna,* II:186). As Anna sees it, a sense of duty motivated her to love the man who treated her so kindly. "When one takes so much, one must give in return what one has to give," she argues (*Anna,* I:263).

The many social authorities in the novel who endorse a simple version of "my station and its duties" find themselves forced to acknowledge this problem. Thus Anna's legal advisers repeatedly remark that Anna was only a child when she made her commitment to Daniel (actually, she was over twenty). Their intent is to suggest that Anna was not a responsible moral agent when she gave Daniel her promise, and that therefore her promise is void. But when Anna's advisers use this argument, they acknowledge her moral obligation to her past. They dare not rely completely on the argument that she need only perform the duties of her new station.

When Anna was a little girl, her mother preached to her the importance of rank. But nothing in Anna's original environment reinforced her mother's lessons—quite the contrary. The ragged child was mocked mercilessly for her aristocratic pretensions. She learned that her noble father had treated her mother with vicious cruelty. Daniel and Thomas Thwaite, the two men whose kindness made her life bearable, were artisans. No wonder Anna learned to hate her rank.

Thus, though Anna is susceptible to the hedonic allure of aristocratic life, her early experiences preclude the possibility that her self-realization can come from accepting her place as a member of the ruling class. To devote herself to the duties of her new position she must renounce her most important moral commitment, her engagement to Daniel. And she must act in opposition to the deepest emotions of her formative years. Her present and past selves will be doubly divided—and divided in a manner that she finds morally unacceptable.

When her advisers tell Anna that she must do her duty in that rank of life to which it has pleased God to call her, she is not convinced by the arguments they offer to support their position. Bradley argues that the man who rejects his station and its duties to seek a higher standard of conduct is probably a deluded egomaniac, on the verge of losing touch with morality altogether. But the terms in which Trollope presents Anna's conflict suggest that he holds a different theory of moral aspiration.

According to Bradley, the moral agent normally faces a clear choice between performing his hereditary duties as defined by the mores of his community and seeking some bizarre (and probably deluded) form of moral elevation on his own. But Trollope suggests that Anna's choice is really a problem in moral interpretation. In order to decide how to act, she must consider both the demands of common morality and the local mores her advisers take so seriously. And in this respect, she is no different from anyone else.

The very authorities who tell Anna to perform the duties of her station know that the matter is more complicated than they admit. Anna's lawyer, Serjeant Bluestone, tells her that she should marry Lord Lovel because "the whole prosperity of a noble and ancient family must depend on what you may do. . . . Here in England the welfare of the State depends on the conduct of our aristocracy" (*Anna,* I:267). But Bluestone is talking through his wig. The narrator reproaches him for his dishonesty: "Oh, Serjeant Bluestone, Serjeant Bluestone! how could you . . . give expression to a sentiment utterly opposed to your own convictions!" (*Anna,* I:267–8).[8] For in nineteenth-century England, hereditary peerage, class distinctions, and political equality were staple issues of an endless debate about the relationship between common morality and particular laws and customs.[9] When Anna's friends assert that the prestige of the aristocracy must be maintained, as if this were a point on which there could be no disagreement, they are simply trying to manipulate her. But Anna knows that this view is only "a fair subject for argument," not an established truth upon which she is bound to act (*Anna,* II:271).

If a person cannot trust social authorities, he should not follow their advice until he has decided, for himself, that their advice is good. And *Lady Anna*'s authority figures, especially its lawyers, are an untrustworthy bunch, as Anna herself comes to realize. They are willing to misrepresent, and in some cases even to lie, in order to achieve their goals: much of the novel is devoted to an investigation of the disagreeable hanky-panky in which they engage. We come to see that Anna cannot trust these manipulative men in opposition to her own interpretive understanding of what common morality demands.

And yet the societies depicted in such novels as *The Eustace Diamonds* and *The Way We Live Now* are far more corrupt than the one described in *Lady Anna*. In terms of the confusion and rottenness that Bradley deplores, indeed, the world of *Lady Anna* is an absolutely average Trollopian world. Even the most dishonest of the novel's lawyers is essentially well-meaning and responsible. For Trollope, then, societies in which "my station and its duties" does not provide an acceptable guide to conduct are the norm—rather than the rare exception that Bradley believes them to be. Interpretive efforts to mediate between morality and mores are inescapable in most, if not all, social worlds.[10]

By now it may sound as if there is no moral ambiguity surrounding Anna's decision to marry Daniel, but this is not the case. A promise *may* be broken, according to common morality, if the conditions that were understood—by both the promiser and the promisee—to limit its scope no longer obtain when the time to perform it arrives. As we saw in Chapter 3, this point also comes up in *The Eustace Diamonds*. It can plausibly be argued that Anna's promise to marry Daniel was subject to a tacit condition: that her social status would be such as to render marriage with a tailor fitting, when the time for the wedding came. But, as it happened, her social condition changed so abruptly that her marriage to a manual laborer became ludicrously unsuitable before it could be celebrated. According to this line of reasoning, then, Anna is exempt from performing her promise (though she cannot be exempted on the ground that she was too young to make a meaningful promise when she accepted Daniel's proposal).

And so it is not surprising that even Daniel himself finds "his mind . . . absolutely divided" about what it is Anna's duty to do (*Anna,* II:101). When Daniel seeks advice from an aging romantic poet, the former revolutionary recommends that he encourage Anna to follow "the usages of this as yet imperfect world" and marry Lord Lovel (*Anna,* II:15). There are moments when Anna herself almost agrees with this pompous sage, who seems to have been modelled on Southey.[11]

Anna has a real moral problem, one not easy to solve. As Trollope noted in *An Autobiography,* the very readers who blamed Anna for marrying Daniel would also have condemned her had she been false to him. Common morality does not offer her (or the readers of her story) unambiguous guidance.

But as the novel progresses, the exigencies of her situation force Anna to hone her casuistical skills. The line of conduct she follows probably respects common morality better than the option she rejects.[12] For when Anna agreed to marry Daniel, they both understood that her legitimacy might well be established at some future time. Because they had this knowledge, the claim that Anna's promise was subject to the tacit condition that her social status would remain unchanged is less convincing than it might otherwise be. Anna "realizes herself" in the course of the novel, overcoming both solicitations to pleasure and the attempts of social authorities to teach her oversimplified moral lessons. But she does this through resistance and independent interpretation—not through the passive acceptance that her advisers (like Bradley) prescribe.

The treatment of the novel's minor characters reiterates the critique of "my station and its duties" that Anna's story suggests. The most "Bradleyan" characters are the Lovels, who—like some of the Tories in Trollope's other novels—do not improve upon acquaintance. Though they embody venerable English values, the deficiencies of their position become evident as their commitments are tested in new situations.

Lord Lovel's uncle, Reverend Lovel, originally believes that Anna is an imposter. He is sure that Daniel Thwaite is "busy in concocting an enormous scheme of plunder. . . . That a Radical should be honest was to him incredible" (*Anna,* I:62). Since he has some evidence to support this opinion, it seems forgivable, although mistaken. A man who thinks that God wants everyone to do his duty in his appointed station has a good reason for disliking radicals. When the narrator blandly remarks that Reverend Lovel is a "thoroughly humane and charitable man," he implies that Lovel's prejudice against such socially disruptive people as Anna and Daniel is not a serious flaw (*Anna,* I:62).

But Reverend Lovel looks less appealing when he refuses to alter his opinions in the face of irrefutable evidence that he has misjudged his radical opponents. After Anna's legitimacy has been established, she and Daniel generously give half her income to the young earl. Asked to accept Anna as his cousin, Reverend Lovel refuses, asserting that "I have always understood that Lady Lovel . . . was never Lord Lovel's wife. For twenty years I have been sure of it, and I can't change so quickly as some other people" (*Anna,* II:259). This traditionalist believes what he believes solely because he *has* believed it; if he let himself think about his beliefs, they would quickly become problematic.

The narrator's initially approving tone increases our surprise as we come to understand how intolerant of difference and disagreement the Lovels really are. When, after all that has occurred, one of the Lovels advises against entertaining Daniel on the ground that "you can never wash a blackamoor white" (and then goes on to mutter "some further remark about negroes," which is fortunately inaudible), it's fairly appalling (*Anna,* II:263–4). The Lovels' commitment to custom has ossified in a most unattractive manner.[13]

One must criticize the mores of one's society, then. But one cannot simply ignore them. *Lady Anna* pokes fun at its most extreme rebels against "my station and its duties" for their intellectual arrogance and for their dependence on the very laws and customs that they pretend to despise—just as it mocks Tories like the Lovels who oppose the slightest alteration in custom or law. Anna's father is a man to whom "all obligations were distasteful . . . and all laws" (*Anna,* I:22). But though he ignores every duty pertaining to his position, old Lord Lovel is far from despising "those [laws] which preserved to him the use of his own money" (*Anna,* I:22).

Without the law, he could not live as he does. Even the form that his "rebellion" takes is determined by tradition—for the reprobate aristocrat is a cultural cliche.

Daniel Thwaite is a decent man, nothing like the old earl, but his radical principles involve him in similar contradictions. A foundationalist reformer, Daniel believes that existing laws can be replaced by "a perfect form of government, or rather of policy, under which all men might be happy" (*Anna,* I:44). But his egalitarian principles are motivated by class hatred, and he attacks only the inequalities by which he suffers, not those which empower him: as a married man, he intends to grasp all the privileges which custom gives to husbands. "For a man with sound views of domestic power and marital rights always choose a Radical," the narrator remarks cynically (*Anna,* II:253).

Daniel's belief that he lives without accepting guidance from the mores of his society proves unwarranted. Where gender is concerned, at any rate, he follows custom to the letter. Nor are his efforts to devise a reformed system of mores for his society especially successful. And so Daniel is probably fortunate that it never occurs to him to question the principles of common morality, as many other nineteenth-century thinkers did. For it's doubtful that he could have improved upon them. It is, in fact, his sincerity as a casuist in the tradition of common morality—not his acumen as a reformer—that wins Daniel the reader's respect.

Lady Anna thus suggests that laws and customs should neither be slavishly accepted, nor harshly rejected. "My station and its duties" is indeed where one ought to start thinking about how to achieve the moral self-realization that some human beings prefer to a life of pleasure. But it cannot be the place where thinking stops. Because local mores and the principles of common morality are often in tension with one another, the integrated moral self must always be constructed out of traditional elements through an active process of interpretation.

6

Moral Responsibility in *John Caldigate*

JOHN BLACKWOOD began publication of Trollope's novel *John Caldigate* in the April 1878 issue of *Blackwood's Magazine*. As the monthly numbers appeared, Blackwood came to dislike the book's eponymous hero, whom he found "cold [and] self satisfied." Trollope agreed that Caldigate's smugness "chokes off the sympathy" that enables readers to identify with fictional protagonists, but he refused to alter the character in any substantial way.[1] For Trollope, there was nothing new about this problem. The romantic heroes in his earlier novels were often less than admirable—and contemporary readers were often annoyed to find such defective young men playing the hero's role.

The most unusual feature of *John Caldigate* is not the nature of its hero, but rather the handling of the character who shares center stage with him. Somewhat surprisingly, this is not the romantic heroine, Hester Bolton, but her mother, Mrs. Bolton. An Evangelical fanatic with an iron will and considerable powers of self-deception, Mrs. Bolton is hardly a likeable woman. But she is a major character who must be taken seriously. In these respects, she differs from Trollope's other Evangelicals.

For in most of Trollope's novels, the important Evangelical characters, like Mrs. Proudie and Mr. Slope in *Barchester Towers,* are caricatures; Evangelicals who are treated seriously and sympathetically, like Lady Macleod in *Can You Forgive Her?* or Mr. Saul in *The Claverings,* are usually relegated to minor roles.[2] In this chapter, I hope to show that the symmetrical moral scheme upon which *John Caldigate* is premised explains why Trollope treats Mrs. Bolton differently from the other low church fanatics who populate his fiction. She mirrors the hero in the amount of attention she receives, as well as in the mixture of censure and sympathy that she evokes, because the moral errors she commits mirror the errors he makes. These errors are related to an important controversy in Victorian ethics: the debate over determinism and the freedom of the will.

In general, Victorian moral philosophers with a theistic bent affirm mankind's God-given freedom of choice. They hold that an appeal to a person's moral aspirations is the best way to influence his or her conduct. And they believe that attributions of moral responsibility make sense. But secular Victorian moral philosophers generally disagree. They argue that conduct is causally determined. They hope to influence behavior by tinkering with the circumstances in which men and women make moral choices according to known psychological laws. And they find the idea of moral responsibility unacceptable. As Jerome Schneewind sums it up, the Victorian intuitionists and idealists "supported their ethical positions . . . by defenses of free will," while "the utilitarians countered with empiricist analyses . . . in favor of determinism."[3]

But this broad-brush account of the free will-determinism controversy needs some qualification. In fact, religious moralists of the Victorian era do not always find it easy to mediate between their view of divine providence and their desire to prove that man is free and responsible. For if God is omniscient and omnipotent, in what sense can man be said to choose his own course of action?

Calvinists solve this problem by concluding that man is not free, that everyone's fate is predestined according to a divine plan. Though the Calvinist position is not a popular one among the most religious of the Victorian moral philosophers, they do acknowledge the conceptual difficulty that the Calvinists sought to solve. F.D. Maurice and Charles Kingsley—influenced by Samuel Taylor Coleridge—offer their own solution to the problem that divine omnipotence poses for theories of human freedom. They argue that man *becomes* free by submitting his own will, enslaved to the corrupt desires of his fallen condition, to the beneficent will of God.[4] These men do indeed rescue some sort of moral liberty, but the condition they describe is not freedom of choice in the usual sense of the phrase.

And some secular Victorian moralists are dissatisfied with a systematic determinism that eliminates the concept of moral responsibility. These moralists notice a tension between their conviction that all actions are causally determined and the indisputable fact that, as Sidgwick put it, the immediate affirmation of consciousness at the moment of volition supports a belief in human freedom. Most of the empirically inclined Victorian philosophers agree that even if this immediate affirmation is mistaken, without it we could not act at all. From this perspective, determinism has no relevance to ordinary life, where we must assume that meaningful choice is possible.

J. S. Mill, indeed, was so uncomfortable with the practical implications of necessitarianism that, a recent commentator argues, he attempted "to modify" this strand of his thought by interweaving it with "ideas of free will and self-development" derived from German idealism.[5] The result was an uneasy philosophical compromise: Mill suggested that education might utilize the laws of psychological development "to inspire a freely willed virtue."[6] In Victorian moral philosophy, then, religious belief is not always linked to a belief in freedom, nor does determinism always imply a complete denial of responsibility.

Trollope's handling of the free will-determinism controversy in *John Caldigate* is illuminated by the analysis offered in the first chapter of Bradley's *Ethical Studies,* published two years before the novel. The chapter is entitled "The Vulgar Notion of Responsibility in Connexion with the Theories of Free-Will and Necessity." Neither Trollope, nor Bradley, couples a belief in freedom of the will with belief in a Christian God. And both suggest that an extreme affirmation of freedom may be no less destructive to a person's sense of moral responsibility than a commitment to determinism. In these respects, Trollope's novel reveals an awareness of the nuances of the contemporary debate.

As a recent book on moral philosophy puts it, Bradley follows Hegel in arguing that philosophical development takes place "through the negation of limited and partial positions, and the retention of them in their negated forms as elements within the whole."[7] In Bradley's chapter, the limited positions to be negated and redefined are free-will theory and necessitarianism. Their more acceptable synthesis is to be found in "the vulgar [i.e. ordinary] notion of responsibility" (Bradley, 1). Since common morality is our "ordinary" morality, it is not surprising that this "ordinary notion of responsibility" simply reaffirms two of common morality's basic premises: that moral agents are free to choose and that choosing to act well is not easy. Because good behavior does not come naturally, we need the guidance and support of morality.

Like Bradley's discussion, the novel introduces, sequentially, the limited positions it will ultimately synthesize. John Caldigate, whose mistaken belief in the freedom of the will constitutes a sort of Hegelian thesis for the novel, is the focus of its first third. Mrs. Bolton, whose determinism offers an antithesis to Caldigate's position, is the focus of the work's middle section. A postal clerk named Bagwax synthesizes the acceptable aspects of free will and determinism. Though he appears for the first time more than two thirds of the way through the book, Bagwax remains very important until it ends.

To reveal the flaws in free-will theory, Bradley chooses to state it in "its clearest form," rather than to treat the toned-down versions of it that have been offered by its "English expositors" (Bradley, 11). According to his paradigmatic version, the will can be called free only if its decisions are uncaused and unpredictable. Free-will theory claims that the "I, in the act of 'I will,' is . . . superior to all its contents, desires, &c., and descends into them only by its own *libertas arbitrii*" (Bradley, 11). An agent who is free in this sense must decide, when faced with a choice, to do one thing rather than another. But no reason can explain this choice, because if there *were* such a reason, the choice would, to some degree, result from its antecedent conditions. And so the self would cease to be completely free. For freedom to exist, choice must be arbitrary. Free-will theory in this pure form holds that "freedom means *chance;* you are free, because there is no reason which will account for your particular acts" (Bradley, 11).

Bradley finds this theory unacceptable for two reasons. First, by ignoring the fact that actions can often be predicted, it denies the reality of character: free-will theory "asserts that the actions are in no case the result of a given character, in a given position" (Bradley, 12). But common sense rejects the view that moral character is radically unstable. Second, this particular version of the free-will theory, unlike most versions, does not support attributions of moral responsibility. Actions must be arbitrary in order to be free, but a person cannot be held responsible for actions that do not flow from his or her character.

The necessitarian theories of "our Westminster Reviewers" in general are equally unacceptable to Bradley (Bradley, 2). Many utilitarian thinkers hold that because there exist laws of character, analogous to those of physical science, it will someday be possible to predict any action whose antecedent conditions are fully known. Necessitarian thinkers assume that "given such a character and such a stimulus, such an act must follow" (Bradley, 50). They believe "character to be inborn and unalterable," so that "we may say that what solicits the character to react alters, but the character does not alter" (Bradley, 51). Since the actor can neither control his inherited character, nor his circumstances, he cannot be held responsible for his actions. According to these philosophers, Bradley claims, "responsibility [and] moral desert" are "horrid figments of the imagination" (Bradley, 2).

Bradley has several objections to determinism. He agrees with Sidgwick that the responsibility ordinary men and women feel for their own actions poses a serious problem to the theory. And he asserts that people are clearly capable of growth and change, though determinists suppose character to be unalterable. Like extreme forms of free-will theory, then, necessitarianism flies in the face of common sense in both its denial of responsibility and its view of character.

In presenting his own position, Bradley synthesizes the valid aspects of these two views and concludes that character is pretty much what the man-in-the-street believes it to be. It is neither radically unstable, as free-will theory argues, nor completely stable, as the determinists claim. Rather, it is "relatively fixed" (Bradley, 52). Free-will theory rightly holds that the will plays an unpredictable role in the never-ending process of character formation. The determinists are correct in stressing the degree of predictability that inborn disposition and social circumstances impose upon this process. As Bradley puts it, "the [raw] material of the character is disposition in relation to circumstances," but the active will is also important (Bradley, 52). Because the will plays a role in forming the moral self, a man must answer for his actions in "the court of conscience," even though he is *not* responsible for the forces with which his will must contend (Bradley, 3).

Because the active will guides character development, this process cannot be predicted with perfect precision. "What I am I have made myself, out of, in relation to, and against my raw material with its external conditions," Bradley writes. As time passes, "the self is more and more determined and realized, and so excludes possibilities, fixes and closes itself; in short, gets hardened. . . . But the fixedness is not more than relative. There is always a theoretical possibility of change, and sometimes a good deal more than this" (Bradley, 52–53).

The action of the systematizing will cannot always be predicted, nor can the "raw materials" of the character ever be systematized into a totally coherent self. Not even the most stable character is completely stable, Bradley suggests, because impulses that are in tension with the systematized, developed character remain a part of the self. In moments of stress, the "underground self comes to light . . . and the result of the volition is uncertain," even in the most consistent individuals (Bradley, 53). The actions of an internally contradictory, inadequately systematized character will be far more difficult to predict.

In Bradleyan language, John Calidgate is one of those men whose character is slow to fix itself, to get hardened, and whose conduct is therefore marked by persistent instability. By disposition, John is a moral chameleon with a taste for pleasure and a susceptibility to the pleasures of female companionship. As a boy, John becomes involved in a romantic entanglement with one of his cousins, an entanglement that he is too weak to resist. When John goes to Cambridge, he gets involved with a fast set and does as his peers do: he lives roisterously, bets on horse races, and is soon in debt.

At this point, John realizes that his moral condition is unsatisfactory: "He had certainly made a failure of his life so far. . . . He had not hitherto chosen the better part."[8] He makes a resolution, his first exercise of active will. He will go to Australia as a gold miner and through self-discipline will regain the money he has squandered. He also resolves that when he returns home, he will woo Hester Bolton, a pure girl from a pious family. "It should be his romance, and he swore that he would cling to it" (*Caldigate,* 21).

John is aware of his own instability and of the need to improve his character through acts of will—hence these rather stiff resolutions. But it is not as easy to systematize the self as the still-youthful John supposes. Character may only be *relatively* fixed, but it is relatively *fixed.* Like the free-will theorists Bradley discusses, John hopefully assumes the primacy of the unconditioned will.

John's disposition puts up more of a fight than he expects. As he makes his way to Australia by boat, John unconsciously adapts himself to yet another social and moral microcosm. "There is no peculiar life," the narrator remarks, "more unlike our usual life, more completely a life of itself, governed by its own rules . . . than life on board ship" (*Caldigate,* 37). The rules include so large an allowance for flirtation that everyone is "more or less in love by the end of the first week" (*Caldigate,* 37). Adaptable and susceptible, John is, of course, more in love rather than less. The woman who attracts him is a widow named Mrs. Smith, of disreputable antecedents. By the end of the voyage, she and John have drifted into an engagement, which John regrets, as he regretted his entanglement with his cousin. The shipboard ambience and his innate weakness for women have caused him to break his vow of fidelity to Hester. His moral self is by no means fully systematized; his will is weaker than he thinks.

The nemesis of your average Australian gold miner is either speculation or drink. But in spite of his youthful surrender to race courses and riotous living, John manages to avoid both these pitfalls. During his stay in Australia, he keeps his resolution to save his earnings and stay sober. Thus he wins his first moral victory, a victory which reinforces his belief that the will can easily master both character and circumstance. Unfortunately, he isn't as successful in overcoming the most serious weaknesses of his disposition, as he is in resisting the lure of gambling and alcohol.

Trollope describes the early months of John's Australian sojourn in great detail, but after John strikes gold, he moves his hero offstage. We learn about the rest of John's adventure only through the brief letters he writes to his father, and not through direct description of the activities in which he takes part. In these letters, John presents himself as an altered character who can easily resist the pressures endemic to life in the bush. The self-satisfied quality that undermined Blackwood's sympathy for John surfaces at this point in the novel.

John's letters portray a writer whose moral self is so thoroughly systematized that he can only pity his less disciplined associates and wonder at their vices. "There is a style of letter-writing which seems to indicate strength of purpose and a general healthy condition on the part of the writer," the narrator remarks, and John writes to his father in this strain (*Caldigate,* 98). But the narrator notes sarcastically that "it need hardly be said that there was no mention . . . of Mrs. Smith" in these upbeat documents (*Caldigate,* 97). And the reader does wonder about her, for when she was last heard of, she and John were still engaged.

Unlike the free-will theorists described by Bradley—who believe that to affirm liberty is to deny causality—John does not espouse a theory whose logic mandates the rejection of moral responsibility. But his belief in the primacy of the will makes it conceptually difficult for him to account for any situation in which his disposition and circumstances win a triumph over his conscious intentions. Although he ought to take responsibility for such situations, he finds ways to evade it.

John returns to England with a fortune and soon becomes engaged to Hester. When the Boltons hear rumors of his shipboard engagement to Mrs. Smith, John flatly denies them. The reader knows that he is lying, but John seems unaware that he is not telling the truth. One possible explanation for this psychological oddity is that John's belief in the will has become a dogma which determines what facts find admittance into his mental universe. Any evidence that confirms his view of his own will as free and omnipotent, he consciously credits. Any evidence that does not, he ejects from his mind. John thus escapes responsibility for his moral failures, without having to question his belief in the power of the will.

When John learns that Mrs. Bolton thinks him unworthy of her daughter, he takes umbrage, telling himself that "there was no just cause for such aversion" (*Caldigate,* 124). Adopting a high moral tone with the Boltons, John marries Hester. Shortly afterward, Mrs. Smith appears in England to claim John as her husband. When John asserts that he never actually married Mrs. Smith, he speaks the truth. But in countering the accusation, John must disclose the whole story of his relationship with her.

The reader now learns that the untruth which John told about his shipboard engagement was not his only lie. He also denied that he and Mrs. Smith lived together as man and wife in Australia—and this revelation comes as a shock, for hitherto the reader has had access only to John's own cleaned-up version of his colonial adventure. We now realize, for the first time, how radically John has had to rewrite his past in order to maintain his belief in himself as a morally perfected being.

When the Boltons hear the story, even Hester's brother Robert, who favored the marriage, expresses disapprobation. John denies angrily that his relationship with Mrs. Smith was "disgraceful to me" (*Caldigate,* 177). "You or anyone else would be very much mistaken who would suppose that life out in those places can go on in the same regular way that it does here," he tells Robert. "Gold beneath the ground is a dangerous thing to touch, and few who have had to do with it have come out much freer from misfortune than myself" (*Caldigate,* 178).

Until this point, John has claimed proudly that his moral victories should be credited to his will—and he has erased those defeats which imply that his will is deficient. But he now must admit that he acquiesced in the prevailing Australian standards of sexual conduct. Since he does not wish to attribute this acquiescence to the inadequacy of his will or to his innate taste for female charms, he tries to dodge the blame he deserves, by attributing his behavior to circumstances alone. And so he changes tack abruptly, arguing that the nature of Australian bush life *compelled* him to make Mrs. Smith his mistress and that neither his disposition, nor his will played any role in the process. A given "deed must issue from my will . . . must be in myself" to be morally imputable to *me,* Bradley argues (Bradley, 6). And this imputability is exactly what John denies. He can thus assert that the episode with Mrs. Smith should be seen not as his own "disgraceful" wrongdoing, but as a "misfortune" caused by regrettable circumstances. After denying responsibility in this way, John refuses "to listen to any fault-findings as to [his] past life" (*Caldigate,* 177).

The undignified conceptual flip-flops in which John engages are probably inevitable, given the untenable belief in the will that he is trying to sustain.[9] He still has a lot of learning left to do. But during the second half of the novel, John gradually accepts responsibility for his own actions.

John's bigamy conviction, though undeserved, constitutes a fortunate fall. Public humiliation forces him to continue the systematization of his moral self, a process which, years earlier, he had prematurely declared complete. Forced to acknowledge that, on several crucial occasions, disposition and circumstances were too strong for his will, John can no longer see himself as a moral being "without a flaw . . . proud in his own strength, and his own rectitude" (*Caldigate,* 190). By the end of the novel, he is able to ask himself, "Though he had been wrongly condemned, had not all this come in truth from his own fault?" (*Caldigate,* 444–5).[10] In Bradleyan terms, John accepts the sobering fact that the struggle against flaws of disposition and external temptations can have no end. The moral self can never be completely systematized. Though people are free to choose, choosing to do right is always difficult.

John's experiences disprove the free-will theory he initially advocates: that character is subject to dramatic transformations because it is the creature of the unconditioned will. This theory is diametrically opposed to the deterministic position passionately espoused by John's enemy, Mrs. Bolton. Her determinism is the Calvinistic sort, not the scientific kind discussed by Bradley. But though their premises are very different, both varieties of determinism assume character to be a constant. Interesting evidence of the affinity between them is offered by the case of the nineteenth-century English historian Henry Buckle. A recent study notes that after Buckle lost his faith, the "residue of [his] early exposure to Calvinism" was transformed into the conviction that "if all the antecedents of the mind of an individual were known, one could predict his behavior."[11] This conviction underlies Buckle's deterministic theory of historical development.

For Mrs. Bolton, there are the sheep and there are the goats. Every man or woman is chosen by God for one fate or the other, and the seemliness of each person's conduct indicates the fate for which he or she is predestined. Mrs. Bolton is not prone to credit abrupt moral conversions—to put it mildly. In her universe, no one changes, and character can be interpreted through signs that are trustworthy because they are given by God. Unlike the scientific necessitarians, who hope that the laws governing human conduct will be fully known at some *future* time, Mrs. Bolton believes that she *already* knows, by revelation, all the laws by which characters can be read and actions predicted.

Mrs. Bolton does not hold herself to a high standard of moral responsibility. Convinced that her piety proves her to be one of God's sheep, Mrs. Bolton concludes that her conduct must be good simply because it is hers. Where John Caldigate avoids responsibility by lying about his actions or denying that they are imputable to his will, Mrs. Bolton avoids it by defining her own acts as blameless, whatever those acts may be. Though she is very hard on the "outside, active sins" which she feels no desire to commit, she does not find the "evil thoughts, [and] hardness of heart" to which she is given in the least "abhorrent" (*Caldigate,* 220). Further, Mrs. Bolton attributes the responsibility for her actions to her creed, which she invariably (and often disingenuously) cites as the ground for her decisions.

Like Bradley, then, Trollope suggests that *both* extreme believers in free will *and* extreme determinists are likely to deny the assumption of responsibility upon which common morality rests. It is their dogmatic assurance—rather than the side that they take in the free will-determinism debate—that results in this denial.

The judgments to which Mrs. Bolton's determinism gives rise are skewed and unreliable. But she has a point in refusing to credit abrupt character transformations. Characters are more fixed than John believes, though less fixed than Mrs. Bolton assumes. When John Caldigate returns from Australia claiming to be a new man, Mrs. Bolton cannot "be brought to think that one who had been so manifestly a goat should cease to be a goat so suddenly" (*Caldigate,* 167). This fanatical woman notices something genuinely incongruous in John's confident self-presentation, even before he is accused of bigamy. Nor is Mrs. Bolton's reasoning after she hears the bigamy accusation completely indefensible, though it proves mistaken. Deciding if a man has done something of which he stands accused is a kind of retrospective prediction: an attempt to determine whether the act imputed to him would have followed from his character and circumstances at the time. When Mrs. Smith appears in England, the facts to which John must admit reveal an extreme split between his public and private selves, or, to put it in Bradleyan terms, an unusually unsystematized self. Where such characters are concerned, prediction is difficult.

The bigamy accusation does not, as John himself claims, oppose "the whole tenor of my life and character" (*Caldigate,* 189). For his life and character to date have not actually had a consistent "tenor" at all. It is not unreasonable for Mrs. Bolton to conclude that this liar and fornicator may well be the sort of man who could commit bigamy, though other evidence suggests the contrary.[12] Mrs. Bolton errs only in assuming that John's character is thoroughly systematized and thoroughly evil, when it is still unsystematized: the mirror image of the error he makes.

Because her moral views incorporate a partial truth, Trollope does not turn Mrs. Bolton into a caricature, like so many of his other Evangelical enthusiasts. But he has some reason to fear that the reader will automatically classify Mrs. Bolton as one of the ludicrous Evangelicals—the Chadbands, Brocklehursts, and Mrs. Proudies—who throng Victorian fiction. Such a response would wrench the book's symmetrical moral scheme out of shape. And so Trollope tries to avert it through the narrator's commentary. For this reason I think N. John Hall is wrong to dismiss as "somewhat perfunctory" the narrator's reiterated demand that readers respect Mrs. Bolton in spite of her violently unattractive personality.[13]

Like John Caldigate, Mrs. Bolton proves capable of change. The learning experience that she undergoes is less dramatic than his, but she does qualify her necessitarianism, and by doing so, moves closer to the position that the novel endorses. Mrs. Bolton's moment of limited moral triumph occurs when she renounces her deterministic view of John as one of those "human beings who had, as it were, lost their souls before death, so that it was useless to think of them otherwise than as already damned" (*Caldigate,* 411–2). She whispers a reluctant acknowledgement that John did not run true to type by committing bigamy, although his youthful profligacy is an established fact. Her admission that John has grown through an exercise of will partially redeems Mrs. Bolton, whose own moral growth undermines her initial position.

Standing at the moral center of the novel is the postal clerk Samuel Bagwax, whose conscientious difficulties occupy much space in its concluding section. Bagwax's sensible response to temptation synthesizes the half-truths incorporated in free-will theory and necessitarianism, just as Bradley synthesizes them in the first chapter of *Ethical Studies*. Bagwax's view of freedom and responsibility is identical to the view assumed by common morality.

After John's bigamy conviction, his lawyer promises Bagwax a trip to Australia to investigate some ambiguous postal evidence which implies that John may be innocent. Bagwax desperately wants to take the journey, but before he leaves he discovers a way to prove John innocent by pure deduction. No one but Bagwax himself knows that the trip is now unnecessary—he can still go, if he keeps silent about the inferences he has made. He must decide whether or not to leave John in prison while he sets off on a junket.

As I noted in Chapter 1, common morality permits a person to conceal information that it would be inconvenient to reveal, except in situations where openness is necessary to prevent a wrong. At first, Bagwax argues that he should not have "to cut the nose off his own face" by publicizing his inferences about the Caldigate case (*Caldigate,* 384). But soon he sees that to postpone John's vindication *is* to acquiesce in the continuance of a wrong. As he thinks of "that young father torn from his paternal acres and cast into a vile prison," Bagwax realizes that he is morally obliged to reveal his discovery (*Caldigate,* 389).

But will Bagwax prove strong enough to follow the guidance of common morality? Fearing that his roving disposition may overcome his will to resist temptation, Bagwax seeks help from circumstances. He reminds himself that he lives in a society which values morality. Because he benefits from its high standards of decency, he tells himself, he has a reciprocal obligation to behave well. To stiffen his vacillating will, Bagwax firmly repeats to himself "Nelson's motto . . . 'England expects that every man this day shall do his duty'" (*Caldigate,* 352). Only then can he resolve to sacrifice his trip.

Indeed, Bagwax repeats Nelson's words so often that they become a running joke in the last quarter of the novel. "Duty," he says on one occasion, in tears at the thought of his lost journey, "Duty! England expects———. D——n it, who's going to whimper?" (*Caldigate,* 393). But Bagwax's Nelsonian mantra is not completely comic, for it reminds the reader that the responsible individual should not trust implicitly the primacy of the will. It is better to do as Bagwax does and seek any adventitious aid that the moral tradition makes available, in performing the difficult task of systematizing the character.[14]

As Sidgwick suggests, moral decision-making implies individual responsibility. But agents need the guidance and support of morality when the will and disposition lock horns. Of course, most men and women would be quite willing to admit this point. Like Bagwax, the average person neither trusts implicitly the strength of the will, nor claims exemption from responsibility on deterministic grounds. This view is, as Bradley observed, the ordinary, the vulgar, view of moral responsibility and it is the view upon which common morality is premised. But *John Caldigate* does not merely assume its validity. The novel offers a skeptical examination of opposing philosophical positions.

7

Cousin Henry and the Role of Expediency in Moral Reasoning

THE UNSTRUCTURED AND SUBJECTIVE consequentialist reasoning that utilitarian theories encourage was more worrisome to Trollope than the danger of rigidity implicit in an unquestioning adherence to moral precepts. But he was aware of the latter danger, as well as the former. The central structuring device in his 1879 novel *Cousin Henry* is its contrast between characters who have too little respect for rules of conduct and those who have too much. Trollope's admirable characters are prone to say *ruat caelum, fiat justitia,* when faced with a moral difficulty. And in general the novelist approves. But *Cousin Henry* looks at some ways in which this impulse can get out of hand.

In late 1876, Trollope had just finished reading "all Cicero's works from beginning to end"; in 1877, he wrote two articles on Cicero for the *Fortnightly;* and by 1879 he had reread most of Cicero's works for the second or third time, preparatory to drafting his biography of the Roman moralist.[1] *Cousin Henry* was thus written at a time when its author was steeped in Ciceronian lore—and, as Ruth apRoberts has noted, *De Officiis* was undoubtedly on Trollope's mind as he conceived it.[2]

I would like to argue that Cicero's influence on *Cousin Henry* is not confined, as apRoberts suggests, to the incident in which Henry Jones conceals his uncle's last will. Ciceronian moral distinctions underlie not merely this element of the plot, but the novel's other subplot as well. They underlie the characterization of Henry Jones, as well as those of the men and women whose behavior contrasts so strikingly with his.

De Officiis centers upon a problem which continued to concern nineteenth-century moral philosophers of every persuasion: the relationship between conduct that is principled or virtuous (honestum) and conduct that is expedient or beneficial in its consequences (utile). A re-examination of the issue in Ciceronian terms would have had obvious contemporary relevance in the 1870s. *Cousin Henry* offers such a re-examination.

Cicero takes the orthodox Stoic position that there can be no real conflict between honestum and utile, arguing that no worldly benefit can outweigh the loss of a clear conscience. "Dishonourableness itself," Cicero writes, "is bitter indeed," too bitter to be compensated, even in the short run, by any imaginable advantage.[3] Cicero is therefore able to assert that, if an action appears to be at once dishonorable (turpe) and beneficial in its consequences, closer examination will reveal an error in *one* of these judgments. Either the action in question is not really dishonorable, Cicero claims, or it is not really expedient. If we carefully examine any action which appears to be both expedient and dishonorable, we will find that one of two dicta *must* apply to it. "It should not be done (i.e., is inexpedient) for the very reason that it is dishonourable," or "It is expedient in such a way that it is not dishonourable" (in which case we may do it).[4]

As we saw in Chapter 4, Trollope does not claim that virtuous conduct is *always* advantageous in either the long or short run. But he certainly agrees with Cicero that it is possible to mistake expedient, but dishonorable conduct for honorable conduct—or to mistake expedient, but honorable conduct for dishonorable conduct. And this is exactly what the characters in *Cousin Henry* do. The novel's protagonist confuses the expedient with the moral, while several rigidly principled minor characters err in concluding that convenient actions must necessarily violate moral norms.

The problem, for all the characters, is to discriminate between situations in which rules of conduct can legitimately bend to the pressures of expediency and situations in which they must remain supreme. The novel takes issue with the three major schools of Victorian moral philosophy concerning the role that rules of conduct and consequentialist reasoning ought to play in moral decision-making, while affirming the way that common morality looks at the question.

Henry Jones is the character who mistakes a dishonorable, but expedient, action for an honorable one. Henry has been the heir to his uncle Indefer Jones for several years. Immediately after his uncle's death, he finds a recent will, bequeathing the estate to his cousin Isabel, inside a book of sermons. Henry doesn't dare to destroy the will, but neither does he tell anyone of it. Living in the same house with the hidden will makes Henry miserable, but he continues to do so. The will is discovered by a clever lawyer who deduces the truth from Henry's guilt-ridden behavior.

In Book III of *De Officiis,* which is concerned with resolving apparent conflicts between honestum and utile, Cicero discusses several cases resembling Henry's. In two of these cases, a man possesses information that it would not be expedient for him to publicize. "Suppose," Cicero asks, "that a good man had brought a large quantity of corn from Alexandria to Rhodes at a time when corn was extremely expensive among the Rhodians because of shortage and famine. If he also knew that several more merchants had set sail from Alexandria . . . laden with corn and heading for Rhodes, would he tell the Rhodians? Or would he keep silent and sell his own produce at as high a price as possible?" A second case raises a similar question. Should an auctioneer selling a house that is unsanitary and ridden with vermin "tell the buyers these things"?[5]

Cicero claims that these cases provoked controversy within Stoicism itself. One Stoic, Diogenes of Babylon, argues that silence is indeed permissible in such situations. According to Diogenes, "to conceal is one thing, to keep silent another. I am not at the present moment concealing from you the nature of the gods . . . if I am not telling you of it; yet to learn that would benefit you far more than to learn the cheap price of wheat. But it is not necessary for me to tell you everything that is beneficial for you to hear."[6] With respect to the second example, Diogenes adds, "What could be more absurd than for the auctioneer to say, 'I am selling an unsanitary house?'"[7]

Predictably, Cicero argues that Diogenes has not drawn the line between innocent silences and guilty concealments in the proper way: "The corn dealer ought not to have concealed anything from the Rhodians, nor the seller of the house from its buyers. For it is not concealment to be silent about anything, but when you want those in whose interest it would be to know something that you know to remain ignorant of it, so that you may profit."[8] Like common morality, Cicero's version of Stoic ethics permits one to keep secrets only if one does not wrong others by doing so. When one *does,* expedient silences become culpable concealments. Henry ought not to keep silent about the will, because he is robbing his cousin by doing so.

Henry Jones is certainly not a good man. As a child, he was an habitual liar; as a youth, he was sent down from Oxford for "some offense not altogether trivial";[9] as a man, he's much too eager to secure the inheritance of his uncle's estate. "To covet other men's goods, to speak evil of his neighbours, to run after his neighbour's wife if she came in his path, to steal a little in the ordinary way . . . these peccadilloes had never oppressed his soul" (*Henry,* 233–4).[10] But oddly enough, even such a man as this has a conscience: it would indeed oppress Henry's soul to be guilty of exceptional wrongdoing. Tampering with a will is no everyday peccadillo—and Henry knows it. He must convince himself that the extraordinary act of keeping silent about the will is justifiable.

Following a line of reasoning similar to that taken by Diogenes, Henry tells himself that, though he left the will "enclosed within the cover of the book, no one could accuse him of dishonesty. He had not placed it there. He had not hidden it. He had done nothing" (*Henry,* 79). Henry argues that it is not his affair to reveal the hiding place of the will—just as Diogenes argues that it is absurd to ask an auctioneer to list the faults of the building he is selling. The men who have been hired to search the house are responsible for finding the will, Henry claims, "It is their business: not mine" (*Henry,* 76). Like Diogenes, Henry asserts that to conceal something actively is different from keeping silent about it. Keeping silent is not a morally significant action and carries with it no guilt. As we have seen, neither Cicero, nor common morality, would assent.

And, indeed, this weak argument does not satisfy even Henry himself. Hence he falls back on a different line of reasoning, according to which he admits that keeping silent is indeed a morally significant act, but claims that this particular silence violates no moral principle. Arguing that his uncle had no valid reason for disinheriting him, Henry suggests that destroying the will "would be . . . no more than an act of rough justice," deserving no condemnation (*Henry,* 233). And if burning the will would be a "just act," then concealing its whereabouts is even more justifiable (*Henry,* 233). But, as Cicero notes in *De Officiis,* it is not just to commit an injustice—even if one does so in pursuit of justifiable revenge. Henry's conduct is unjust to Isabel, whether or not Indefer did Henry an injustice by disinheriting him. The Pauline principle, of course, makes Cicero's point in more general terms: one may not do evil in order that good shall come of it.

Thus Henry makes two attempts to prove that his conduct falls into Cicero's category of acts that are expedient and not truly dishonorable. That both attempts fail is demonstrated by his uneasy alternation between them. Although Henry continues to tell himself that honesty does not require him to surrender the will, he remains uncertain about what to do. Since he thinks that he has settled the issue of principle in his own favor, Henry must fight out his inner conflict on the basis of pure expediency.

This endeavor does not go smoothly. Throughout the long and painful middle portion of the novel, Henry remains in a state of total paralysis, unable to act and utterly miserable. His desires—for revenge on his uncle and for the enjoyment of the property—are evenly balanced against his fear of the law. He also fears eternal punishment, in the event that God should happen to judge his conduct less leniently than he himself does.

A correct assessment of the moral issue raised by his discovery of the will would have yielded a clear directive to surrender it, but Henry's attempt to choose a line of conduct on the basis of expediential considerations gets him exactly nowhere. This, of course, is a problem with consequentialist moralities, as Victorian moral philosophers of all persuasions understand. The consequences of any action we may contemplate are hidden in the mists of time, but the relationship of that action to a set of antecedent moral principles is easier to ascertain. Victorian utilitarians are almost as keenly aware of this as their intuitionist and idealist opponents. It is one reason why they find rule utilitarianism attractive.

It's no surprise that a man like Henry, who fools himself about what honestum requires and who is guided by utile alone, should come to moral grief. But it is surprising that the novel's most principled characters—Indefer, Isabel, and Isabel's manly suitor William Owen—should all be brought by an excess of principle into states of paralysis resembling the one to which Henry is reduced by his utter lack of moral starch.

The reasons why Indefer gets into this condition are different from those which account for Isabel and William's moral difficulties.[11] When the novel opens, Indefer Jones has been in a state of painful uncertainty about his estate for many years. He can't decide if he should leave it to his nephew, the direct male heir on whom the estate would be entailed, if it were entailed, or to his niece, who has been like a daughter to him and who is infinitely more admirable than Henry. "Inclination," for which we may read "expediency," prompts Indefer to leave the estate to Isabel whom he loves and wants to benefit—but "conscience" tells him that Henry must have it (*Henry,* 1).

It may seem odd that Indefer's conscience tells him to enrich the disreputable Henry at the expense of the highly reputable Isabel, but his views concerning the inheritance of land explain this anomaly. Though the estate is not entailed, Indefer thinks that "it was simply an accident that the power of disposing of the property should be in his hands. It was a religion to him that a landed estate in Britain should go from father to eldest son, and in default of a son to the first male heir" (*Henry,* 9). If Englishmen began to ignore this principle, "Britain would be ruined" (*Henry,* 9). So important is the principle of male heirship to Indefer that it outweighs all the considerations that support Isabel's claim; he believes that it is his duty to respect the custom of primogeniture by acting as if the estate were entailed.

In his indecision, Indefer takes successive actions that cancel one another out. Several years before the opening of the novel, he made Isabel his heir. Unable to deal with the guilt of having disobeyed his principles, he changes his will in Henry's favor. But a visit from Henry reanimates Indefer's dislike and he alters his will yet again (the new will is the one that Henry finds). Nothing but death can end Indefer's moral conflict, a conflict as insoluble as the one Henry undergoes.

In Ciceronian terms, Indefer makes the error of thinking that he is morally obligated to choose an inexpedient action in a situation that actually leaves him free to heed expediential considerations without dishonor. Common morality certainly does define a number of actions as absolutely impermissible, no matter how dire the consequences of refusing to perform them seem likely to be. But why has Indefer classed the trivial action of bequeathing his estate to the next female heir, rather than to the next male heir, as conduct of this sort?

The episode in *Cousin Henry* that deals with Indefer's moral conflict is based upon the Stoic distinction between the "law of nature" and the "law of nations"—or, to put it in the terms I have been using throughout this study, between the widely applicable principles of common morality on the one hand and the customs and laws of particular societies on the other. Indefer's moral difficulties result from his failure to make any distinction between the law of nature and the law of nations, between moral prohibitions and the demands of custom.

As we saw in Chapter 2, a milder version of the error into which Indefer falls ensnared several moral philosophers of the intuitionist and idealist persuasions. Because he believes that abstract moral universals must be fleshed out through the social arrangements of particular communities, Whewell concludes that "the Morality of the individual depends on his not violating the Law of his nation" (*Elements,* I:83). And as Mill observed, Whewell holds that "mere custom is of almost equal authority with express enactment" in defining moral obligation (Mill, *Essays,* 269). Maurice, Green, Bradley, and the evolutionary utilitarians Spencer and Stephen share Whewell's conviction that a person's duty arises from the specific social relations into which he or she was born—in ordinary circumstances, at any rate. Because these philosophers argue that mores define duty, they have trouble building into their moral theories a mechanism through which customs can be criticized or altered.

Unlike moralists who believe that the details of duty reside in the organic customs of particular communities, common morality finds nothing sacrosanct in any existing set of property arrangements. As Alan

Donagan puts it, "property is not in itself a moral institution. In the Hebrew-Christian tradition, many forms of it are considered morally permissible and many not" (Donagan, 95). Permissible forms of property are those which do not transgress inviolable moral precepts; impermissible ones (like slavery or serfdom) do. From the perspective of common morality, the existing property rights in *any* society are subject to criticism. Even if the property customs of a society are morally permissible, there are many other permissible customs which that society might decide to adopt in their place.

I noted in Chapter 1 that permissible customs give rise to limited obligations under common morality: only if a custom is stable and widely accepted, can its violation be said to disappoint legitimate expectations in an unacceptable manner. In most situations, some individual choice in deciding how closely to adhere to custom is tacitly allowed. In this space, morality offers no clear directives; the conflicting claims of expediency and customary rules must be negotiated case by case as individuals consider what duty requires them to do.

Trollope's novels contain many characters who are most conscientious, but who, like Indefer Jones, do not discriminate between what morality commands and what custom recommends. It causes these characters acute moral anguish to disobey any rule, however trivial, that possesses authority in their social world. In *The Duke's Children,* the Duke of Omnium believes it is his duty to prevent his daughter from marrying a commoner even if by doing so "he would doom her to death, or perchance to madness."[12] When mores are mistaken for morals, a rigid resolution to do what duty demands, regardless of consequences, can be most deleterious. This is an error to which conservatives are peculiarly prone (though politically liberal, the Duke of Omnium is quite conservative in his social preferences).

Indefer Jones is both conscientious and conservative. Since his estate is not entailed, it is only his sense of what custom demands that prevents him from bequeathing it to Isabel. But there is considerable disagreement within the novel about what custom does demand in such a situation.[13] No one except Indefer himself thinks him obligated to leave the estate to the natural male heir. Henry does not expect it and feels wronged only after Indefer makes a will in his favor—and then publicly humiliates him by revoking it. The servants, the tenants, and the neighbors all prefer Isabel to Henry as a prospective heir.

This disagreement derives from the relative force given by Indefer and his associates to the words "natural" and "male" in the phrase, "the natural male heir." For Indefer, male is the significant term here; for the others it is natural. And they think that Isabel, patrician in manner, upstanding in conduct, as familiar with the estate as a son of Indefer's could possibly be, is the natural heir. Shifty-eyed Henry, a "disreputable clerk from London," is merely male (*Henry,* 274). But for Indefer, "male" outweighs everything else.

Indefer and his neighbors differ about what custom recommends because they differ in their attitudes toward custom itself. Indefer's lawyer, Mr. Apjohn, says that his client does "not understand the root of that idea of a male heir. The object has been to keep the old family, and the old adherences, and the old acres together. . . . But in this case, in sticking to the custom, he would have lost the spirit, and . . . gone against the practice which he wished to perpetuate" (*Henry,* 273). Apjohn advocates a critical, flexible attitude toward custom. The present efficacy of a custom like primogeniture in promoting the end which it originally served is open to evaluation. Such an evaluation involves balancing the consequences of maintaining the custom against those of refusing to comply with its demands.[14]

Cousin Henry endorses Mr. Apjohn's view of custom through its analysis of the reasons why Indefer's neighbors think about the inheritance as they do. As a result of historical changes of the kind which underlie most alterations in custom, these bystanders have concluded that the natural heir to a landed estate need no longer be male. The British women's movement, which began in the late 1840s, had significantly improved the position of women by the time *Cousin Henry* was written. Trades and professions had been opened to women; their educational opportunities had been expanded; the first Married Women's Property Act had been passed. In the late 1870s, it was no longer plausible to argue that no woman could handle a landowner's duties. Only someone who felt obliged to maintain every custom in the form in which it was originally established, could contend that "male" was still more important than "natural," whatever it might once have been.

And so it is probably no accident that Isabel is an exceptionally manly woman, and Henry an exceptionally effeminate man—exceptional even for Trollope's novels, where powerful women and ineffectual men abound.[15] Isabel is "different from other girls" in a number of ways (*Henry,* 34). She is fearless, decisive, self-reliant, able to repress her emotions, above resorting to the slightest feminine pretense, and (as we shall see shortly) sexually aggressive. She easily performs a squire's duties. "She knows every man, woman, and child about the place," says her uncle proudly (*Henry,* 27).

Henry, on the other hand, has all the traits that Victorians coded as feminine: he's timid, eager to please, manipulative, indecisive, unable to conceal his feelings. Other people see Henry as disturbingly feminine. Mr.

Apjohn tells him not to sit "whining like a woman" (*Henry,* 159) and compares him to "a little girl who pauses and blushes and confesses all the truth before she half murmurs her naughty fib" (*Henry,* 278). The contrasting characterizations of Isabel and Henry prove that the gentlemanly qualities of an ideal landowner and biological maleness don't necessarily go together in the modern world—though they may have done so when women's opportunities were more restricted.

As an authoritative social practice, primogeniture's time was running out in the late 1870s.[16] And according to common morality, customs that do not enjoy wide acceptance may be disregarded on the basis of expediential considerations. Indefer is therefore mistaken in thinking that honestum requires him to leave the estate to Henry. He is free to follow the dictates of utile, "to indulge his own heart," by making Isabel the heir, without compromising his virtue (*Henry,* 9).

Because he fails to distinguish between custom and morality, Indefer does not allow sufficient weight to expediential considerations in choosing an heir. Isabel and her lover William also maneuver themselves into a seemingly insoluble dilemma by imagining a conflict between principle and expediency, where no conflict exists. But the reasons why they make this error are different.

In Book I of *De Officiis*, Cicero writes that a brave and great spirit "lies in disdain for things external, in the conviction that a man should admire, should choose, should pursue nothing except what is honorable and seemly, and should yield to no man, nor to agitation of the spirit, nor to fortune."[17] But such a spirit has its own unfortunate tendencies. As Cicero puts it, "it is a hateful fact that loftiness and greatness of spirit all too easily give birth to wilfulness and an excessive desire for preeminence."[18] Although it is one of Cicero's four central virtues, greatness of spirit can thus come into conflict with justice, the most important virtue of the group.

If the subplot of *Cousin Henry* involving the concealed will was suggested by the casuistical examples in Book III of *De Officiis,* and if the episode concerning Indefer's inability to choose an heir is premised on Cicero's distinction between natural law and the law of nations, it seems equally possible that the subplot concerning Isabel and William's romance was suggested by the discussion of greatness in Book I. For Cicero's description of the great-spirited man fits both Isabel and William—but especially Isabel.

Unlike her uncle, Isabel understands the distinction between morality and mores, though she doesn't always draw the line in the appropriate place. She has no objection to behaving unconventionally, as she does by attending Indefer's burial in defiance of the custom excluding women from such events. But Isabel is grimly determined to obey the rules of morality as she understands them, let the consequences to herself be what they may. Thus she swears "to herself a thousand times that she would not covet [Indefer's] house and property. . . . even though she should be stricken with absolute poverty" (*Henry,* 181).

But like Cicero's lofty-spirited man, Isabel, "sedulous in every duty. . . . had, perhaps, learnt too thoroughly her own superiority, and was somewhat apt to look down upon . . . other people" (*Henry,* 118). Selfless rectitude becomes a source of passionate pride. In fact, "she gloried . . . in the hardship of her position" when disinherited by her uncle (*Henry,* 38).[19] This taste for moral sacrifice often leads Isabel to deem actions honorable simply because they are inexpedient. The only action which cannot be attributed to interested motives, after all, is one that undermines the actor's own interest. Isabel therefore feels most glorious when acting in direct opposition to her own desires. And in his passion for sacrifice, William is Isabel's counterpart, though we learn less about his motives. A bizarre moral purism results.

When William first proposes to Isabel, she is still her uncle's heiress, and she knows that he will disapprove because William comes from a plebeian background. Feeling "bound to regard such an offer in reference to . . . the obedience which she owed to her uncle" (*Henry,* 17), she refuses it, though she loves William dearly.[20] With her usual self-destructive rectitude, Isabel doesn't tell her uncle that she loves William, lest this information make it painful for him to forbid the marriage.

William, who would not have proposed at all had he known that Isabel was an heiress, withdraws, mortified to have placed himself in a position where he can be suspected of interested motives and as reluctant to ask Isabel to disobey her uncle as she is to do so. Such scrupulous deference to the wishes of the older generation in marital matters is unprecedented among Trollope's young lovers. Though they generally wait for parental approval before tying the knot, they press for it if it is not immediately forthcoming. But Isabel and William are unable to reject such a golden opportunity for self-denial.

After Indefer's death and Isabel's supposed disinheritance, William renews his proposal. But no—now Isabel is sure that "not even to secure her happiness would she allow him to think that she accepted him because of her altered circumstances" or become a burden on his slender resources (*Henry,* 37).[21] Carrying her contempt for consequences to its highest pitch, she asks her lover, "What does it matter whether there be a little more suffering or a little less?" (*Henry,* 138). Some of Isabel's remarks verge on moral hysteria: she claims that it would be "inexpressibly base" for a penniless girl to marry a clergyman with a smallish income (*Henry,* 130). When the lost will is discovered, William hastily withdraws his suit. Because neither lover can bear the thought of making a beneficial marriage, when William is on, Isabel is off—and vice versa.

This ludicrous stalemate is reminiscent of Indefer's paralyzed inability to choose an heir and Henry's inability to reveal or destroy the hidden will. No wonder Isabel's pragmatic father thinks with irritation that she and William are "self-willed, obstinate, and contradictory" (*Henry,* 218). He is sure that "some stupid notion" of a highly ethical sort will prevent them from accepting any solution to their problem, so passionately do both fear their own advantage (*Henry,* 265). As Cicero noted, greatness of spirit can be in tension with the demands of justice.

Many utilitarians reject Sidgwick's claim that it is just as moral for an agent to seek his own advantage as it is for him to seek the advantage of all mankind. Even if, as psychological hedonists, they believe that individuals always choose the most pleasurable course of action available, they acknowledge that the pleasure sought can be more or less self-regarding. The utilitarians as a group cannot therefore be charged with promoting the selfishly expediential reasoning that characterizes Henry, but the indeterminacy of expediential calculation is as serious a problem for them as for him. Henry's reasoning has much affinity with that of Victorian rule utilitarians who argue that in certain unusual cases of moral decision-making, consequentialist calculation ought to override the prohibitions of common morality.

Isabel and William, on the other hand, commit an error that characterizes intuitionism and idealism. Philosophers of these schools leave little space for ordinary prudence because they assume that in every situation of choice, morality demands that the highest and purest course of action be followed. Whewell, for example, argues that although some actions appear to be morally indifferent, they "have really a character of good or bad. They may form or foster *Habits*." The indulgence of selfish desires must therefore be avoided" (*Elements,* I:308). Like Isabel and William, Whewell thinks that the expedient is wrong because it is expedient—even if it is not wrong for any *other* reason. The wide scope that common morality leaves for the pursuit of one's own interest within a structure of moral constraints has been virtually eliminated—and common sense revolts. Moralizing everything, *Cousin Henry* suggests, isn't all that much better than moralizing nothing. To identify the inexpedient with the just is, in a sense, to be guided by expediency alone.

But Isabel seems to undergo an eleventh-hour conversion on this point. After regaining the estate, she plots to overcome William's scruples. Pressing her body against him, she demands that he kiss her and he can't resist—though for a moment he hopes that if he can just bring "his collected thoughts" to bear on the moral issues involved, he will find it "possible to refuse" (*Henry,* 269). After this embrace, morality seems to require that William marry the woman he has treated with such familiarity, even if she is an heiress. And so he does.

The weakness William displays in kissing Isabel is utterly out of character, but perhaps that's the point. Their insoluble problem can be solved only if William and Isabel change their modus operandi—they must stop moralizing the inexpedient and think sensibly about the future. No sooner has William kissed her, than Isabel begs him to "say that you are happy. Tell me that you are happy. Do you think that I can be happy unless you are happy with me?" (*Henry,* 270). The woman who once took such pride in her disdain for consequences, who remarked proudly "that she cared but little for her own misery," has changed her moral tune for the better (*Henry,* 177).

Several critics of *Cousin Henry* have been puzzled by the intense hostility with which Indefer and Isabel treat the vacillating, opportunistic Henry. Since Henry is guilty of little active wrongdoing, their hatred seems so disproportionate as to have aroused the suspicion that Trollope intended some sort of ironic reversal at their expense. Thus Robert Polhemus argues that Henry is a persecuted everyman figure, driven to commit a crime because his relatives' "bourgeois respectability" will not tolerate his innocent peculiarities.[22] This characteristically 1960s reading ignores the serious character flaws that turn Indefer and Isabel against Henry, but Polhemus is right, I think, to assert that the novel generates much sympathy for Henry and keeps the reader at a distance from Indefer and Isabel. The reason for this, I would argue, is that Henry's moral error is so similar to the one his relatives make: if he mistakes the expedient for the honorable, they mistake the inexpedient for the honorable. Why shouldn't the reader's sympathies be divided?

Like common morality, *Cousin Henry* suggests that consequentialist reasoning ought to play a significant role in moral decision-making, provided that calculations of advantage are confined within a constraining structure of principles. The novel thus offers an implicit critique of the intuitionist, idealist, and utilitarian positions concerning the role of expediential considerations in moral reasoning. If utilitarianism grants insufficient authority to moral rules, intuitionism and idealism make insufficient allowance for considerations of personal advantage.

8

Dr. Wortle's School and the Consistency of Common Morality

LIKE SOME of Trollope's other novels of the 1870s and 1880s, *Dr. Wortle's School* (1881) takes as its premise an extraordinary situation that could easily serve as a casuist's hypothetical case. Mr. Peacocke is an Englishman, a clergyman, a classical scholar, and a decent fellow. While teaching at an American university, he falls in love with Ella Lefroy, whose degenerate husband has deserted her. Peacocke and Ella combat their love, as propriety and morality command, avoiding one another and hiding their feelings. But when Peacocke hears that Ella's husband has died on the frontier, he sets forth to investigate the rumor. After finding evidence that confirms Lefroy's death, Peacocke marries his widow.

Six months later, Lefroy reappears briefly—then vanishes again. The evidence in which Peacocke trusted turns out to have been faked. The marriage is bigamous. What ought the Peacockes to do? They consider separating, but decide to remain together. They go to England, where they pretend that they are legally married. At first their deception succeeds, but while Peacocke is teaching at Dr. Wortle's school for boys, the truth comes out.

There are several ways that a casuist working within the tradition of common morality might analyze the Peacockes' problem. It could be argued, for example, that the Peacockes faced a genuine moral dilemma when they discovered that their marriage was not legal. According to this line of argument, the Peacockes would violate at least one of common morality's exceptionless prohibitions by choosing *any* of the courses of action open to them. Only by disregarding both the prohibition against adultery *and* the prohibition against lying, could Peacocke continue to live with his wife while concealing the irregularity of their relationship. But in leaving her, or in living with her while acknowledging openly that they are not legally married, he would break a freely given promise to protect and cherish her.

As we saw in Chapter 1, the prohibitions of common morality are derived from its central principle of respect for the autonomy, rationality, and humanity of others. But because adultery does not necessarily imply a failure of such respect, the prohibition against it can be viewed as a commandment addressed specifically to Christians as Christians, rather than as a rule of common morality, binding upon all. Ella Peacocke seems to look at the issue in this light—and a number of Victorian men and women did so as well. Like G.H. Lewes, Ella has been deserted by her spouse and can argue that he has no further claim on her. "Duty to [Lefroy] she could owe never," she asserts.[1] Like the highly moral (but not conventionally Christian) George Eliot, Ella will not admit to being "vicious or impure" because, under exceptional circumstances, she has promised marital fidelity to a man who cannot legally become her husband (*Wortle,* 43).

Most of the characters in *Dr. Wortle's School* disagree violently with Ella on this point. As Christians, they don't much care if the prohibition against adultery is religious or moral—they accept it as absolute in either case. But as a friend of the Leweses and a talented casuist, Trollope himself might be expected to endorse the view that an exceptionless ban on adultery forms no essential part of morality.[2] And indeed he does present Ella's position very sympathetically. Because of this sympathetic presentation, the reader is prepared to take the charge seriously, when one of the novel's more liberal moralists calls its staunchest supporter of an absolute prohibition against adultery a "strait-laced, fanatical, hard-hearted bigot" (*Wortle,* 100).

Even if one accepts Ella's view that her adulterous relationship violates no principle of common morality, one must still acknowledge that the Peacockes' dishonesty in pretending to be legally married does so. But if they had refused to tell this lie, Ella would have suffered ostracism, while Peacocke would have found it virtually impossible to earn a living as a schoolmaster, the only job at which he can command more than a starvation wage. In order for Peacocke to keep his vow to cherish and protect Ella, their lie, as well as their continued adultery, seems to be necessary.

But if Peacocke had broken his vow to cherish Ella by separating himself from her, it can be argued that he would have violated the prohibition against breaking a freely given promise. On this reading of the situation, although Peacocke's vow became legally void as soon as the flaw in the marriage was discovered, the moral responsibilities that were created by the union remained. Peacocke had lived with his wife for some time;

their intimacy had created emotional, economic, and social obligations that could not simply be annulled. According to this line of argument, then, the Peacockes found themselves in a situation of true moral perplexity upon learning that their marriage was bigamous: each option available to them involved the violation of a moral prohibition.

This is the way in which the independent and pugnacious Dr. Wortle analyzes the Peacockes' problem when he hears their story. He acknowledges that Peacocke was required to respect the prohibitions against adultery and lying by separating himself from Ella. "I cannot defend him by strict laws of right and wrong," Wortle concludes (*Wortle,* 134). On another occasion, he admits that "Mr. Peacocke should not have brought the woman there, into [Wortle's own] school, as his wife. There had been deceit" (*Wortle,* 101).

But Wortle also recognizes the obligation to one another that the Peacockes' vows created. He argues that after living together as man and wife, Peacocke "was right to cling to her, and she was bound to obey him" (*Wortle,* 138). In the end, Wortle simply does not know what morality demands in so unusual a situation. He can only say that in similar circumstances, he would have followed the prompting of his heart and "clung to [his wife,] let the law say what it might" (*Wortle,* 88).

Because Wortle cannot resolve the dilemma created by the Peacockes' bigamous marriage, he concludes that there must be a serious incoherence in the moral principles according to which he has analyzed it. Apparently, the moral system by which he lives may mandate that an action be done and not be done—simultaneously. Wortle decides reluctantly that situations sometimes arise in which "the common rules of life seem to be insufficient for guidance" (*Wortle,* 213). In such situations, people can never be sure that they are acting rightly. After deciding that he himself would have done exactly what Peacocke did, Wortle remarks uneasily, "But I might have been wrong . . . I might have been wrong" (*Wortle,* 88). Wortle feels that he has two consciences in the matter, one pro-Peacocke and one anti-Peacocke, and that he cannot mediate between them. "Even when he counselled himself to yield to his conscience [by condemning the Peacockes and sending them away from his school], his very conscience,—a second conscience as it were,—revolted against the first" (*Wortle,* 92).[3]

If the Peacockes did indeed face an insoluble moral dilemma upon learning that their marriage was bigamous, does its occurrence really convict morality of internal inconsistency, as Dr. Wortle hesitantly concludes? In considering this question, the novel obliquely refutes a serious charge levelled against the ordinary man's morality by several contemporary philosophers: that it stands in need of systematization, because its principles generate contradictory imperatives. Utilitarians pursue this line of argument with particular vigor, but it also appears in the work of thinkers like Martineau and Maurice, who adopt a motive-based approach to moral judgment.

In *Utilitarianism,* Mill argues that any self-consistent moral system must lay down "some one fundamental principle or law . . . or if there be several, there should be a determinate order of precedence among them; and the one [fundamental] principle, or the rule for deciding between the various principles when they conflict, ought to be self-evident" (*Utilitarianism,* 206). This, Mill claims, morality as most people understand it fails to do. The rules defining just conduct, for example, though by far the most "immutable, ineffaceable, and unmistakable" part of morality (*Utilitarianism,* 251), are still no more than a morass of mutually exclusive considerations. The notions of rewarding desert, of setting a salutary example, and of encouraging amendment are combined promiscuously in the usual view of justice. Neither a single underlying principle, nor a master rule for ordering these considerations can be found. In many circumstances, moral agents will find that conflicting conceptions of justice mandate conflicting courses of action.

Sidgwick argues that the rules of morality do not offer coherent guidance in difficult situations. Indeed, he devotes nearly one fourth of his *Methods of Ethics* to demonstrating that traditional conceptions of virtue do not generate clear axioms that can be applied to moral decision making, the claims of some intuitionist philosophers notwithstanding. When moral prescriptions are left vague, Sidgwick argues, they easily win general acceptance, but as soon as one tries to define them, contradictions arise.

Sidgwick thinks that because the rules of morality conflict with one another, each one necessarily carries with it a copious and confusing list of ad hoc exceptions. "Even where we seem able to educe . . . a more or less clear reply to the questions raised in the process of definition [of a moral concept], the principle that results is qualified in so complicated a way that its self-evidence becomes dubious or vanishes altogether," he remarks (*Methods,* 342–3). In the course of his protracted attack upon the claim that morality can provide a self-consistent guide to conduct, Sidgwick lists dozens of situations in which it prescribes that a certain action be done and not be done.

Thus Sidgwick argues that one generally accepted moral rule directs "that the duties of the domestic relations must yield to the duty of law-observance." From this it follows that "a son ought not to aid a parent . . . in escaping the punishment of a crime" (*Methods,* 302). Yet rules concerning the deference due to parents prescribe the opposite course of action. What ought the son of a criminal father do? Heaven only knows, says Sidgwick, who shares Mill's view that the ordinary person's morality does not provide a "determinate order of precedence" among its principles that can resolve such conflicts of duties.

The issue of moral perplexity was by no means new to philosophy when Mill and Sidgwick took it up. The possibility that genuine conflicts of duty could occur had been discussed for centuries by moralists and theologians working interpretively within the tradition of common morality. Nor had this possibility invariably been dismissed. Thus St. Gregory the Great asserts that the suggestions which Satan puts to men "are linked together by cunning devices . . . inasmuch as it happens that [when] they make an effort to escape a sin, they avoid that one only by [falling into] another snare of sin" (Quoted in Donagan, 144).

But St. Thomas Aquinas argues that St. Gregory missed an important distinction: the distinction between cases of perplexity that follow the commission of a misdeed and cases of perplexity not consequent upon any wrongdoing. Aquinas claims that situations of moral perplexity which are *not* consequent upon previous wrongdoing cannot arise within Christian morality. And he claims that the examples of moral perplexity devised by casuists prove the truth of his assertion. A casuist might argue, for example, that a man who has promised a gang of killers that he will join them in a murder faces an insoluble moral dilemma. He must either break a freely given promise or he must kill, though both of these actions are absolutely impermissible. But Aquinas points out that had this man not promised to commit a prohibited action in the first place, no moral dilemma would exist.

Most interpreters of common morality side with Aquinas against St. Gregory, arguing that it is in the nature of some wrongs to entangle those who commit them in further wrongdoing. The fact that moral perplexity follows the commission of misdeeds does not convict common morality of the internal inconsistency that would be implied by the occurrence of situations in which *innocent* people cannot avoid wrongdoing. In order to defend itself against the charge of internal inconsistency, all that a moral system needs is a principle for dealing with this kind of perplexity. And common morality does offer one. It is a basic premise of this tradition that, as Donagan puts it, "wrongness . . . does not have degrees"—any action which is defined as impermissible being impermissible absolutely. But according to the tradition "impermissible wrongs are more or less grave" in their consequences (Donagan, 152).

And so the principle for dealing with perplexity following upon misconduct is that, when *some* wrong must be committed, one should choose the wrong that is least grave in its effects. Since no instructions for weighing the gravity of wrongs are offered, the principle is not a very satisfactory one in practice—all the ambiguities of consequentialist calculation are likely to make themselves felt as people struggle with such decisions. But no moral system is obligated to save wrongdoers from the need to make problematic choices.

According to this account, then, common morality *does* possess the metaprinciples for ordering its substantive commands that Sidgwick and Mill accuse morality, as it is ordinarily understood, of lacking. In cases of perplexity following upon misconduct, the principle that one should choose the lesser evil provides some guidance. And in other situations, the Pauline principle—that one may not do evil so that good shall come of it—functions much more acceptably as an ordering device.

Trollope understood and accepted the line of argument that I have just sketched out. In his travel book, *The West Indies and the Spanish Main* (1859), he suggests that it is the nature of wrongdoing to generate situations in which every available course of action is morally problematic. Such a situation developed in the West Indies, where enslavement had destroyed the negroes' will to work. If immigration into the islands were permitted, the demoralized former slaves would suffer from the competition of more active immigrants. But if immigration were restricted, wages would remain so high that former slaves could live (as they preferred to do) by working only a few hours a day. In that case, no economic advancement for *any* of the inhabitants would be possible. From a moral perspective, neither alternative was completely satisfactory. Trollope concludes that, although Britain has cleansed herself from the crime of slavery, "the mere fact of doing so has not freed [her] from [her] difficulties. Nor was it to be expected that it should. The discontinuance of a sin is always the commencement of a struggle."[4]

Trollope's 1879 novella, *An Eye for an Eye,* suggests that genuine cases of moral perplexity *inevitably* arise from prior wrongdoing. In this tragic story, Fred Neville, the heir to an earldom, seduces an innocent girl of obscure parentage under a promise of marriage. Though he later decides that such a marriage will disgrace his family, he knows he should not break his promise. When Fred complains to his brother that "there are times in which it seems impossible that a man should do right," his brother decides charitably "not [to] remind [Fred] that these dilemmas *always* come from original wrong-doing."[5] The novella offers its readers no reason to doubt this generalization.

Among the characters in *Dr. Wortle's School,* only Dr. Wortle himself sides with Mill and Sidgwick by suggesting that the Peacockes' dilemma reveals an internal inconsistency in morality. The other characters offer two competing interpretations of what the Peacockes' moral problem implies. Though they are very different, both of these interpretations implicitly exonerate *common* morality (though *not,* I shall argue below, ordinary morality as it is conceptualized by Mill and Sidgwick) from the charge of simultaneously prescribing incompatible actions.

The first interpretation of the Peacockes' moral problem is offered by the Peacockes themselves. No one else in the novel accepts their casuistical analysis of the issue, as we shall see shortly. The Peacockes believe that their moral dilemma is the kind of perplexity that follows misconduct and that it ought to be solved by choosing the least damaging course of action available.

If the Peacockes do indeed face a dilemma of this sort, we must note that their perplexities differ in one respect from those that beset Fred Neville. Peacocke and his wife find themselves in a moral dilemma because they have committed bigamy—an act that is indisputably wrong. But they themselves were not originally culpable for having done so, because they did not do so intentionally.

As we saw in Chapter 1, certain principles of common morality determine the rightness or wrongness of actions, while others determine the culpability or innocence of the individuals who perform those actions. Peacocke was unaware that he was entering a bigamous union, for he thought that Ella was free to marry. According to the precepts that guide judgments of guilt, Peacocke would be culpable only if his ignorance resulted from want of due care in investigating the situation (Donagan, 130). Since Peacocke conducted a very thorough investigation of Ella's marital status by travelling west in search of her husband, his ignorance was not culpable. Peacocke's enemies tacitly acknowledge the authority of this principle when they attempt to magnify his guilt by claiming falsely that "no inquiry was made at all. . . . He couldn't have cared very much,—nor she" (*Wortle,* 120).

Unlike the protagonists of *The Fixed Period* and *Mr. Scarborough's Family,* the Peacockes are not moral freethinkers. In judging the Peacockes' later behavior, it is important to remember that they followed the guidance of convention to the letter, until the moment when they discovered that their marriage was not legal. Only when they find themselves, quite innocently, in a drastic case of moral perplexity consequent on the commission of a misdeed, do they choose a course of action that their associates find questionable. Only then do they take on the guise of moral rebels. But even then the Peacockes are not really the rebels that others believe them to be. They are simply trying in their own way to obey the directives of common morality. And Peacocke wishes to obey the directives of Christianity as well, though Ella, as we have seen, differs from him in this respect.

Peacocke—who, like Trollope himself, is a highly sophisticated casuist—agrees with Dr. Wortle that he faced a choice of impermissible actions upon learning that his marriage was bigamous. Peacocke was sure that it would be wrong to desert Ella. But after deciding to remain with her, he admits grimly that this course of action probably involved wrongdoing as well. "If it were a crime, then he would be a criminal. If it were a falsehood, then would he be a liar," he tells himself (*Wortle,* 43). Up to this point, Peacocke and Wortle agree. But from here on, Peacocke's analysis diverges from Wortle's. In such a dilemma, Peacocke believes, morality does provide a directive: to determine *which* of the impermissible courses of action available will have the least damaging consequences. And so he tells his wife "that it may be well to choose one sin in order that another may be shunned" (*Wortle,* 64).

Peacocke understands that because "a woman with a misfortune [of a sexual nature] is condemned by the general voice of the world," Ella will become a social outcast if he leaves her (*Wortle,* 43). Of the evils facing them, her predictable "ruin" seems to him the most grave. To protect her at all costs is "my duty as well as my pleasure," he asserts (*Wortle,* 64). Unlike Wortle, neither of the Peacockes wavers in the belief that they have chosen a defensible course of conduct, because, according to their analysis of the situation, common morality *clearly* sanctions their actions.

Some might say, of course, that selfish motives of which he is not fully aware have caused Peacocke to mistake pleasure for duty, expediency for obligation, in choosing to remain with his beautiful wife. For he certainly adores her. But Trollope is, I think, concerned to close off this possibility by proving that Peacocke is a man of great rectitude, whose account of his own motives can be taken pretty much at face value. Travelling through the wild west, Peacocke refuses to load the pistol he carries. He has resolved not to shoot under any circumstances, because, as he explains, "little as I wish to be murdered, I should prefer that to murdering any one else" (*Wortle,* 270). Since common morality does permit the use of deadly force where deadly force is necessary to prevent murder, Peacocke goes beyond what it requires in making this decision. When so scrupulous a man says that he has chosen to stay with a woman who is not legally his wife because leaving her is a graver wrong than remaining, his claim deserves consideration.

Peacocke is right that a separation would have had a terrible effect on Ella. What she would have experienced had he left her can be inferred from what happens when he goes to search, a second time, for evidence of Lefroy's death. During Peacocke's absence, Ella remains at Wortle's school, but gives up her job caring for the pupils' sheets and towels, lest even this contact with her impurity taint their morals. The outcry aroused by her mere presence is so great that the school is nearly ruined. But the danger with which her presence threatens the school's survival also suggests that the Peacockes radically underestimated the harm that lying about their marital status could cause their associates.[6] Even when undertaken at the behest of common morality, then, consequentialist calculations yield an indeterminate result.

The remaining characters in *Dr. Wortle's School,* en masse, offer an analysis of the Peacockes' moral problem that departs radically from the line taken by Wortle and the Peacockes. For, according to this communal consensus, no dilemma whatever resulted from the Peacockes' initial error. Among the three alternative interpretations of the Peacockes' situation that the novel offers, this one receives the clearest and fullest exposition. Because the communal view conceptualizes the Peacockes' problem as *most* problems are conceptualized in the tradition of common morality, its advocates have a better grip on it than Wortle and the Peacockes have on the rather arcane arguments they are trying to work out.[7]

The community claims that the Peacockes faced a simple choice governed by the usual moral precepts when they learned that they were not really married, because the vows that they made at the alter were contingent upon the assumption that they were contracting a valid union. As I noted in earlier chapters of this study, when a tacit assumption upon which a promise is contingent proves false, common morality regards the promise as void. According to this line of argument, then, Peacocke's vow to cherish Ella remained in force only until they discovered the illegality of their union. Afterwards, no moral principle would be violated by their separation.

In such a situation, there is no valid reason for the Peacockes to disobey the exceptionless prohibitions of common morality. These prohibitions may or may not include a ban on adultery, but certainly do include a prohibition against lying, as well as one against doing evil so that good may come of it. The characters who analyze the issue in this way argue that "every day passed together [by the Peacockes] as man and wife must be a falsehood and a sin. There would be absolute misery for both in parting;—but there is no law from God or man entitling a man to escape from misery at the expense of falsehood and sin" (*Wortle,* 32). Do right though the heavens fall, in other words. And in common morality this is indeed the correct prescription, except in cases of genuine moral perplexity where only a choice of wrongs is available.

The community's position is plausible and it is never proved to be mistaken. But neither is the equally plausible position taken by the Peacockes.[8] Different as they are, the novel makes no real attempt to decide between these two analyses of the moral problem it raises. Passages of narrative commentary endorse now one view, now the other, almost at random. By refusing to reject either, Trollope implies that both positions fall well within the realm of legitimate interpretive disagreement.[9]

The only interpretive possibility that is unambiguously ruled out in *Dr. Wortle's School* is the possibility that a conflict of duty *not* resulting from prior misconduct has arisen within common morality. Thus, although the novel does not settle the interpretive issue raised by the Peacockes' bigamous marriage,[10] it does defend the moral tradition against its contemporary critics. Mill and Sidgwick underrate the coherence of this tradition, of course, because they fail to discriminate clearly between morality and custom. In describing "ordinary" morality, both philosophers roll the principles of common morality and various local mores together into one huge, undifferentiated mass of precepts. But unless its principles are distinguished from the prescriptions of custom, the logical structure of common morality becomes difficult, if not impossible, to discern.

The novel's happy ending is premised upon an uneasy compromise at the level of plot. This compromise allows both sides to claim the victory, but fails to settle their moral dispute. Peacocke's second trip west produces conclusive evidence that Lefroy is now dead; he and Ella can and do remarry. Morally, however, nothing has really changed. For if the Peacockes had not been "saved" by the accident of Lefroy's death, they were resolved to remain together. If they were sinners before their second marriage ceremony, they are unrepentant after it has been performed. Although the Peacockes appear to have accepted the community's moral standards, in actuality they have not renounced the views that offended it in the first place. Indeed, Ella remains certain that when Peacocke is "called to his long account," he will "stand there pure and bright, in glorious garments . . . because he has done to others as he might have wished that they should do to him," a veritable saint of common morality (*Wortle,* 211).

Yet few of Trollope's readers would have disagreed with Whewell's claim that for forgiveness to be possible, "the transgressor must *repent*. . . . There can be no remedy of the evil without this" (*Elements,* I:257). The community in *Dr. Wortle's School* seizes the excuse offered by their second marriage ceremony to readmit the Peacockes. But unless the community has changed its mind about their original crime, it should, in consistency, continue to shun these unrepentant wrongdoers.

Thus the central issue in moral interpretation raised by *Dr. Wortle's School* is not fully resolved, either conceptually or at the level of plot. Once again we see that even within a structured moral tradition, the definition and application of principles is a task in which ultimate agreement can never be achieved. But the question concerning moral consistency that the novel raises *is* resolved: although common morality offers only a minimal guide to conduct, the guidance it provides is self-consistent. And—as Mill's and Sidgwick's failure to find coherence in a code that combines morality and mores suggests—a minimal code can more easily achieve self-consistence than a detailed and inclusive one. The novel thus implies that the Victorian desire for a comprehensive *and* logically coherent morality will never be realized.

9

Reason and Reform in *The Fixed Period* and *The American Senator*

IN *The Fixed Period* (1882), Trollope takes issue with rule utilitarians like Mill, Bain, and Sidgwick, who argue that moral principles are simply the instrumental means by which human happiness can be attained. For these thinkers, the precepts of common morality are authoritative only if reason cannot improve upon them. When more felicific rules can be devised, rule utilitarianism dictates that they should be followed—even though the new rules may be strikingly different from those they replace. Following Bentham, many nineteenth-century utilitarians argue that legislation should compel individuals to promote the greatest happiness of the greatest number by mandating alterations in existing rules of conduct.

The Fixed Period takes a look at what might happen if a utilitarian reformer tried by law to restrict the scope of a basic precept of common morality. Could he convince people who are not committed to the greatest happiness principle as the criterion for evaluating rules of conduct that the change he proposes is really a change for the better? Would people obey the law mandating such a change? These questions were frequently discussed by rule utilitarians during the Victorian period and were of the utmost importance to their project of moral reform. For if people stubbornly refuse to alter the moral precepts by which they live, utilitarianism promises no practical results whatever.

As a cautious utilitarian, Sidgwick argues that attempts to tamper with the rules of an existing morality are indeed prone to failure. Perhaps "the new rule, though it would be more felicific than the old one," would not be "so likely to be obeyed." Or perhaps the new rule may "require a greater intellectual development, or a higher degree of self-control, than is to be found in an average member of the community," and if it does, its introduction would be a mistake (*Methods,* 481). These dangers, Sidgwick thinks, constitute "an important rational check upon such Utilitarian innovations on Common-Sense morality as are of the . . . destructive kind" (*Methods,* 483). But Sidgwick finally concludes that, under optimal circumstances, attempts to substitute improved alternatives for existing moral rules can succeed and should therefore be made.

Common morality, as I noted in Chapter 1, holds that it is impermissible for one rational human being to use force against another. From this general prohibition may be derived the specific prohibition that it is impermissible to kill another person, except in response to that person's own life-threatening violence (Donagan, 83). In *The Fixed Period,* which is set in the imaginary country of Britannula in the year 1980, President John Neverbend's attempt to limit the scope of this prohibition by introducing euthanasia of the elderly degenerates into a protracted comic debacle, worse than the worst possibilities Sidgwick imagines. Through this bizarre tale, Trollope questions two central assumptions of utilitarianism: that neutral reason can devise improved substitutes for existing moral rules and that the rules it devises can be put into practice by means of legislation.[1]

Neverbend's attempt to alter common morality fails not only because his claim to speak for reason proves hollow, but also because moral concepts are so deeply woven into the texture of ordinary thought and speech that he cannot extract them. Neverbend is unable to find a locus outside morality from which to mount his attack upon it, although he shares the conviction that reason provides such a standing ground with many Victorian foundationalists. In *The Fixed Period,* common morality cannot be criticized effectively from an "external" perspective, because that morality itself provides the concepts and the terms which are morally meaningful to those whom such criticism must convince. The novel works this idea out in great detail.

Let us begin our discussion of *The Fixed Period* by considering the curious fact that it is the only one of Trollope's novels with a first-person narrator. The third-person narrators Trollope employs in other novels often discuss the moral issues those novels raise. Indeed, the typical Trollopian narrator is a kind of interpretive moral philosopher, who articulates concepts that will help readers judge the characters and actions in his story. Given the necessary indeterminacy of interpretation, it is not surprising that Trollope's narrators rarely provide definitive solutions to the interpretive problems they define, that their analyses cannot simply be accepted at face value. Nor is it surprising that the principles they apply are invariably those of common morality itself.

In *The Fixed Period,* however, the *relatively* authoritative third-person narrator is absent. And the intelligent characters whose sophisticated commentary on moral questions sometimes supplements that of Trollope's narrators are absent as well. Though Trollope certainly understands how common morality would judge Neverbend's outrageous proposal for euthanasia of the elderly, none of his characters in *The Fixed Period* possesses such an understanding. Thus, although *The Fixed Period* derives most of its interest from the examination of a single moral issue, it does not offer its readers the sophisticated moral analysis that Trollope's novels often provide. It is a book about the way *ordinary* people think about moral issues. But why write a book about a moral problem which no one in that book fully understands? This is, to say the least, an unusual project.

As earlier chapters of this study argue, morality for Trollope is largely a matter of action. By learning how to behave in a variety of situations, people come to grasp (though perhaps not very clearly) the principles that guide their conduct. But mastering a set of abstract moral precepts performs a less important educative function. As a seventeenth-century English moralist put it, "if thou *art* this, thou hast *seen* this."[2] By populating *The Fixed Period* with unsophisticated and morally inarticulate, yet thoroughly decent, men and women, Trollope dramatizes his belief that common morality is more important as a practice than as a theory. And if the authority of a moral practice does not derive from its theoretical validity, the foundationalist approach to moral philosophy must be woefully misguided.

Sidgwick suggests that utilitarian moral innovations can succeed under optimal conditions—and the conditions were indeed optimal when Neverbend convinced Britannula to enact the fixed period law. For the colony had just been founded by a group of vigorous emigrants from New Zealand to whom old age seemed a distant prospect. But as the novel opens, the first victim, Gabriel Crasweller, is approaching his sixty-seventh birthday. At that age, he must be "deposited" in the state-owned "college" for the elderly, where he will spend twelve quiet months preparing for a painless death on his next birthday. To Neverbend's surprise, almost no one enjoys this prospect: neither Crasweller, nor the other aging Britannulans, nor the government of Great Britain, which granted the colony her independence, but still feels responsible for her conduct. Opposition to the fixed period mounts; the British reannex the nation.[3]

As Neverbend discusses his scheme with its increasingly vocal opponents in a desperate attempt to salvage it, they offer many arguments against euthanasia. But they prove uniformly unable to provide a persuasive analysis of the moral issues involved. Mrs. Neverbend's manner of arguing against the fixed period may remind the reader of Samuel Johnson refuting Berkeley by kicking the stone: "It's all very well for the Assembly [to pass laws], but when you come to killing poor Mr. Crasweller in real life it is quite out of the question."[4] Common morality for Mrs. Neverbend needs no more proof than the existence of the physical world.

Sir Ferdinando Brown, sent to govern the reannexed colony, claims that the fixed period falls under common morality's prohibition against suicide. "Is not this self-slaughter, this theory in accordance with which a man shall devote himself to death at a certain period?" (*Fixed,* 137). Because Britannula's elderly are so frantically unwilling to die, this analysis is unconvincing—though when an elected legislature decides to kill its constituents, there is a certain artificial sense in which such killing might be described as "self-inflicted."

The British sailor Lieutenant Crosstrees comes closest to formulating the issue correctly, when he says that it is not permissible to kill the weak: "There is a prejudice about killing an old man, or a woman. Young men don't matter. . . . The Parliament in England might order a three months old baby to be slain, but could not possibly get the deed done. . . . Strength is very strong, but it is not half so powerful as weakness." (*Fixed,* 166–7). Closer, but still not correct.

Confused by the fact that young men are permitted, or even compelled, to risk death in war, Crosstrees concludes that common morality permits strong people to be killed for the good of the community, though weak ones may not. Fortunately, we need not go deeply into the morality of war to prove him mistaken. It will suffice to note that common morality forbids men to fight in an unjust cause. If their cause is just, soldiers may risk their lives to repel the enemy. But they may not be asked to submit to outright execution. To kill a young man for the advantage of his own community is no less absolutely prohibited than the killing of an old man under the same circumstances.[5]

When Neverbend advocates the fixed period, then, he must convert men and women who are stubbornly committed to common morality although they are not highly skilled as casuists. Because he is addressing such an audience, the arguments that Neverbend offers in support of the fixed period are curiously mixed. His main argument, as we shall see shortly, is purely utilitarian. It appeals directly to the economic gains that euthanasia will bring. But Neverbend obviously fears that utilitarian persuasions alone cannot convince people who do not accept the greatest happiness of the greatest number as the end which morality should promote. The way in which he supplements the utilitarian argument for euthanasia shows him to be intuitively aware that he must make his case in terms of concepts drawn from common morality itself.

It is tempting to justify the use of force by claiming that those who are to be forcibly constrained are not fully rational, for constraint becomes morally allowable whenever this is the case. Yielding to this temptation, advocates of slavery have argued that Negroes are too stupid to live productive lives unless they are forced to obey the orders of Caucasians. Victorian opponents of women's rights offered similar arguments in support of their position.

By denying that the elderly are rational agents who may not be subjected to force, then, Neverbend can suggest that common morality permits the legal innovation he proposes—or, to put it another way, that it is not really an innovation at all. He cites the "faineant imbecility" of senescence as the reason why the elderly, like madmen and children, should be forcibly constrained for their own good (*Fixed,* 2). "The relief to be brought to the aged was the one argument [for euthanasia] to which no reply could be given," Neverbend argues (*Fixed,* 3).

Neverbend, however, does not merely decide that the elderly would be better off subordinated to their more rational juniors—he decides that they would be better off dead. And this claim is both horrifying and unprecedented. But we must remember that common morality's prohibition against killing is merely a specific application of its prohibition against the use of coercive force. Neverbend's line of reasoning, then, attempts to justify his proposed restriction of the prohibition against killing without directly challenging the more general prohibition against the use of force to constrain rational agents—though his argument that the elderly are too irrational to control their own lives remains unconvincing.

In addition to offering a defense of euthanasia in terms of principles drawn from common morality, Neverbend claims that empirical social science can demonstrate euthanasia's desirability by proving that it promotes the greatest happiness of the greatest number. He provides an elaborate economic analysis showing that the resources saved by euthanasia will keep Britannula "out of debt, make for us our railways, render all our rivers navigable, construct our bridges, and leave us shortly the richest people on God's earth" (*Fixed,* 3–4). None of euthanasia's opponents is able to prove this analysis mistaken.

But Neverbend does not dare to make his analysis of euthanasia's felicific effects the basis of a *direct* challenge to the prohibition against doing evil for a good purpose. He prefers to argue that no evil is involved.

Though Neverbend never mentions the Pauline principle, he thus reveals an unconscious reluctance to violate it. The way that Neverbend makes his case, then, demonstrates the power of common morality to structure moral debate in any community where it prevails, even if the debate is initiated by a utilitarian. But there is a second reason why Neverbend finds it impossible to discuss the fixed period in purely utilitarian terms: the principles of common morality are rooted in language. Neverbend's attempt to shift the discussion of euthanasia to a point outside the conceptual field of common morality fails because that field is conterminous with language itself.

Like Jeremy Bentham, whom he resembles in many ways, Neverbend senses that ordinary language is the enemy of the consequentialist reformer. "Bentham," Whewell remarks, "finding in the . . . common language of men a recognition of the supreme distinction of right and wrong . . . is extremely disposed to quarrel with the terms which imply this distinction; while at the same time he cannot really . . . avoid using the terms which apply [the traditional moral analysis] . . . he so vehemently condemns in others."[6] Neverbend falls into the same trap.

In its moral sense, the word "murder" means the intentional killing of an innocent person. The word "execution" refers to the punishment of a guilty one, as does the word "imprisonment." The word "euthanasia," which I have applied to the fixed period, and which Neverbend himself uses several times, doesn't really fit this startling project of mass extermination. In fact, no English word describes the fixed period: the killing of a large group of victims—many of them in excellent health—in their own interest. The word is absent from Britannula's language because the concept is absent from her moral tradition. Or vice versa.

Neverbend realizes that he must invent new words for this new concept of benevolent mass murder, words whose positive connotations will counteract the negative connotations of the terms that most Britannulans reflexively use. The elderly will not be imprisoned, but rather deposited in a college, if Neverbend has his linguistic way. They will not be killed, but will experience a fixed period. Neverbend's son Jack tacitly protests the awkwardness of the last locution by turning the noun "fixed period" into a verb—remarking breezily that few Britannulans actually want "to fix-period old Crasweller" (*Fixed,* 151).

But Jack's slangy adaptation is the closest that any of Neverbend's neologisms come to entering the ordinary speech of Britannula. On the contrary, Neverbend is continually nettled by the stubborn adherence of his people to the old terms, growing "very angry" when he is accused of trying to "lock up old Crasweller, and . . . put an end to him" (*Fixed*, 15). The word that surfaces most often is, of course, the word "murder."

Neverbend argues that this term cannot apply to the fixed period because "murder, to be murder, must be opposed to the law. This thing was to be done by the law" (*Fixed*, 4). But here, as so often, Neverbend reveals an inadequate understanding of the tradition he hopes to reform. The term "murder," after all, has *both* a legal and a moral meaning, and its legal meaning is not necessarily primary. As we have just seen, Neverbend hopes to alter a moral prohibition by passing a law limiting its scope, but his assumption that law simply overrides morality when the two practices conflict is mistaken. Although many eighteenth- and nineteenth-century utilitarians share Neverbend's belief that the law should enforce obedience to the dictates of the greatest happiness principle, even where those dictates conflict with common morality, common morality (as I noted in Chapter 1) stubbornly claims primacy over law and custom. And that is why a law mandating killing which falls under the moral definition of murder will prove difficult to enforce.

Lieutenant Crosstrees comes close to pointing this out when he says that no one would actually kill a baby, even if the law required it—but, as usual, he doesn't quite manage to clarify the issue. The other characters don't even try to refute Neverbend's argument that murder is solely a legal term, but they register their disagreement by continuing to use it in its moral sense. When Neverbend requests his wife to stop using the "odious word" murder, she replies tartly, "English is English, Mr. President" (*Fixed*, 49).

The Fixed Period suggests that the English language itself teaches Britannula how to live by the principles of common morality. Because those principles are part of the deep structure of their speech and thought, it does not really matter that the Britannulans cannot describe them in the abstract or deploy them with much casuistical skill. Its link with language offers an explanation for common morality's stability and longevity: one cannot attack the assumptions upon which it rests without using terms which invoke the distinctions one hopes to eliminate.

The way Trollope characterizes Neverbend's own style of moral reasoning underscores the point that morality triumphs because it is ubiquitous. Neverbend, a less systematic utilitarian than Bentham, is happy to use traditional moral concepts where their use is not inimical to his *idee fixe*, the fixed period project. The moral tradition he claims to despise has tremendous power over his thought. Whewell found it amusing that Bentham could not rid his prose of moral terminology—and *The Fixed Period* presents the comic spectacle of a utilitarian who invokes justice, rights, and virtue, except when his monomania requires him to denounce those concepts as irrational.[7]

Neverbend claims that the elderly should be doomed to death on the basis of rational calculations of economic interest. But when the British navy appears to abolish the fixed period, Neverbend thinks the Britannulans should be "prepared to die" (*Fixed,* 10) resisting this act of "gross tyranny" (*Fixed,* 8). Here he appeals to justice to provide grounds for a gallant resistance that is certainly not in Britannula's interest. When Crasweller—quite reasonably, if we consider only the material aspects of his situation—tries to gain another year of life by lying about his age, Neverbend deplores his friend's dishonesty.

In his attempt to make euthanasia a reality, Neverbend encounters the opposition of a populace stubbornly committed to the principles of common morality. Sidgwick advises the utilitarian reformer who confronts such resistance to follow his own principle of calculation. He should beat a prudent retreat if his innovation does not "meet with support and sympathy" (*Methods,* 484). Neverbend frequently considers doing this as his own doubts multiply and opposition builds, but he always convinces himself to go on with his scheme. His commitment to his reform rests in part on his moral theory, in part upon emotional forces of which he is naively unaware.

Neverbend sees himself as a pioneer of moral science, resembling other great discoverers like "Columbus and Galileo" (*Fixed,* 87). His moral theory is based upon "inductively established" psychological propositions which he shares with Bentham, whose friends liked to call him the "Newton of legislation."[8] For Bentham, all opposition to the greatest happiness principle should be attributed to what he contemptuously terms "the Principle of Caprice."[9] Those who affirm existing morality do so because their education has instilled an irrational attachment to it.

Neverbend also believes that people obey the rules of common morality for this reason: "When I say educated I mean prejudiced," he remarks dismissively (*Fixed,* 51). Traditional wisdom simply prevents people from using reason to solve moral problems. In their attack on tradition, Bentham and Neverbend are less cautious than such rule utilitarians as Mill and Sidgwick, who suggest that existing moral precepts shouldn't be altered too cavalierly, because they encapsulate "the whole unanalysed experience of the human race" (Mill, *Essays,* 147).

Since morality is a matter of education and habit, Neverbend concludes that it is infinitely malleable. Any precept of common morality can be altered, provided that people can be weaned from their thoughtless adherence to it. Neverbend thinks that there are two ways in which this weaning process can be accomplished: reason or some combination of guile and force.

At first, Neverbend believes that indisputably reasonable arguments can convince his people to accept euthanasia. Their "feelings . . . would be taught at last to comply with reason" (*Fixed,* 4), he asserts optimistically.[10] And by reason, Neverbend means simply the sort of utilitarian analysis he and Bentham both favor—though, as we have seen, he cannot avoid mixing traditionally moral argumentation into this analysis.

But in *The Fixed Period,* neutral rationality is shown to be a figment of the foundationalist imagination, for it falls victim to the effects of emotion. Neverbend understands that common morality is largely a matter of feeling, but he does not see that feelings enter (and must necessarily enter) into his own putatively rational thought processes. The powerful emotions involved in the euthanasia debate determine the stand that Neverbend takes, just as they determine the reactions of his opponents. It is, on both sides, essentially a question of "killing the father." Most of Neverbend's utilitarian arguments for euthanasia deplore the stranglehold on economic power possessed by elderly *men,* and indeed all the prospective victims of euthanasia mentioned by name in the novel are male.

When the fixed period law was enacted, Neverbend and his fellow settlers were sons unconsciously acting out an oedipal fantasy that must have seemed as harmless as it was pleasant. But thirty years later these sons have become fathers. Neverbend himself remains passionately committed to euthanasia as his own ticket to the immortality of fame. But the other Britannulan elders no longer find it appealing that fathers should be slaughtered to make room for their sons—though many of those sons now find the prospect attractive.

Two comically extreme oedipal triangles, which occupy center stage in the novel, reveal the psychological forces involved in the fixed period debate. Neverbend is annoyed that his wife prefers her son to her husband. He complains sourly that Mrs. Neverbend is "beyond measure solicitous for all good things to befall that scapegrace Jack Neverbend, for whom she thinks that nothing is sufficiently . . . grand" (*Fixed,* 38). Feeling his oats, Jack becomes Neverbend's opponent in the fixed period battle—and Neverbend finds it more difficult to surrender his scheme because he is so unwilling to be defeated by his son.

In the novel's second oedipal triangle, Crasweller's daughter is engaged to Abraham Grundle, who supports the fixed period because it offers him speedy access to his prospective father-in-law's fortune. Grundle demands that the Britannulan parliament carry out the fixed period law—

and this leads to a renewed discussion of the measure. In this debate all semblance of objectivity disappears as the members record their age-related preferences and Grundle "altogether carrie[s] with him the younger . . . part of the House" (*Fixed,* 39).

But though Grundle wants to kill the father, Crasweller's daughter Eva opposes the fixed period. Father-son antagonism determines which sides Jack Neverbend and Grundle choose in the fixed period debate, while the bond that links fathers to daughters and mothers to sons determines the position Eva and Mrs. Neverbend take. Arguments—however factual—have nothing to do with it.

In addition to suggesting that conflicts over moral issues are always driven by emotion, Trollope uses the fixed period debate to demonstrate that utilitarian calculations concerning these issues can never be impartial. *The Fixed Period,* like Newman's *A Grammar of Assent,* suggests that the reasoning by which we settle practical matters proceeds from premises that are necessarily disputable because they are grounded in personal experience. Though utilitarian calculations about such matters may appear to be factual, someone has ordered the facts according to his own idiosyncratic judgment of their significance.

As a son, Neverbend denied that the wisdom of age could benefit society. His "impartial" argument in favor of euthanasia rested on the unexamined assumption that the elderly make no economic contribution whatever. Had he been emotionally inclined to put a price on the wisdom of age at that time, his calculations would have come out differently. But when Jack Neverbend opposes the fixed period, Neverbend is outraged that his son is displacing him, and his arguments suddenly veer off in a new direction. "I, the father, have to submit to you the son; . . . I the thoughtful man to you the thoughtless boy," he tells Jack indignantly (*Fixed,* 115).

In fact, Neverbend is hoisted by his own utilitarian petard. As a father, he cannot resist deploying arguments about the wisdom of age against his son. But by doing so he proves that his own calculations in support of euthanasia rest upon questionable assumptions. And the novel does indeed make it clear that Crasweller at sixty-seven is a superb businessman—why not tot up the life experience of such a man on the plus side of the balance sheet?

Grundle's calculations are equally dubious. When the fixed period is debated in parliament, Grundle insists "with all the vehemence of youth" on the horrors of old age. "Had you heard the miseries of rheumatism, gout, stone, and general debility pictured in the eloquent words of five-and-twenty,—you would have felt that all who could lend themselves to perpetuate such a state of things must be guilty of fiendish cruelty,"

Neverbend comments approvingly (*Fixed,* 39). But the ailments of senescence do not seem as horrifying to the Britannulan fathers, who are in the process of adjusting to them, as they seem to their vigorous sons. If these fathers were to calculate the savings in suffering to be gained by eliminating such ailments, their bottom line would not resemble Grundle's.

The point here is not that Neverbend and Grundle just happen to be biased, but rather that consequentialist calculations concerning complex issues cannot be *other* than biased. Like many utilitarians, as I noted above, Neverbend thinks that reason provides a perspective outside common morality from which the felicific value of its rules may be evaluated. *The Fixed Period* suggests that this proves false—in part—because reason is the servant of feeling. The exceptionless prohibitions of common morality, of course, aim to constrain the influence of feeling within the bounds of justice.

Because he thinks that morality is a matter of habit, Neverbend hopes, after his appeal to reason fails, that his moral innovation will take root if it can be maintained temporarily by guile or force. At this point, Neverbend hopes to trick the first victims into compliance by offering them attractive apartments in the fixed period college. When that too fails, he hopes that the law can enforce compliance until the Britannulans become "accustomed to the fashion of depositing the aged" (*Fixed,* 81)—when, he is certain, all opposition will evaporate. He imagines himself as "a shepherd driving sheep into a pasture which was distasteful to them," while telling them, "Eat, O sheep, and you will love the food in good time" (*Fixed,* 114).

Moral innovators must often have recourse to such "unattractive politics," Michael Walzer suggests, when their legislative reforms encounter resistance from those who are committed to the morality they wish to replace.[11] But one cannot use force unless one has control of the big guns and that is not the case with Neverbend. The 250-ton steam swiveller—*The Fixed Period*'s equivalent of a nuclear device—belongs to Great Britain. Threatened by this fearsome weapon, Neverbend has to surrender his plan. Had he not been forced to do so, things might have turned ugly in Britannula.[12]

If G.E.M. Anscombe is correct that Sidgwick was the first English moralist willing, on consequentialist grounds, to set aside the prohibition against murder,[13] then the issue of euthanasia was indeed topical when Trollope published *The Fixed Period*—further evidence that the novelist was in close touch with Victorian ethical debates. But it also is worth noting that, in refuting the utilitarian claim that basic moral precepts can sometimes be amended, *The Fixed Period* predicts the twentieth century with startling accuracy.

Like Neverbend, the Nazis hoped to diminish the authority of the prohibition against murder through a combination of moral and economic arguments. They tried to prove that their victims deserved to die *and* that killing them would be advantageous to the community. Neverbend's college, with its huge crematorium, segregates euthanasia from the public eye, just as the concentration camps tried to make genocide invisible. Both Neverbend and the Nazis tatooed their victims with identifying marks. The euphemisms facilitating the "final solution" changed the German language as Neverbend hopes to alter English in order to make the "fixed period" acceptable. But in the end, neither Neverbend nor the Nazis succeeded in altering the shape of common morality.[14]

Like *The Fixed Period, The American Senator* (1877) examines the experiences of a well-intentioned critic who thinks he can transform a society by the efforts of his own unaided reason. But unlike Neverbend, Senator Elias Gotobed never challenges the principles of common morality itself. The senator hopes to rationalize only the *details* of British custom and law. Gotobed believes himself to be the sort of trained, sophisticated analyst who plays a central role in the theories of moral progress developed by Victorian philosophers as different from each other as Whewell and Mill.

Because his project is more modest, we might expect Gotobed to succeed where Neverbend fails. But this is not the case. For *The American Senator* suggests that custom and law resist attacks that invoke only the "neutral reason" upon which the senator (like Neverbend) relies. Because the senator's reason is no less biased than Neverbend's—though it is biased in a different way—his critique of English mores proves almost as unconvincing as Neverbend's critique of a basic rule of common morality.

Like most Victorian moral philosophers, Gotobed thinks of reason as a reliable, uniform faculty, which all men share and which culture does not influence. But Trollope does not endorse this view of reason. He makes it clear that, although Gotobed claims to speak from a universal perspective, his response to British mores is naively ethnocentric.

The manner in which Gotobed defines the word "rational" is itself culturally determined. In the senator's lexicon, this term refers either to social arrangements that are systematic and uniform or to social arrangements that guarantee unrestricted liberty to the individual, especially where property rights are concerned. Since Gotobed believes that American laws are characterized by their systematic logic, and since American culture is indeed individualistic both in its values and in its property arrangements, Gotobed's use of the key word "reason" simply reveals his bias towards American procedures.[15]

The American norms which Gotobed celebrates under the name of reason turn out to underlie virtually all the criticisms of British mores that he articulates. Gotobed believes, for example, that there can "be no possible motive"[16] for the beloved British sport of foxhunting, because this sport—unlike the far more rational American trotting race—does not place one individual in direct competition with another.[17] That farmers permit the hunt to ride over their crops because, in England, private property implies public responsibilities only increases Gotobed's distaste for the pastime. Primogeniture is to Gotobed "damnable and cruel" because it prevents individuals from freely determining the fate of their own property (*Senator,* II:545). Parliament is an absurd institution because the electoral districts which return its members are not uniform in size.

The senator is no better able to free his critique from the influence of culture than Neverbend was to eliminate the influence of emotion from his utilitarian calculations. And so Gotobed's criticisms of British laws and customs by no means succeed in proving them to be in tension with universal reason (as he himself believes). Nor do most of his criticisms prove that these mores are in tension with the principles of common morality. The senator proves primarily that English arrangements are in tension with American arrangements. He uses one set of national mores as the basis for his attack on a different set of national mores.[18] It is not surprising that the British are not particularly interested in what he has to say.

But there is a second reason why Gotobed's criticism misfires: he doesn't understand English mores very well. And in this respect, Gotobed's problems as a reformer are the mirror image of Neverbend's difficulties. Because common morality is the core morality of Western civilization, the discussion of moral issues in a Western nation cannot easily be moved to a point outside its conceptual field, as Neverbend ultimately discovers. Mores, however, are by definition local. They can easily be criticized from an external perspective. And Gotobed does indeed survey British mores from outside their own conceptual field—the difficulty with his critique is that he stands too *far* from that field. Gotobed is so detached from the local mores he would like to alter that he cannot accurately identify their moral deficiencies.

The senator arrives in England with some powerful preconceptions about what he will find there. Theories of national character were popular in the nineteenth century, and the senator is well aware of the character assigned to Englishmen. As Mill puts it, the British "distrust everything which emanates from general principles" (Mill, *Essays,* 164). England—to quote Mill again—was reputed to be "the native country of compromise"

(Mill, *Essays,* 191), where institutions dating from various periods coexist without regard to logic.

Gotobed turns his sojourn in England into a vigorous search for evidence that will support this theory and demonstrate the superiority of America's recently designed institutions. His primary interests are political representation and class—and in the former area, the anomalies he is looking for are numerous. But where class is concerned, Gotobed isn't so successful in discovering evidence to support his view that anachronistic customs prevent the lower orders from achieving the level of prosperity enjoyed by the American worker.

"Just feudalism!" says Gotobed triumphantly, when he is told that game-preserving aristocrats decide how much compensation will be paid to the farmers whose crops their pheasants have eaten. But in order to reach this pleasing conclusion, the senator must distort the details of a custom that is more complex than he realizes. Any farmer who is dissatisfied with the damages awarded him can in fact submit his case to arbitration—and if still unsatisfied can sue to increase his award. These mores do not fit the prearranged theoretical grid which Gotobed superimposes upon them.

The two subplots that occupy most of *The American Senator* have nothing to do with the British customs with which Gotobed is obsessed: they concern the sale of women in marriage. One of the heroines, the penniless beauty Arabella Trefoil, internalizes the view that women are nothing more than merchandise. The other heroine, Mary Masters, the equally penniless daughter of an attorney, must combat her family's cruel attempts to force her into a loveless marriage. Neither woman has any way, outside marriage, of earning a place in society. Here are mores which are truly in tension with the precepts of common morality.[19] But the senator fails to grasp this point.

Although he spends a lot of time with Arabella, Gotobed overlooks the evidence of a moral problem in which he is not interested. Towards the end of the novel, after persistently ignoring Arabella's plight and her increasingly distraught response to it, the senator states his opinion of her. Arabella could, he says, "be sprightly enough; but at times there seemed to come a cold melancholy upon her," and he adds that, she "always gave me the idea of being a good type of the English aristocracy" (*Senator,* 475).

Gotobed here turns a problem of gender into a problem of class, and then dismisses it in a sentence. Arabella's cold melancholy offers no evidence to support his theory that the English aristocracy suffers from an ennui unknown to the bustling citizens of a democracy. Rather it is evidence of the immoral way British mores objectify *women* and restrict their freedom

(Arabella's fickle suitor, Lord Rufford, does not suffer from melancholia—indeed he is as happy as the proverbial clam). Thus *The American Senator* shows us an inept social critic who exaggerates the evils he expects to find, while overlooking abuses that he is not prepared to encounter.

But there's nothing surprising about Gotobed's failure: any outsider will probably find that his own preconceptions interfere with his understanding of an alien society. In fact, it is extremely difficult to comprehend another culture well enough to come up with a persuasive plan for improving its mores. James Kincaid is, I think, correct that *The American Senator* offers an "anatomy," or descriptive classification, of rural English society, from top to bottom.[20] The society thus revealed, like any other, would take a long time to understand.

The American Senator opens with five long chapters that describe the history, social structure, and inhabitants of the town of Dillsborough in stupefying detail. This peculiar narrative strategy is Trollope's way of showing the reader how much knowledge and study are needed to get inside any social world, even the relatively simple world of provincial Dillsborough. No wonder that the senator fails to comprehend even those aspects of British society, like the class system, in which he is most interested; no wonder he largely fails to see where the real injustices lie. Predictably, his ill-informed lecture on "The Irrationality of Englishmen" starts a riot.

The approach to *The American Senator* which I have just developed explains a feature of the novel that puzzled its earliest reviewers, who complained that the love plots have no discernable relationship to the senator's activities. *The Times* thought the senator "an excrescence on the work to which he gives his name,"[21] while *The Athenaeum* and *The Examiner* suggested that Gotobed should have been omitted altogether, so detached is he from the rest of the story.[22] But if Trollope is trying to show that the detached criticism of a foreign rationalist must be irrelevant to the tradition he hopes to reform, we can explain the novel's schizoid plot structure as something other than a failure of art.[23]

The American Senator presents a grim picture of misguided foreigners and complacent natives—all of whom fail to see what is wrong with British society. For the novel's English characters, immersed in their rich social world, are no better able to criticize its mores than the senator is. People can live comfortably with unjust customs until a powerful moral argument reveals their injustice, and no one in *The American Senator* manages to make such an argument. Although the social problems *The American Senator* analyzes are solved on an individual level by a fairy-tale ending that saves Mary and Arabella from disaster, they are not solved on a social level—where they are never directly addressed. The novel does indeed offer a critique of the position of Victorian women in terms of the principles of common morality, but this critique is articulated only by the narrator's commentary and by the structure of its painful romantic subplots.

Many of Trollope's other novels suggest that criticism based upon the principles of common morality provides a mechanism through which mores can change, though such change is likely to be slow and intermittent. In *He Knew He Was Right,* for example, the characters gradually feel their way toward a moral critique of the customs that limit women's autonomy. English laws and English mores, as one of these characters remarks, treat a woman like "a dog," rather than a responsible human being, and therefore stand in need of reform.[24]

Such criticism, as *The American Senator* pessimistically suggests, may not always be forthcoming. But people like the senator, who think that mores can be criticized effectively from the perspective of universal reason, are simply misguided. Thus *The American Senator* supplements *The Fixed Period*'s analysis of the difficulties that arise when a utilitarian tries to reform common morality. In their different ways, these two novels argue that the rationalist projects of reform advocated by so many Victorian moral philosophers are fundamentally flawed.

10

Morality without Rules in *Mr. Scarborough's Family*

The Fixed Period and *Mr. Scarborough's Family* (1883)—written during the last two years of Trollope's life, when his health was failing—have much in common. Both focus upon the displacement of the old by the young and the anticipation of imminent death. In these two books, Trollope seems to be reminding himself that even in the shadow of death the moral life continues. Each novel features an elderly hero, passionately committed to achieving a surprising moral goal before he dies.

The Fixed Period deals with a reformer who hopes to make euthanasia of the elderly the law of his land. John Scarborough shares Neverbend's contempt for existing laws, customs, and moral precepts, but not his desire to reform them by political means. Only in his own conduct does Scarborough put the moral innovations he advocates into practice.

Owner of an immense estate, Scarborough "of all things . . . hate[s] most the entail" that denies him the power to decide its fate.[1] "If a man has a property he should be able to leave it as he pleases," he asserts (*Scarborough*, 389). Soon Scarborough extends his hatred of entails to the law as an institution, concluding that it consists of "a perplexed entanglement of rules got together so that the few might live in comfort at the expense of the many. . . . Taxation was robbery, rent was robbery, prices fixed according to the desire of the seller and not in obedience to justice, were robbery" (*Scarborough*, 194). Viewing law as the servant of the long purse, Mr. Scarborough concludes that he can "do better than the law" in deciding how to dispose of his property (*Scarborough*, 188).[2]

Scarborough feels no greater respect for the unwritten laws of custom and common morality than for the laws enforced in courts of justice. He makes no distinction between morality and mores, which he lumps together under the general heading of "convention" and rejects as a congeries of outdated prejudices too superficial, self-contradictory, and absurd for a sensible man's guidance. "In seeking my duty, I look beyond the conventionalities of the world," he remarks with lofty self-satisfaction (*Scarborough*, 544–5).

Having rejected law, custom, and common morality as guides to conduct, Scarborough must make his moral decisions in accordance with some other principle. Somewhat surprisingly, given his cynical and rationalistic bent, he finds this principle in a version of motive-based intuitionism, and not in the economic calculation favored by Neverbend and other utilitarians. In fact, the moral theory that Scarborough develops closely resembles the theory articulated by F.D. Maurice in his 1868 book, *The Conscience: Lectures on Casuistry*.

As we saw in Chapter 2, Maurice argues that simple human sympathy is a better guide to decision making than the most sophisticated rules of conscience ever devised. People can *generally* express this sympathy by performing the duties implied by their position in a given social order. For this reason, agents should not ask themselves what the rules of morality require, but rather, what they must do to "fulfil [their] relations to this man or that set of men" with whom their lot is cast.[3] However, Maurice acknowledges that there are circumstances under which moral agents should ask themselves a different question.

For unlike F.H. Bradley, whose views concerning the social nature of moral obligation he otherwise shares, Maurice believes that corrupt societies are by no means rare. Such societies pressure their members to behave in unacceptable ways—and so their commands must be questioned, whether those commands take the form of unjust laws, inhumane customs, or perverse moral rules. In corrupt societies, "relational" human sympathy motivates resistance to tradition, not compliance with the lessons it teaches.

Maurice therefore concludes that moral conflict can sometimes take the form of a struggle "between the opinion of the majority and the 'I ought not' of a single man. . . . The 'I ought not' . . . is protesting against a disorder, which however long it has been [socially] sanctioned . . . is a disorder still."[4] In such situations, human sympathy—not guided as in ordinary times by "Decrees or Statute," custom, or conventional moral precepts, but informed directly by a God "who is right and seeks to make [the conditions of human existence] right"—can alone direct moral conduct.[5]

Scarborough arrives by the same route at more or less the same conclusion. For, as I noted above, Scarborough is firmly convinced that he inhabits an immoral society, one of those societies where, according to Maurice, resistance to tradition becomes a duty. The "gross injustice" of

English society, Scarborough claims, makes it impossible for decent men to observe its laws and customs (Scarborough, 73).[6]

And like Maurice, Scarborough believes that unfettered human sympathy provides the best moral guide available to the inhabitants of such a society. For Scarborough, as for Maurice, motive alone counts in judging the moral status of actions and the guilt or innocence of the agents who perform them. "All virtue and all vice were comprised by [Scarborough] in the words 'good-nature' and 'ill-nature,'" the narrator remarks (*Scarborough,* 194).[7] Scarborough, as we shall see shortly, violates not merely custom, but the precepts of common morality as well. He feels no guilt about these violations because he is certain that his motives are pure in the eyes of God. If you love, you may do what you will—and Scarborough is sure that he is a loving man. "Lying there on the very brink of eternity," remarks a friend when Scarborough is on his deathbed, "he is quite content with himself, because he thinks that he has not been selfish" (*Scarborough,* 157).

Like Maurice, then, Scarborough advocates a morality of pure benevolence. His experiences therefore enable Trollope to test the widely held Victorian view that common morality is unsatisfactory because it assigns a relatively small role to benevolence as a constitutive element of good moral conduct. By extension, Scarborough's behavior tests the many Victorian ethical theories that judge actions right or wrong not in terms of their relationship to moral rules, but according to the ends they promote.

Scarborough puts his moral theory into practice by developing an elaborate plan through which he can circumvent the law of entail. He marries his wife twice—once before the birth of his elder son, Mountjoy, a second time before the birth of his younger son, Augustus. Depending on which marriage he conceals, he can "prove" either son to be his legitimate heir. In this way, Scarborough hopes to regain the power of which the entail deprived him, and perhaps to demonstrate that he can improve upon the law by following his own good impulses. More will be said shortly about the fate of Scarborough's plan.

It would be only too easy for a supporter of common morality like Trollope to undercut an innovative moral foundationalist like Scarborough by revealing that he is mistaken about his own motives. After all, a man who permits himself to evade the law may well lie to himself about his motives for doing so. One obvious danger in establishing "love and do what you will" as the sole moral rule is that this will happen: sympathy cannot function as the central principle of an ethical system if it can easily be impersonated by malice. But Trollope does not pursue this strategy, stressing repeatedly that Scarborough is an unusually loving man who really does think about moral issues in the relational terms Maurice recommends.[8]

The narrator's final assessment validates Scarborough's own version of his motives: "In every phase of his life [Scarborough] had been actuated by love for others. He had never been selfish, thinking always of others rather than of himself. Supremely indifferent he had been to the opinion of the world around him, but he had never run counter to his own conscience" (*Scarborough,* 567). I shall argue below that this hagiographical assessment can't quite be accepted at face value—could even a saint maintain so high a level of selflessness as is here attributed to Scarborough? But it remains substantially accurate.

Trollope also could have discredited Scarborough by suggesting that he is unwilling to act upon his radical views when such action proves personally inconvenient. But in fact, Scarborough does endeavor to "right" the "wrongs" caused by the law of entail in particular and by property law in general at some expense to himself. Before deciding to disinherit Mountjoy, he forgoes many pleasures in order to amass a fortune for Augustus. And he atones for his possession of private property by being extremely "kind to many people, [by] having a generous and an open hand" (*Scarborough,* 194).[9] Scarborough is indeed more beneficent than many men who consistently obey the rules of common morality.

Of course Scarborough violates no moral precept by saving money for his younger son or by giving away his income. But when he challenges the law of entail, he must lie and steal in order to succeed.[10] At this point, Trollope might have undercut Scarborough by showing the custom he opposes by these morally prohibited methods to be unambiguously desirable. But in 1882 many people shared Scarborough's view of entail as an arrangement that had once helped to maintain the great estate as the central social institution of agrarian England, but that, with industrialization, had become a pointless restriction on individual freedom. Unlike slavery, entail is not a custom that violates the precepts of common morality. But neither is it one that morality mandates. Its desirability—as *Cousin Henry* and *The American Senator* also suggest—can and should be debated.

Because Scarborough really is both benevolent and intelligent, Maurice's theories receive a very fair trial through his actions. But in spite of Scarborough's sincerity and the problematic nature of entail and primogeniture, his project turns out badly. The notion that the moral life is best lived within the confines bounded by law, custom, and common morality is affirmed as emphatically as we would expect it to be, in spite of Trollope's affection for his renegade hero.[11] We will next examine the reasons for Scarborough's failure.

It never becomes clear exactly what Scarborough intended when he married his wife twice. What actually happens is this: Scarborough, fatally ill, learns that Mountjoy has borrowed money at ruinous rates of interest to pay his gambling debts. On Scarborough's death, the estate must be sold to cover Mountjoy's promissory notes. To save the estate, Scarborough produces evidence of his second marriage, making it appear that Augustus is the heir. Now Mountjoy's notes, secured only by his interest in the estate, are worthless. At this point, Scarborough plans to leave Augustus, fraudulently, in the position of eldest son.

But Augustus soon alienates his father, who changes course once again. Scarborough buys back Mountjoy's supposedly worthless notes from the creditors for a small sum and then produces evidence of his first marriage—proving Mountjoy legitimate. When his father dies, the estate goes to Mountjoy, who returns to the gambling tables where he is sure to lose it.

The first thing to be noted about Scarborough's plot is that his motives alter in the course of executing it. His original intention is to "do his duty by his children" in a spirit of pure affection (*Scarborough,* 521). But when he acts to prove Mountjoy illegitimate, he is no longer motivated solely by the desire to save the estate for one of his sons. He is also moved by unacknowledged annoyance at the way Mountjoy's actions have negated his own authority. Mountjoy has taken his inheritance and spent it in his father's lifetime—acting as if his father were already dead.

When Augustus repeats the offense, telling Scarborough "to die out of the way," so that he can enjoy the estate, Scarborough takes "his revenge, very bitter of its kind. Augustus should be made to feel that he . . . [is] not to be laughed at in his last days," that he is still powerful (*Scarborough,* 566). "I think that you have behaved damnably, and that I have punished you," he tells Augustus triumphantly, from his deathbed (*Scarborough,* 545).

As the narrator notes, the pain of knowing, in old age, that one's heirs regard one as a burden is simply a fact of life. It is love for himself, "for which an old man is always hankering, for which the sick man breaks his heart; but which the old and sick find it so difficult to get from the young and healthy. It is in nature that the old man should keep the purse in his own pocket, or otherwise he will have so little to attract" (*Scarborough,* 550). The tricks that Scarborough plays to evade the entail do not, in fact, enable him to express his love for his sons more effectively than he could otherwise have done. They merely allow him to play an illegal—but otherwise quite conventional—version of old age's age-old will game.

Trollope's last three completed novels, *The Fixed Period, Mr. Scarborough's Family,* and *An Old Man's Love* (also written in 1882), are all meditations upon the appalling emotions that the rejection of the old by the young evokes. *Mr. Scarborough's Family* suggests that in the face of death the intense passions of family life tend to turn ugly—even where basically unselfish fathers like John Scarborough are concerned. Rules of inheritance embodied in law and morality discourage property owners from treating their heirs unjustly, under the influence of these passions. Generous men, men for whom "love and do what you will" is often a safe guide to conduct, need rules for such moments of emotional stress.

A second reason why Scarborough's plan goes awry is that he does not make sufficient allowance for the context within which he must execute it. Law, custom, and common morality form the matrix of his acts, and though he can disobey their dictates, he cannot negate their effects upon the people he is trying to influence. His attempts to *live* by an unconventional moral code interact with these resilient social practices in ways that he does not foresee. In my discussions of *The Fixed Period* and *The American Senator,* I noted that characters who try to *reform* the morality or mores of an entire society encounter a similar problem. Many Victorian philosophers of an innovative bent understand this problem very well indeed (Sidgwick, for example, never loses sight of it for a moment), but Maurice minimizes its importance.

Though Scarborough early empowers himself to upset the entail, his plan will work only if he conceals it until the moment for executing it arrives. He must therefore raise Mountjoy as his legitimate eldest son. And he must raise both sons in a world that takes legality, legitimacy, and heirship quite seriously. Mountjoy grows up, courted by all, proud of "his birth and position and fashion," as well as of the wealth he expects to inherit (*Scarborough,* 511).

It is naive of Scarborough to think that a man raised as Mountjoy has been would submit tamely to the announcement that he is illegitimate. Scarborough himself feels no allegiance to such "conventionalities" as legitimacy. He thinks that "to be illegitimate would be . . . nothing unless illegitimacy carried with it loss of property" (*Scarborough,* 6). But Mountjoy's name and his mother's reputation are as important to him as the material value of the estate he has already squandered. Instead of being pleased that the estate will remain in the family, Mountjoy is angry that his father has robbed him of his remaining social and moral assets. His feeling for tradition surprises his father, but it is actually quite predictable.

Scarborough's plan to benefit his sons alienates Augustus as well. When Scarborough informs Augustus that he is now the heir, Augustus is not grateful, but indignant. Since Scarborough cannot tell Augustus that his legitimation is a fraud designed to benefit him at the expense of Mountjoy's creditors, Augustus believes that he was saved from losing his rights only by an accident which made it inconvenient for his father to carry the injustice to its intended conclusion. He gives his father no credit for relational benevolence of the sort celebrated by Maurice, but zeros in on the purely legal wrong which he believes that his father planned to do him.

Augustus flatly rejects the distinction between law and justice on which Scarborough bases his "right" to disobey the law of entail. "The making of all right and wrong in this world depends on the law," he asserts indignantly, adding that his father "did choose to marry my mother before I was born, but did not choose to go through that ceremony before my brother's time. That may be a trifle . . . but because of that trifle [the estate] will be my property, and his attempt to rob me of it was just the same as though he should break into a bank" (*Scarborough,* 45).

Of course Augustus denies that justice can be separated from law. It is clearly in his interest to do so—at least at *this* point in the story, when he believes that he has always had a legal claim to the estate. Scarborough's conduct enrages both Mountjoy and Augustus, because the traditions he scorns tell them who they are and define their rights. Yet Augustus's feeling for legality proves no less surprising to Scarborough than Mountjoy's feeling for custom.

There is a third reason for the failure of Scarborough's fatherly endeavors. The repulsive selfishness that makes Mountjoy and Augustus so unwilling to forego, out of charity to their father, one jot or tittle of the advantages they can claim under custom and law is the recognizable product of the moral upbringing they received from him.

As we have seen, Scarborough doesn't believe in rules of conduct, but only in unfettered benevolence. Hence he is logically precluded from teaching his sons to obey the precepts of common morality, to respect the law, or even to defer to the mores of their society. Scarborough is not anxious for his sons' "welfare," conceived conventionally as including their moral development, but only for their "happiness" (*Scarborough,* 2). He expresses his love by promoting their enjoyments, and in this his practice is consistent with his theory. "I let my two boys do as they pleased," he says, "only wishing that they should lead happy lives. I never made them listen to sermons or even to lectures" (*Scarborough,* 390). Nor, obviously, is Scarborough able to set his sons a personal example of respect for law or morality.

Thus, although Mountjoy and Augustus turn out to be more deeply attached to the customs and laws from which they benefit than their father expected, they never learn that inconvenient laws apply to *them* or that moral precepts must be obeyed even when obedience requires a sacrifice. There is a certain symbolic fitness in the fact that Mountjoy, an incompetent but inveterate gambler, does not see that the laws of probability which doom him to lose cannot be evaded. And it seems equally apropos that Augustus should turn out a textbook example of utterly hedonistic calculation. The legally and morally repressed, one might say, returns here with a vengeance.

But why should Scarborough's sons fail to imitate the personal example of generosity that their father undoubtedly *does* set for them? We must, I think, conclude that good nature is not a sufficiently structured guide to action to be efficacious for the instruction of children. From this perspective, it is not surprising that Mountjoy and Augustus grow up "alike in their selfishness," despite having an unselfish parent (*Scarborough,* 76). His sons reveal unattractive possibilities latent in the moral theory which Scarborough exemplifies in a very attractive form.

Outside the family, Scarborough's refusal to consider the legal, social, and moral context in which he acts also creates problems. To convince Mountjoy's creditors that he is illegitimate, Scarborough abuses the trust of his own lawyer, Mr. Grey. If Grey can be convinced that Augustus is the heir, Scarborough reasons, his reputation for probity will help to convince the creditors. And so Scarborough makes Grey the unwitting party to a fraud, a fraud which is revealed when Scarborough produces the proof of his first marriage.

Deeply compromised, Grey retires from his law practice, a broken man. In a world that respects rules, the consequences of covert disobedience cannot be confined to the sinner himself. "[Scarborough] has treated me," Grey says, "as no one should have treated his enemy; let alone a faithful friend. . . . [He] has used me . . . simply as a machine" (*Scarborough,* 530). Deference to common morality's central principle of respect for others would have prevented Scarborough from using any human being as a tool in his pursuit of a "higher" moral life.

After his death, a friend claims that nobody could "make an apology for [Scarborough] without being ready to throw . . . all morality to the dogs. But if you can imagine for yourself a state of things in which [no]

. . . morality shall be thought essential, then old Mr. Scarborough would be your hero" (*Scarborough,* 567–8).[12] Good nature like Scarborough's is admirable, perhaps even heroic. But by itself it does not constitute a morality. And only in an unimaginable "state of things" could it suffice as a guide to conduct.

The main plot of *Mr. Scarborough's Family* is parallelled by two subplots concerning elderly men who also are having trouble with the younger generation.

Peter Prosper's estate is entailed on a nephew, Harry Annesley, who pays his uncle scant respect. Prosper is hurt that his heir has no use for him, except as a source of acres. "How happy you would all be if I were dead, and Harry were living here in my place," he tells Harry's mother, echoing Scarborough's complaints about Augustus (*Scarborough,* 497). It may be worth noting that Harry shares his first name with Trollope's older son, whose infrequent visits home are a subject of complaint in Trollope's later letters.[13]

Although Prosper's motives for wishing to disinherit his heir are identical to Scarborough's, he is a much less loving and self-aware man. But he is also more principled: he would never take the sort of fraudulent action in which Scarborough delights. Prosper respects law, morality, and custom with equal fervor. If he is to disinherit Harry, he must have a moral pretext for doing so. He finds this pretext when Augustus Scarborough accuses Harry of telling a lie. Prosper makes a hasty plan to marry in the hope that a son will cut Harry out of the entail. He can thus revenge himself on his nephew, he thinks, without behaving in an immoral or ungentlemanly manner.

Prosper intends to obey the rules of common morality, but he is so stupid that he can't figure out what they require of him. As Harry's father puts it, Prosper "intends to be a good man. If it were brought home to him that he were doing a wrong he would not do it. He would not rob; he would not steal; he must not commit murder, and the rest of it. But he is a fool, and he does not know when he is doing these things" (*Scarborough,* 239). A smart man who scorns conventional morality may act unjustly—and so may a fool who wants to do right in the most conventional sense. But things turn out better for Prosper than for Scarborough and not only because he lives while Scarborough dies.

The structure of ordinary moral reasoning constrains Prosper's conduct within acceptable bounds, despite the fact that he doesn't have a very good grasp of that structure. To disinherit Harry for having told a single lie is so excessive that even the foolish Prosper eventually sees that he must not do it. At first he attempts, comically, to maintain his right to cast Harry off by exaggerating the significance of his sin: "You told . . . a deliberate untruth. This is what the plain-speaking world, when it wishes to be understood as using the unadorned English language, which is always the language I prefer myself, calls a lie;—a LIE!" (*Scarborough,* 238).

But several people tell Prosper that this incident occurred under circumstances that rendered it innocent, for Harry lied to an enemy who was obviously pumping him, when a woman's reputation might have been compromised by his telling the truth. After hearing this, Prosper is afraid to continue. A man who respects ordinary morality will probably—precisely because he *is* conventional—obey its dictates as interpreted by others, even if he cannot work out their rationale for himself. And this may save him from committing flagrant wrongs.[14] So Prosper forgives Harry, breaks off his own intended marriage, and decides, in a burst of generosity, to refurnish his house to receive Harry's bride. Since Harry is not without a conscience, he realizes that he too has been wrong and resolves to show "gratitude and kindness to poor Uncle Prosper" (*Scarborough,* 497).

The Scarborough plot ends sadly. Though Scarborough's fraud preserves the property, only his timely demise saves him from seeing Mountjoy squander it a second time. But the Prosper plot ends comically with marriage and reconciliation.[15] Trollope might once again have had Cicero in mind in creating the stupid, conscientious Prosper and the clever, unprincipled Scarborough. For in *De Officiis,* Cicero writes that "justice without good sense will be able to do much; [but] without justice, good sense will avail not at all."[16] As for good feeling, well, in family life it comes and goes, to be depended on neither in the presence of moral principles, nor in their absence.[17]

The novel's second subplot looks at what happens when good sense and good principles unite in the *absence* of much good feeling. Like Scarborough and Prosper, the elderly Mr. Grey is troubled by ungrateful young dependents. But they are his nieces—not his own child, Dolly, with whom he has a close and loving relationship.

The bond between Dolly and Mr. Grey is essentially moral. In their discussions of the issues of conscience raised by Grey's legal work, Dolly advises her father to manage his firm "with an integrity which among lawyers might be called Quixotic" (*Scarborough,* 312). When Grey is disgraced by his unwitting involvement in Scarborough's shenanigans, Dolly consoles herself by reflecting upon his innocence: "To have been high above [all base tricks],—for him and for her,—was not that everything?" (*Scarborough,* 533).

Dolly and her father are as intelligent as Scarborough and as sincere in their commitment to common morality as Prosper. "When it had once been brought home to [Dolly]," the narrator claims, "that duty required her to do this thing or the other . . . the thing would be done . . . let the result be what it might" (*Scarborough,* 150). What the Greys lack—as moral agents—is generalized benevolence of the sort celebrated by Maurice, though this deficiency is far more marked in Dolly than in her father.

Out of a pure sense of obligation, Grey voluntarily undertakes the support of his sister, Mrs. Carroll, her drunken husband, and her six noxious daughters. A "thin-skinned and irascible" man (*Scarborough,* 150), Grey regards his sister's family as a nuisance which, like "the gnats of the world," must simply be tolerated (*Scarborough,* 166). There is little love lost between him and them. As for Dolly, she hates the Carrolls "with an almost unholy hatred. . . . She could not do other than hate them" (*Scarborough,* 147).

Dolly's theories concerning the role of love in ethics are diametrically opposed to Maurice's. She believes that benevolence is neither the central constituent of good moral character, nor the central motive to good moral conduct.[18] In fact, she asserts that hatred of those who do not deserve to be loved plays an important role in morality.

Though her father is not particularly kind-hearted, Dolly nonetheless finds his good nature excessive. Not entirely in jest, she argues that Grey ought to "hate Uncle Carroll's idleness and abominable self-indulgence worse" than he does (*Scarborough,* 166). If he hated Carroll as Carroll deserves to be hated, Grey might end the donations which his brother-in-law spends on drink and confine his largesse to the rest of the family, who are not totally beyond redemption. Unrestrained generosity can easily become injustice. This, to be sure, is an obvious point, but it is one that Scarborough and Maurice both overlook.

There is more than a touch of incestuous feeling between Dolly and her father. When he asks her if there is anyone whom she'd like to marry, she answers "You" without the slightest hesitation (*Scarborough,* 317). She is happiest when sitting on Grey's bed, in her dressing gown, sharing in an orgy of midnight . . . *moralizing*. But although Dolly's adoration renders the Greys' relationship quite disturbing—the reader may well wonder if *this* is the kind of love for which "an old man is always hankering"—it does not negate the value of their moral bond.

And that is probably the point: the Greys' principles control the powerful and potentially destructive emotions to which they, no less than other men and women, are subject. Neither Dolly's intense hatred of the Carrolls, nor her strange love for her father actually does any harm.[19] Having decided that they are morally bound to care for the Carrolls, Dolly and her father do it with dogged determination. An intelligent sense of obligation produces a more consistent line of conduct than that achieved by Scarborough, though he is more benevolent than Grey and far more loving than Dolly.

As the novel closes, Grey, having given up his profession and realized that the Carrolls will never do much to repay the sacrifices he has made for them, tells his daughter, "You at least will be left to me" (*Scarborough,* 599). Perhaps this is not much to show for a life of moral effort. But in the light of Scarborough's experiences with *his* heirs, we can't discount it completely.

What line of conduct will best subdue the greedy or resentful feelings that approaching death arouses? In considering this question, *Mr. Scarborough's Family* rejects Maurice's ethic of good nature in favor of a grim commitment to the rules of common morality.

CONCLUSION

Three "Moral Trollopes"

THIS BOOK revisits territory that was first mapped out by Ruth apRoberts's study *The Moral Trollope* in 1971. Observing that several of Trollope's novels focus upon a perplexing moral problem, apRoberts argues that their treatment of these problems is "casuistical." For most of us, "casuistry" means the application of abstract moral principles to the solution of concrete "cases of conscience." But apRoberts uses the word in an idiosyncratic sense—for unlike the casuist of ordinary speech, *her* casuist uses cases of conscience to invalidate the abstract principles of morality. If we look at the complex moral choices that people face, apRoberts claims, we see that no conceivable set of precepts could be nuanced enough to resolve them. Casuistry must therefore involve the "careful, detailed consideration of the circumstances" surrounding each moral problem, rather than the endeavor to decide it according to general rules (apRoberts, 42).

ApRoberts believes that Trollope's art is casuistical in this sense. She asserts that his novels often present us "with a case in which the moral ambivalence is striking." In such cases, "some theory, some precept, some generalisation is being invalidated. And there are in this, implications of very great importance. May it be that *any* theory or precept can be invalidated, in *some* case?" (apRoberts, 39). Through this sort of casuistry, Trollope pursues a "more serviceable" morality than "the simplistic [systems] of the abstract philosophers" and "the Sunday schools" (apRoberts, 44). "The ethical ends of Trollope's art appear to be best served by his situation-structure," apRoberts writes, "He is always recommending, by means of his cases, a more flexible morality. His stance is that of what we now call Situation Ethics" (apRoberts, 52).

In *Situation Ethics* (1966), the theologian Joseph Fletcher argued "that all general, abstract laws of morality had to give way to whatever actions seemed most loving in a given situation." Fletcher's book was published at a propitious moment. For situation ethics, as Fletcher's 1991 obituary in *The New York Times* remarks, "resonated widely" in the 1960s, "a decade marked by discontent with conventions and established authorities."[1] Situation ethics certainly resonated for apRoberts, who argues that both F.D. Maurice and Trollope see moral issues from its perspective.

Maurice's motive-based moral theory does indeed have much in common with Fletcher's morality of love. But what of that bearded, Victorian flower child—so reluctant to accept the guidance of tradition—whom apRoberts calls the "moral Trollope"? Is this alter ego of Joseph Fletcher still a persuasive portrait of the novelist in the 1990s?

Though the conclusions of my study could hardly be more different from those reached by apRoberts, I share her view that Trollope's "position consists in 'antisystematism,' and that it is a deliberate, considered position" (apRoberts, 65). Trollope certainly *is* an antiphilosophical moralist. He certainly *does* dislike ethical systems that regulate every aspect of human conduct. But according to apRoberts, Trollope the moralist had only two theoretical options: to judge cases of conscience according to the rules of an inadequate, simplistic system or to approach them on an ad hoc basis, guided primarily by human sympathy. I have argued in this study that Trollope had a third option, the judgment of unique cases in terms of a moral tradition neither tyrannical, nor comprehensive, nor simplistic.

Common morality is not a "Sunday school" morality that offers a pat prescription for every moral ailment. It distinguishes between durable, but minimal moral principles and the shifting, but detailed mores that govern particular communities. Its principles are often the means by which Trollope demonstrates that the precise prescriptions for conduct which systems of mores *do* offer are rigid or inhumane.

Because apRoberts (like some of the Victorian philosophers discussed in this book) makes no distinction between morality and mores, she fails to see this. Many of the repressive principles of conduct that she correctly believes to be under attack in Trollope's novels are customary norms that *violate* common morality. ApRoberts argues, for example, that the cruelty with which society punishes the fallen heroine of *The Vicar of Bullhampton,* while letting her lover escape unscathed, tells us that we should always bend "principle to pity" (apRoberts, 123). But for me this episode implies that the British custom of treating male and female sinners differently—on the consequentialist ground that sexual license in women is more threatening to social order than license in men—must bend to the moral principle of impartial justice. Rightly surmising that Trollope rejects *some* rules of conduct accepted by his society, apRoberts wrongly concludes that he rejects them *all.*[2]

A second misconception concerns interpretation. Using the precepts of common morality to solve moral problems is not a mechanical task. To decide what these principles require in an ever-changing world involves nuanced interpretive reasoning that pays close attention to the case at hand—exactly the kind of moral reasoning that apRoberts correctly finds characteristic of Trollope's novels. ApRoberts argues that casuistry can be responsive to the individual case only if it dispenses with the guidance of rigid principles. Following her general line of argument, Christopher Herbert suggests that the "moral system driving [Trollope's] fiction is reducible to no rigid calculus, but always remains fluid and problematical."[3]

ApRoberts, Herbert, and other critics who share their view of Trollopian ethics fail to grasp the distinction—central to common morality—between judgments of actions, judgments of responsibility, and judgments of character. And so they find only a shapeless fluidity in situations which common morality's tripartite principles can actually reduce to a high degree of casuistical order. Trollope's moral reasoning is persuasive *because* common morality provides him with standards by means of which satisfactory judgments can be reached. If his casuistry were guided only by a vague principle of sympathy, it is hard to see from whence its highly nuanced consistency could have come. As James Kincaid puts it, "in the end, situation ethics are just not delicate or complex enough."[4]

ApRoberts suggests that *all* moral rules are repressive. But the prohibitions of common morality seem less vulnerable to this charge than those of some other moral systems. Because common morality is premised upon a view of man as a free and rational creature, it enjoins respect for human autonomy. Its positive injunctions are neither numerous nor specific. Its prohibitions *are* numerous and specific, but attempt only to prevent people from mistreating one another as they pursue their own self-chosen ends. It makes better sense to look at common morality as an attempt to guarantee the freedom of all, than to see it as a restriction on the freedom of some. Its prohibitions limit autonomy in the interests of autonomy itself.

ApRoberts claims that, like Trollope, Cicero works to invalidate ethical generalizations by addressing "himself not to those easy cases like murder or theft . . . but to the difficult ones, the moral dilemmas, where the course of virtue is obscure" (apRoberts, 69). It is true that *De Officiis* considers many difficult moral problems. But by employing the notion of "honestum," or principle, Cicero solves every case he considers with little delay. In order to claim Cicero as an ally whose ethics are based upon "*humanitas* or charity," apRoberts must minimize the importance of honestum (apRoberts, 123).[5] In fact, the basic premise of Stoic morality—

that reason can deduce immutable moral principles from the nature of man—is the polar opposite of the premise underlying situation ethics.

Unlike Cicero, Trollope never suggests that the moral law is grounded in reason. On the contrary, both *The Eustace Diamonds* and *The Fixed Period* imply that the authority of common morality rests upon its acceptance and *not* upon a truth claim that might conceivably be invalidated. But though Trollope makes no foundational claim for common morality, when we look at the cases of conscience his novels pose, we find that its principles guide the firm judgments that always accompany the sympathy he generates for his moral rebels. When Lady Mason, the protagonist of *Orley Farm,* forges a codicil to her husband's will, her outrage at his unjust treatment of their child is a mitigating circumstance. But though Trollope knows that Lady Mason is not an evil woman, she is nonetheless guilty of theft, a crime which she must repent—as she acknowledges by returning the property to the original heir.[6]

Shortly after the publication of *The Moral Trollope,* a spate of essays responding to its central thesis appeared.[7] And during the 1970s and 1980s, several book-length studies of Trollope's art, focused upon other concerns, considered the issues raised by apRoberts's volume. But the treatment of Trollopian ethics in these articles and books is invariably brief. They generally leave such key terms as "morality" and "moral relativism" undefined, and they do not make a sustained effort to relate Trollope's ethical thought to that of the Victorian period.[8]

In *The Unofficial Trollope,* for example, Bill Overton points out that critics who present Trollope as a "situation ethicist" can do so only "by silently editing out, or by rationalising much that is discordant" with this position.[9] Overton also suggests that Trollope's morality stresses the observance of constraints, rather than the pursuit of desirable ends, and that he is out of step with his contemporaries in this respect. Trollope's characters ask themselves only, "'How do I maintain myself in the world with integrity?'," while the characters in George Eliot's more typically Victorian moral universe wonder, "'What is it in life that is absolute and fundamental?'," Overton writes.[10] But he does not develop these excellent points any further.

Like Overton, Kincaid rejects apRoberts's claim that Trollope is an early advocate of situation ethics. He concludes that Trollope's morality is "tied to situations, but only because situations test and make solid an ethical code that would otherwise remain abstract and superficial. . . . Even the passages of circumstantial pleading always move away from the special case to the general principle, not in the other direction."[11] Absolutely. But concerning the nature of these general principles, Kincaid remains somewhat noncommittal.

The Gentleman in Trollope: Individuality and Moral Conduct, Shirley Letwin's vigorous challenge to apRoberts's portrait of Trollope-as-situation-ethicist, was published in 1982.[12] Letwin argues that Trollope's novels take issue with a theory that she calls the morality of "the self-divided man." This theory, she believes, "has dominated civilized thought since ancient times" (Letwin, 37). It is premised upon the notion that "a human being is an unstable compound of two elements struggling for supremacy, each connected to a different kind of being" (Letwin, 37–38). These two elements are passion and reason. "[Passion] belongs to life on earth, where people need bread, feel want, taste grief, and all things alter, decay, and perish. [Reason] links men to a realm beyond mortality, where everything has a fixed place in an eternal unity" (Letwin, 38).

Such a view of the human condition implies a view of morality according to which the imperatives of an overarching order, discoverable by reason, discipline the unruly passions of the individual. This order may be merely social, but it also can be conceived in cosmic terms. Thinkers who see the moral life as a struggle between reason and passion may side with the passionate individual in his struggle against restraint, or they may side with the social or cosmic order in its struggle to repress individual selfishness.

But Trollope sees neither the human condition, nor moral development, in the terms proposed by this theory of the self-divided man, Letwin argues. His view of morality does not split off an authentic, passionate, rebellious self from a reasonable, submissive, but inauthentic, social self. Rather, Trollope realizes that the self has no existence prior to or separate from the forces that give it form. And these forces are largely social. "In the arts, disciplines, skills, manners, habits, institutions, conventions, traditions, and rules that constitute civilization," Letwin writes, "men find the limits that can shape their experience. They learn to make distinctions and connexions in what is presented to them and so to make their world meaningful. A man is then what he learns to be" (Letwin, 62). Since the self is a social creation, there need be no schism between its authentic desires and society's demands.

It is the purpose of Letwin's study to reconstruct the traditional code that informs judgment and conduct in Trollope's novels. Letwin calls this code "the gentleman's morality," though she is careful to assert that "gentleman" is essentially a moral term, which need not refer either to a male or to a member of the upper classes. But if the word "gentleman" is taken in a moral—rather than a social—sense, "the gentleman's morality" can mean nothing more than "the morality of those whose morality this morality is." As we shall see shortly, Letwin does in fact retain some of the social connotations of the term "gentleman" in her description of the gentleman's morality—without fully acknowledging that she has done so.

Letwin argues that the gentleman's code is an English creation, connected with a characteristically national "fidelity to traditional ways of doing things" (Letwin, 55). She asserts flatly that "the history of the word makes it impossible to doubt that a gentleman is a character whose native habitat is England" (Letwin, 21). And Letwin appears to believe that her attempt to describe the gentleman's morality in abstract terms is the first such attempt ever made. "What has made the relation of the gentleman's morality to [Trollope's] novels . . . so elusive," she writes, "is that . . . the bearers of the morality have been unaware of it" (Letwin, 56). Letwin proposes to reveal the principles of this code by analyzing the conduct of Trollope's most admirable characters. "To understand what a gentleman is we must make explicit the grammar of a language which has been spoken without being identified," she writes. "We need examples . . . of the variety of usage allowed by the language. And there is no better source for such examples than Trollope's novels" (Letwin, 57).

But when Letwin offers a summary of the code that she has reconstructed by these methods, it sounds very much like common morality itself—with a somewhat incongruous overlay of upper-class etiquette. From the "fundamental postulate" that "men are not for eating" (Letwin, 67), which she acknowledges to resemble the golden rule (Letwin, 68), Letwin derives a list of moral guidelines that would sound very familiar to the reader of this study were I to repeat them in detail. Men must respect themselves; they must respect others; they may not use their fellow man as "instruments," and so forth (Letwin, 68). Along with these bedrock moral precepts, however, goes a stress on style and sophistication that seems class-related—as in the claim that "a gentleman's integrity gives him a kind of fixity [which] makes him resemble a work of art" (Letwin, 68).

Like common morality, the gentleman's code as described by Letwin "sets conditions to be observed in the pursuit of [men's] business; it does not dictate what that business shall be" (Letwin, 63). And like some versions of common morality, the gentleman's morality does not rest upon a foundational claim. Gentlemen think about moral issues in terms of this code because they learned in childhood to think about moral issues in terms of this code—and not because the code can be justified by reason. An adherent of this traditional morality denies that it "can be proved to be the only true [morality]. It is in this sense a sceptical morality" (Letwin, 67).

It is, of course, reassuring to me that the code Letwin reconstructs from evidence provided by Trollope's novels turns out to be a skeptical, constraints-oriented code that closely resembles common morality. For I believe that an antifoundationalist version of common morality is indeed the morality these novels ultimately affirm. I hope that this congruence may suggest that neither Letwin, nor I, is very far off base.

But though I accept Letwin's description of Trollopian ethics as generally accurate, it seems to me that Alan Donagan's account of common morality in *The Theory of Morality* casts doubt on two of her claims concerning the relationship between the gentleman's morality and the western ethical tradition: that this morality is peculiarly English and that its structure has never been described. I am frankly at a loss to understand why Letwin overlooks the obvious similarities between "the gentleman's morality" and the much-discussed central core of Stoic-Hebrew-Christian morality.

The main differences between Letwin's description of Trollopian morality and my own account derive from her identification of it with the code of the English gentleman in all its details. Because she believes that this local ethic *is* the moral code of Anthony Trollope, Letwin makes no distinction between rules of conduct that are central to common morality and the customs of the Victorian upper classes. Where apRoberts's moral Trollope holds that *neither* morality nor mores need be obeyed, Letwin's mandates obedience to *both*.

In both its epistemological basis and its stress on the community as a source of moral value, Letwin's account of Trollopian morality bears some resemblance to my account of Victorian idealism. And this resemblance is no accident. Letwin's philosophical mentor, Michael Oakeshott, whose influence pervades *The Gentleman in Trollope,* offers a sophisticated, secular reworking of the idealist position articulated in religious terms by Green and Bradley. According to this skeptical version of idealism, *all* knowledge is organized by the mind itself. There is no way of getting beyond the world as experienced through socially transmitted categories of perception and judgment to some sort of ultimate reality; no indisputable truths about morality, or indeed about anything else, can be reached. Oakeshott and Letwin offer an idealism deprived of the reliable, though incomplete, guidance that, according to the Victorian idealists, the "universal spirit" provides.

In its epistemological skepticism, this version of idealism closely resembles Trollopian ethics. But in another respect the two diverge: for skeptical idealism is even more likely than religious idealism to emphasize the importance of mores in a manner that Trollope found unacceptable.

Skeptical idealism offers no universal spirit to consult if community standards become corrupt or confused. And indeed, Letwin never considers the possibility that such a situation might arise: her brand of idealism offers no appeal beyond community standards to anything whatever. In *The Gentleman in Trollope,* this emphasis on the centrality of custom has some unfortunate consequences.

First, it prevents Letwin from realizing that absolute moral prohibitions are central to Trollopian ethics. Letwin believes that *all* traditional rules and norms are authoritative for Trollope, but that none is *completely* authoritative. Letwin writes that gentlemen "will recognize that rules mean different things in different circumstances, and that, if in some contexts firmness about rules is more important than achieving perfect justice, in other contexts, since rules are abridgements of a practice, they should be ignored" (Letwin, 69). Of course, Trollope's most sophisticated moral agents sometimes decide to obey rules and sometimes decide to violate them—but their decisions are not dictated, as Letwin implies, by the nature of the decision-making "contexts" in which they find themselves.

Instead, such decisions are dictated by the nature of the rules involved. The rule against eating soup with a teaspoon may be disobeyed for reasons of expediency, but not the rule against murder. Abridgement from practice may well be the method by which the rules of common morality were originally articulated, but in deontological moralities rules so arrived at have an absolute authority which is independent of their derivation.[13] And the morality to which Trollope grants his allegiance is certainly a deontological morality. *Ruat caelum, fiat justitia* is not a subject for humor in any of his novels, though its misapplication by conservatives who mistake custom for morality can be grimly comic.

The second consequence of Letwin's failure to distinguish mores from morals is an inability to offer a clear account of moral criticism. Letwin asserts that "subscription to rules, even when they remain unaltered, [need not] prevent change. On the contrary, it makes accommodation to change easier by providing a steady way of attaching the new to the old" (Letwin, 63). But in this passage, Letwin seems to be confusing changes in the rules of conduct *themselves* with changes in their *applications* necessitated by changed social circumstances. She sounds as if she is offering an account of both phenomena, but her remarks actually relate only to the latter. Like Michael Walzer, Letwin sees that it is not easy to offer a moral critique of the traditions which have shaped one as a moral being. But her failure to discriminate among the elements that make up a society's moral inheritance commits her to the view that it is no less difficult to identify a satisfactory position from which to criticize local custom than it is to find one from which to criticize morality itself.

Because he refuses to criticize the mores of his society, Letwin's moral Trollope is far more backward-looking than mine—a true conservative, rather than an advanced conservative liberal. Her traditionalist Trollope, who takes the nuances of upper-class conduct as seriously as he takes the prohibitions of common morality, stands almost as far to the right of my moral Trollope, as apRoberts's situation ethicist stands to his left.[14] The persistent disagreement among his critics about whether Trollope is a conservative or a progressive may stem (in part) from a failure to see that by using traditional precepts of common morality to criticize local mores, he can be both at once.

It is Letwin's purpose to contrast Trollopian ethics with the "self-divided morality," which she believes has dominated western ethical thought for millennia; she is less interested in placing Trollope's moral thought in its historical context. But she does say a few words on the latter subject, arguing that German philosophy appealed to many Englishmen in the 1830s and 1840s because it looked "beyond the joys and sorrow of human life to a higher reality" (Letwin, 48). Letwin suggests that the desire to integrate individuals "into a higher unity," which brought German thought into vogue (Letwin, 50), was "reinforced by other imports, such as Comtist positivism, as well as by native inventions like Social Darwinism," that also located human behavior within some larger theoretical context (Letwin, 49).

This account of the dominant Victorian approach to ethics seems to me excellent as far as it goes, but it does not go very far. Having identified the Trollopian moral code as something very much like common morality itself, and having hinted at the incompatibility between Trollope's moral thought and that of his era, Letwin lays down her pen, her task completed. In a way, my study begins where hers leaves off.

Like Letwin, I think that a traditional, yet skeptical, morality is the morality of Trollope's novels. But I also wanted to know how his fictional formulations of moral issues were affected by the prevailing climate of thought in Victorian England, so antithetical to his own approach. I discovered that Victorian moral philosophy did indeed leave a deep impression upon Trollope's novels, though he never wavered in his adherence to common morality. Should moral principles or consequentialist calculations serve as the basis for moral judgment? Should morality or mores guide action? Are human beings free and morally responsible? Should foundationalism replace interpretation as the primary mode of moral philosophy? These issues in Victorian ethics help to structure many of Trollope's later novels.

But Trollope rarely sides *with* a moral philosopher, unless that philosopher happens to be attacking another philosopher's theories. From Trollope's deontological perspective, a utilitarian theory demanding that every action promote universal happiness is no more objectionable than an intuitionist or idealist theory demanding that every action forward moral development or the purposes of the universal spirit. *Lady Anna, John Caldigate,* and *Cousin Henry* all imply, through plot and characterization, that schools of Victorian moral philosophy, generally thought antagonistic to one another, make similar errors in treating various key issues.

"Abundant as was [Trollope's] gift for satire on conduct and manners," writes Bradford Booth, "he had no talent for satire on *ideas*."[15] Many critics agree with Booth that Trollope is unable to dramatize abstract ideas successfully in his fiction. But why do these critics fail to note that Trollope's novels undeniably do dramatize an elaborate, internally consistent set of moral concepts? The answer to this question may be embarrassingly simple: because common morality is so deeply familiar to them, critics do not grant the status of "ideas" or "abstractions" to the moral concepts which Trollope's novels employ and defend. Booth's tacit assumption that "conduct and manners" (for which we could probably substitute the terms "morality" and "mores") are unrelated to "ideas" supports this hypothesis.

My choice of the philosophical heuristics that organize my analyses of particular novels is admittedly arbitrary. I need not, for example, have focused my discussion of *John Caldigate* upon Bradley's formulation of the free-will determinism issue—another philosopher's might have done equally well. Nor is Green the only thinker whose critique of psychological hedonism could have provided a point of departure for my analysis of *Lady Anna*. The heuristics are arbitrary, because the novels I discuss do not respond to particular philosophical works. But they do respond, at a relatively specific level, to contemporary trends in moral philosophy. Kincaid remarks that Trollope's novels invariably "set themselves squarely against the . . . linear and progressive views which dominate nineteenth-century thought."[16] And this generalization applies with special force to the linear and progressive views that dominate Victorian ethics.

Does Trollope believe that those views pose a serious threat to the survival of common morality? Yes and no. The novels analyzed in this study suggest that he finds the philosophical challenges to common morality mounted by his contemporaries to be conceptually unimpressive. On a practical level, however, he sometimes seems anxious about the fate of morality. Several novels suggest that creeping consequentialism—with its emphasis on the bottom line—characterizes the increasingly commercial England of Queen Victoria. This development could ultimately undermine the authority of common morality, despite its long history as an established practice and its internal consistency as a perspective on human conduct.

NOTES

1 Anthony Trollope and Common Morality

1. As Shirley Letwin puts it, "the common reader . . . accepted the same morality [as these novelists] and therefore felt completely at home with them." Shirley Letwin, *The Gentleman in Trollope: Individuality and Moral Conduct* (Cambridge, Mass.: Harvard University Press, 1982), 56. Quotations from *The Gentleman in Trollope* are cited in the text using the following abbreviation: Letwin. Although the novel is not the only genre whose practitioners can appeal to moral concepts that their audiences share, the realism of many eighteenth- and nineteenth-century English novels made it easy for the reader to judge their characters according to the morality that guided his or her own daily life. The reader of Shelley's *Prometheus Unbound* could not use his own moral code to judge the conduct of its mythic characters in a simple, direct manner. But the reader of *Pride and Prejudice* could judge Elizabeth Bennet in exactly this way.

2. Bernard Harrison, *Henry Fielding's "Tom Jones": The Novelist as Moral Philosopher* (London: Published for Sussex University Press by Chatto & Windus, 1975), 122.

3. To expose the weaknesses of moral sense theory in *Sense and Sensibility,* Austen employs a similar strategy: she lets Marianne Dashwood try to live by it.

4. Alan Donagan, *The Theory of Morality* (Chicago and London: University of Chicago Press, 1979), 1. Quotations from *The Theory of Morality* are cited in the text using the following abbreviation: Donagan.

5. Anthony Trollope, "The Fourth Commandment," *The Fortnightly Review* XVII (15 January, 1866): 536.

6. Ibid.

7. Ibid.

8. For an interesting discussion of the complicated attitudes toward Jews that emerge from *The Way We Live Now,* see Paul Delany, "Land, Money, and Jews in the Later Trollope," *Studies in English Literature* 32 (1992): 765–87.

9. Anthony Trollope, *The Life of Cicero* (New York: Arno Press, 1981), 1:35.

10. A.O.J. Cockshut, *Anthony Trollope: A Critical Study* (London: Collins, 1955), 22.

11. William Whewell, *Lectures on the History of Moral Philosophy in England and Additional Lectures on the History of Moral Philosophy* (Bristol: Thoemmes, 1990), 59.

12. Michael Walzer, *Interpretation and Social Criticism* (Cambridge, Mass.: Harvard University Press, 1987), 32.

13. Anthony Trollope, *Barchester Towers and The Warden* (New York: Modern Library, 1950), 402. Quotations from *Barchester Towers* are cited in the text using the following abbreviation: *BT*.

14. My account draws heavily upon Alan Donagan's *The Theory of Morality,* which describes Stoic-Hebrew-Christian "morality as traditionally understood" by "theologians and philosophers whose work has won acceptance as authoritative" over a period of centuries (Donagan, 29). In fact, Donagan's formulations of its central principles are very similar to those that I would have suggested, had I attempted to reconstruct common morality solely on the basis of evidence provided by Trollope's novels. And this is not surprising, for Trollope understands the tradition of moral discourse described by Donagan very well indeed.

15. Anthony Trollope, *Phineas Redux* (New York: Oxford University Press, 1986), 9. Quotations from *Phineas Redux* are cited in the text using the following abbreviation: *PR*.

16. Anthony Trollope, *Travelling Sketches,* 97. Quoted in Arthur Pollard, *Anthony Trollope* (London, Henley, Boston: Routledge & Kegan Paul, 1978), 182.

17. This is also the way David Skilton sees Carbury's moral failure: "Trollope is condemning Felix Carbury for his total lack of human life—for his zombie-like existence." Skilton, *Anthony Trollope and his Contemporaries* (London: Longman, 1972), 94.

18. Anthony Trollope, *The Small House at Allington* (London: J.M. Dent & Sons, 1909), 23. Quotations from *The Small House at Allington* are cited in the text using the following abbreviation: *SH*. Shirley Letwin goes somewhat too far in asserting that Trollope's moral code downplays benevolence: "If it means pursuing self-sacrifice, altruism is a sin rather than a virtue for a gentleman because he feels obliged to respect his [own] selfhood," Letwin writes. She says that "to be constantly active on behalf of the future is not, for a gentleman, a virtue, but a vice." Letwin, *The Gentleman in Trollope,* 70, 69. What about Plantagenet Palliser's desire to bestow the blessing of decimal coinage on future generations, one might ask in response to Letwin's second claim?

19. This distinction between prohibitions and injunctions must be qualified in one respect. For it is possible to state prohibitions as injunctions, and vice versa. The prohibition, "Do not steal," for example, may also be stated as an injunction, "Give every man his due." For this reason, many moralists have chosen to distinguish moral precepts from each other in terms of their specificity, rather than by calling one set of precepts "prohibitions" and the other set "injunctions" (as I have done and shall continue to do). Some commands (such as "Give every man his due") can be performed to the letter, but others (like "Develop your powers") are vague.

20. Trollope, *The Life of Cicero* (New York: Arno Press, 1981), 1:27.

21. But the relation between intention and responsibility is complicated. The consequences of an act cannot be called intentional unless the actor aimed to promote them. Common morality is often thought to hold people responsible for

all the foreseen consequences of their voluntary actions, even if they did not intend those consequences. But the matter has been much disputed. The doctrine of "double effect" is sometimes thought to exempt agents from responsibility for acts which were foreseen, but not intended.

22. Robert Tracy argues that Trollope distinguishes clearly between the moral quality of an action and the moral character of the actor: Trollope "is always prepared to present as favorably as possible a character who has done something wrong out of some good motive, while admitting that the act itself is ultimately wrong." Tracy, *Trollope's Later Novels* (Berkeley, Los Angeles, London: University of California Press, 1978), 60–61.

23. James Kincaid makes a similar point: "Unlike most moral comedies, where . . . the reader is asked to sharpen his critical faculties, [in *Barchester Towers*] we are especially asked not to be so eager to judge." Kincaid, *The Novels of Anthony Trollope* (Oxford: Clarendon Press, 1977), 35.

24. Trollope certainly thinks that when morality and law diverge, so much the worse for law. A.O.J. Cockshut remarks that "the immorality of normal legal procedure was a permanent bugbear for Trollope." Cockshut, *Anthony Trollope,* 166. Coral Lansbury asserts that "the law is subject to criticism only because there is this discrepancy between the law as it is in fact and what the moral right indicates it ought to be. Trollope's works provide a continuing confirmation of this attitude." Lansbury, *The Reasonable Man: Trollope's Legal Fiction* (Princeton, N.J.: Princeton University Press, 1981), 46. And R.D. McMaster notes that Trollope's "displeasure with the law is usually that it departs from . . . basic principles of truth and justice." *Trollope and the Law,* (London: Macmillan Press, 1986), 119.

25. Anthony Trollope, *An Autobiography* (Oxford: Oxford University Press, 1950), 291.

26. Quoted in Bill Overton, *The Unofficial Trollope* (Totowa, N.J.: Barnes & Noble, 1982), 149.

27. Anthony Trollope, "Kafir Land," *The Fortnightly Review,* New Series, CXXXIV (1 February, 1878):198.

28. Ibid., 205.

29. Frances Power Cobbe, *An Essay on Intuitive Morals: Being an Attempt to Popularize Ethical Science* (Boston: Crosby, Nichols, & Co., 1859), 4.

30. Anthony Trollope, *Phineas Finn* (London, Oxford, New York: Oxford University Press, 1973), II:178–79.

31. A.O.J. Cockshut points out that Harding is an unusually negative moral exemplar: "In the Barsetshire novels, Mr. Harding is used as a moral touchstone for the other characters. To give this function to one character in a novel is not, of course, uncommon; what is, is the way he is portrayed. The typical character of this sort is Robert Elsmere, an active hero who influences everyone by his zeal. . . . But Harding is . . . weak, troubled, and lacking in energy." Cockshut, *Anthony Trollope,* 151.

32. Because common morality assumes the supreme value of the individual, Geoffrey Harvey's claim that Trollope's "belief in the supreme value of the individual

and his right to self-determination demands a moral relativism" is not convincing. Harvey, *The Art of Anthony Trollope* (London: Weidenfeld & Nicolson, 1980), 16.

33. Anthony Trollope, "The Rose of Cheriton," *The Fortnightly Review,* New Series, II (1 February, 1867):253.

34. As Kincaid puts it, "Trollope is resolute in rejecting the myths of sacrifice and redemption." Kincaid, *The Novels of Anthony Trollope,* 57.

2 Common Morality and Victorian Ethics

1. Leslie Stephen, *The Science of Ethics* (London: Smith, Elder, & Co., 1882), 91.

2. Jerome Schneewind, *Sidgwick's Ethics and Victorian Moral Philosophy* (Oxford: Clarendon Press, 1977), 90.

3. Ibid., 91.

4. Thomas Hill Green, *Prolegomena to Ethics* (Oxford: Clarendon Press, 1899), 53. Quotations from the *Prolegomena* are cited in the text using the following abbreviation: Green.

5. John Henry Newman, *An Essay in Aid of a Grammar of Assent* (Notre Dame, London: University of Notre Dame Press, 1979), 239.

6. Ibid., 320.

7. See Walzer, *Interpretation and Social Criticism,* 21.

8. Jerome Schneewind, ed., *Moral Philosophy from Montaigne to Kant: An Anthology* (Cambridge: Cambridge University Press, 1990), I:3.

9. John Stuart Mill and Jeremy Bentham, *Utilitarianism and Other Essays* (New York: Penguin, 1987), 257. Quotations from this collection are cited in the text using the following abbreviation: Mill, *Essays*.

10. Schneewind, *Sidgwick's Ethics and Victorian Moral Philosophy,* 230.

11. Whewell, *Lectures on the History of Moral Philosophy,* 113.

12. John Grote, *An Examination of the Utilitarian Philosophy* (Bristol: Thoemmes, 1990), 273.

13. Henry Sidgwick, *The Methods of Ethics,* 7th edition (Indianapolis and Cambridge: Hackett Publishing Co., 1981), 2. Quotations from *The Methods of Ethics* are cited in the text using the following abbreviation: *Methods*.

14. Walzer, *Interpretation and Social Criticism,* 7.

15. *Utilitarianism,* reprinted in J.S. Mill, *The Logic of the Moral Sciences* (London: Duckworth, 1987), 218. Quotations from *Utilitarianism* are cited in the text using the following abbreviation: *Utilitarianism*.

16. Skilton's remark that Trollope often annoyed contemporaries because "he was descriptive while his critics sought for [a] prescription" for every social ill, applies well to his treatment of moral issues, where he describes and applies existing distinctions, but never proposes utopian innovations. Skilton, *Anthony Trollope and his Contemporaries,* 78.

17. Anthony Trollope, *La Vendee* (London: Ward & Lock, 1878), 22.

18. Alexander Bain, *Moral Science: A Compendium of Ethics* (New York: American Book Co., 1869), 26.

19. Stephen, *The Science of Ethics*, 102. Stephen's peculiar moral theory of interracial competition (with the European "race" poised to win) is obviously the product of a colonial era.

20. Ibid., 154.

21. F.H. Bradley, *Ethical Studies* (London: Oxford University Press, 1962), 2nd edition, 101–2. Quotations from *Ethical Studies* are cited in the text using the following abbreviation: Bradley.

22. It should be noted that utilitarianism maintains the sharp division made in common morality between judgments of actions and judgments of responsibility. Utilitarians judge actions by the consequences they actually have, while the guilt or innocence of agents is judged by the consequences that they foresee in acting.

23. F.D. Maurice, *The Conscience: Lectures on Casuistry* (London and Cambridge: Macmillan & Co., 1868), 109. Quotations from *The Conscience* are cited in the text using the following abbreviation: Maurice.

24. William Whewell, *The Elements of Morality* (New York: Harper & Bros., 1854), 1:162. Quotations from *The Elements of Morality* are cited in the text using the following abbreviation: *Elements*.

25. Grote, *An Examination of the Utilitarian Philosophy*, 354–5.

26. Frances Power Cobbe, *An Essay on Intuitive Morals: Being an Attempt to Popularize Ethical Science* (Boston: Crosby, Nichols, & Co., 1859), xiv.

27. Sidgwick, *Lectures on the Ethics of T.H. Green, Mr. Herbert Spencer, and J. Martineau* (London: Macmillan & Co., 1902), 356.

28. James Martineau, *Types of Ethical Theory* (Oxford: Clarendon Press, 1885), II:179.

29. Skilton attributes to the same motive the desire of many Victorian critics that novels teach the highest moral lessons: "The critical demand for a basis of moral security within a work of art undoubtedly stems from anxiety about change in all areas of life." Skilton, *Anthony Trollope and his Contemporaries*, 74.

30. Anthony Trollope, *Phineas Redux*, 178.

31. John Sutherland, "Trollope and *St. Paul's* 1866–70," in Tony Bareham, ed., *Anthony Trollope* (Plymouth and London: Vision Press, 1980), 128.

32. Anthony Manser, *Bradley's Logic* (Totowa, N.J.: Barnes & Noble Books, 1983), 20.

33. Schneewind, *Sidgwick's Ethics and Victorian Moral Philosophy*, 5, 6.

34. Ibid., 6.

35. Quoted in Manser, *Bradley's Logic*, 10.

36. T.H.S. Escott, *Anthony Trollope: His Public Services, Private Friends, and Literary Originals* (Port Washington, N.Y.: Kennikat Press, 1967), 256.

37. See for example, Stephen Wall, *Trollope and Character* (London, Boston: Faber & Faber, 1988), 271, or Overton, *The Unofficial Trollope*, 175. Eliot herself felt that there was something lax about Trollope's moral views. In a letter to Charles

Bray, she comments that Trollope clings to "whatever is, *on the whole,* and without fine distinctions, honest, lovely, and of good report." Quoted in R.C. Terry, ed., *Trollope: Interviews and Recollections* (London: Macmillan Press, 1987), 137.

3 Morality and Social Advantage in *The Eustace Diamonds*

1. Grote, *An Examination of the Utilitarian Philosophy,* 143.

2. As P.D. Edwards puts it, in Trollope's later novels, the "gentry are everywhere selling out to adventurers and vulgar financiers. Class barriers and moral standards are crashing in unison." Edwards, *Anthony Trollope: His Art and Scope* (New York: St. Martin's Press, 1977), 168. For a different view of the relationship between honesty and class in Trollope's fiction, see John Kucich, "Transgression in Trollope: Dishonesty and the Antibourgeois Elite," *ELH,* 56:3 (Fall 1989):593–618.

3. Anthony Trollope, *The Eustace Diamonds* (New York: Penguin Books, 1969), 283. Quotations from *The Eustace Diamonds* are cited in the text using the following abbreviation: *Eustace*.

4. Edwards remarks that in *The Eustace Diamonds* "manufacturing sensations, in wilful disregard of commonsense and common honesty, has become a nationwide industry." Edwards, *Anthony Trollope,* 174.

5. Several critics have compared Fawn to the exemplary gentlemen in Trollope's early novels. Kincaid remarks that in *The Eustace Diamonds* "Mr. Harding's nearest descendent is gentle Lord Fawn. . . . [But he] is nearly an idiot, cast adrift in this environment." Kincaid, *The Novels of Anthony Trollope,* 203. Andrew Wright sees Fawn as "a caricature of Plantagenet Palliser." Wright, *Anthony Trollope: Dream and Art* (Chicago: University of Chicago Press, 1983), 92.

6. Kincaid, *The Novels of Anthony Trollope,* 204.

7. On this point I take issue with Juliet McMaster, who reads the novel as an allegory in which "character after character is revealed in the light of his allegiance to truth and falsehood." McMaster, *Trollope's Palliser Novels: Theme and Pattern* (London & Basingstoke: Macmillan Press, 1978), 90. Though I am indebted to McMaster's discussion, I see the novel in less static terms. I would argue that *The Eustace Diamonds* does not merely offer a typology of truthfulness and dishonesty, but also a typology of what can *happen* to people in a dishonest world.

8. Among the critics who say that Lizzie *is not* a product of her society are McMaster, who writes that she embodies a "natural . . . love of the lie," McMaster, *Trollope's Palliser Novels,* 78; Wall, who asserts rather belligerently that Lizzie's conduct "is not seen by Trollope (as it is by some of his modern critics) as symptomatic of some pervasive social malaise," Wall, *Trollope and Character,* 264; and Pollard, who stresses "the gap between ordinary human behaviour and Lizzie's constant assumption of roles," Pollard, *Anthony Trollope,* 90. Those who argue that Lizzie *is* a social product include Overton, who writes of "the lying and dishonesty which the novel says are epidemic in fashionable life," Overton, *The Unofficial Trollope,* 165;

Polhemus, who notes that "the society of *The Eustace Diamonds* turns rotten with public-relations mentality," Polhemus, *The Novels of Anthony Trollope,* 172; and Kincaid, who claims that "Lizzie is a judgment on the world," Kincaid, *The Novels of Anthony Trollope,* 209.

9. As Overton puts it, Lizzie is "an innocent who tries to succeed in society with only a superficial knowledge of the rules of the game. It's the men who hold all the cards." Overton, *The Unofficial Trollope,* 173. Cockshut remarks that Lizzie's "wickedness is the wickedness of a child," compared to Becky's sophisticated scheming. Cockshut, *Anthony Trollope,* 187.

10. Both Pollard and Cockshut conclude that Lucinda's response to Sir Griffin is evidence of a "definite sexual abnormality." Pollard, *Anthony Trollope,* 91; Cockshut, *Anthony Trollope,* 195. I'd argue that the "abnormality" here is in Pollard's and Cockshut's attitudes, not in Lucinda's. They assume that any woman who is repelled by a man—even a stupid, ugly sadist like Sir Griffin—must be suffering from a sexual problem.

11. Critical opinion is divided with respect to Frank. Kincaid says that Frank "does more than touch pitch lightly; he wallows in it." Kincaid, *The Novels of Anthony Trollope,* 203. McMaster remarks dubiously that though Frank "may be a rather feckless Redcrosse Knight . . . perhaps the choice of his name, 'Frank,' does . . . suggest his quest for honesty." McMaster, *Trollope's Palliser Novels,* 85. Wall thinks that the narrator endeavors to "deflect censure from . . . Frank" by encouraging the reader to "enter imaginatively into Frank's self deceptions." Wall, *Trollope and Character,* 263.

12. Bradford Booth attributes the gloomy mood of this love story to a failure of Trollope's art: "The soil is exhausted, the fruit is dry—there is no springtime freshness in the air." But I think this sense of claustrophobia is intentional. Booth, *Anthony Trollope: Aspects of His Life and Art* (Bloomington: Indiana University Press, 1958), 91.

13. Frances Power Cobbe, *Studies New and Old of Ethical and Social Subjects,* 279.

14. The Victorian critic Richard Hutton argued that outline "'is a result of comparison,—moral outline of moral comparison. You cannot compare without an implied standard.' And it is this standard that must somehow be embodied in the work of art." Quoted in Skilton, *Anthony Trollope and his Contemporaries,* 67. Trollope offended critics like Hutton because he did not embody the "implied moral standard" of every novel in at least one exemplary character. I believe that Trollope refused to create idealized characters, because his readers were already familiar with common morality: the "implied moral standard" of every novel he wrote. He knew that he could appeal to this moral standard without explicitly embodying it.

15. Anthony Trollope, *South Africa* (London: Dawsons, 1968), 2:188.

16. Overton remarks that in *The Eustace Diamonds,* "Trollope's relaxed, easy-paced narrative is perfect for conveying the . . . steady deliquescence of principle, under the influence of what everyone says or does." Overton, *The Unofficial Trollope,*

171. Christopher Herbert argues that *The Eustace Diamonds* satirizes "not active vice but a general worldly dulling of moral sensitivity. Even people of relatively good character . . . take for granted that strict moral principles are quaint anachronisms at best." Christopher Herbert, *Trollope and Comic Pleasure* (Chicago: University of Chicago Press, 1987), 161.

4 Morality and Individual Advantage in *Phineas Redux*

1. McMaster and Kincaid both argue that *Phineas Redux* focuses upon the issue of poetic justice. In this novel, says McMaster, "plot and subplot, action and incident and character are arranged to reiterate the proposition that . . . virtue is not rewarded." McMaster, *Trollope's Palliser Novels,* 73. Kincaid writes that "the novel is dominated by Phineas's sense of injustice. . . . Where is the previous coherence that had recognized his virtue and rewarded him with all that good luck [in *Phineas Finn*]?" Kincaid, *The Novels of Anthony Trollope,* 210. I find these critics' remarks illuminating, but I hope to improve upon their readings by explaining *why* it is that the world of *Phineas Redux* does not always reward virtue. The novel offers a complex analysis of this question.

2. Wall also thinks that Slide believes himself to be acting morally when he defames Phineas. Wall argues that "Trollope's transition from a hostile external view of an abuse to a not unsympathetic inquiry into the psychology of the person guilty of it [in this episode] reminds us again of the way in which his fiction veers away from the abstract principle and towards the particular case." Wall, *Trollope and Character,* 165. I think that Wall is mistaken here. The fact that Slide acts so badly while believing that he is acting well emphasizes the inadequacy of the "abstract" consequentialist principles which guide his moral reasoning.

3. Anthony Trollope, *Phineas Redux* (New York: Oxford University Press, 1986), I:249–50. Quotations from *Phineas Redux* are cited in the text using the following abbreviation: *Redux.*

4. Several critics remark upon Phineas's susceptibility to this particular sanction. Wall, for example, notices his "hypersensitivity to public opinion and his deep need to be in good standing with the world." Wall, *Trollope and Character,* 170.

5. Cicero, *On Duties,* ed. M.T. Griffin and E.M. Atkins (Cambridge: Cambridge University Press, 1991), 23.

6. I think that Kincaid underrates the support Phineas receives from his friends. "Where are his friends?" Kincaid imagines Phineas asking himself as his "sense of injustice" increases. Kincaid, *The Novels of Anthony Trollope,* 210. But Wall argues that Phineas's friends are exceptionally devoted: "The testimony in court as to Finn's character . . . is deeply consoling because it transcends the reticence normal in Trollope's society." Wall, *Trollope and Character,* 169. According to R.D. McMaster, such testimony would not have been offered at a Victorian murder trial, because "at common law, the character of a defendant was in general irrelevant to his guilt of a

criminal charge." McMaster, *Trollope and the Law,* 63. Perhaps Trollope violated legal procedure in this incident in order to emphasize the loyalty of Phineas's closest friends.

7. R.D. McMaster is certainly correct that in his handling of the Tankerville election "Trollope avoids reducing what may seem to us a clear-cut moral issue to a matter of black and white." Ibid., 100. But this does not imply that Trollope reduces the issue to a uniform shade of gray: the moral principles involved are clearly distinguished from the customs which are in tension with them.

8. As Juliet McMaster puts it, "the reader who looks for the triumphant vindication after the trial ordeal is left instead with the same kind of distaste and disillusion that he has in reading other tales with bitterly qualified happy endings." McMaster, *Trollope's Palliser Novels,* 77.

9. As Wall aptly observes, "Laura has the humiliation of realizing that promises of restraint and self-sacrifice are one thing to make and another to keep. Unhappiness has made her capable of a cheapness of which she would never formerly have been guilty." Wall, *Trollope and Character,* 157–8. Kincaid notes that the narrator of *Phineas Redux* "develops a distinct impatience for Lady Laura's immersion in her grievances." Kincaid, *The Novels of Anthony Trollope,* 215.

10. James Martineau discusses this character type in similar terms: "A bad man, without conscience, you cannot call a fool for not acting as if he had one. He neglects no element of happiness about which he cares. . . . Compunction he escapes by his insensibility; the sentiments of others are indifferent to him, so long as he holds his place among companions on his own level; and, short of . . . the direct punishments of human law, there is nothing to restrain him, on prudential grounds, from following the bent of his predominant inclinations." *Types of Ethical Theory,* Vol. II:71.

5 Moral Interpretation in *Lady Anna*

1. Thus, though the theory he calls "my station and its duties," is one of the partial positions that Bradley—in Hegelian fashion—ultimately transcends by incorporating it into a more inclusive synthesis, he does not in fact qualify it to any significant degree.

2. Skilton writes that "the logic of certain novels begins from the assumption that some particularly interesting event has occurred or situation arisen." *Mr. Scarborough's Family, The Fixed Period, Dr. Wortle's School,* and *Lady Anna* are all novels of this sort. Skilton, *Anthony Trollope and his Contemporaries,* 98. The events and situations in these novels prove interesting because of the way they test contemporary moral theories.

3. Anthony Trollope, *Lady Anna* (Leipzig: Bernhard Tauchnitz, 1873), I:10. Quotations from *Lady Anna* are cited in the text using the following abbreviation: *Anna.*

4. The *Saturday Review* thought it "cowardly" that Trollope downplayed the class difference between the lovers by failing to write a scene in which Daniel plies his lowly trade. But perhaps Trollope thought that these references to the stink of

a laborer's sweat demonstrate that Daniel suffers under a real social handicap. Quoted in Wall, *Trollope and Character,* 309.

5. Anthony Trollope, *Hunting Sketches* (Hartford, Conn.: Edwin Balentine Mitchell, 1929), 26.

6. J. Hillis Miller, Introduction to Anthony Trollope, *Lady Anna* (New York: Arno Press, 1981), viii. According to Tracy, Anna marries Daniel because she thinks she "can be happier" with him than with the earl. Tracy, *Trollope's Later Novels,* 144. Though he takes a different tack, Pollard also misses the role of Anna's antihedonic choice in the novel's thematic scheme. Unlike Miller, Pollard finds Daniel less attractive than Lord Lovel: "There is more than rank and wealth in Lord Lovel, and there is more also than a handsome manner and appearance." But Pollard sees it as a defect in the novel's art that Anna does *not* marry the more pleasant of her suitors. Because she chooses "a sullen tailor" as her husband, Trollope cannot "sustain and establish a sympathy with Lady Anna," Pollard claims. Pollard sees that Anna is *not* a hedonist, but thinks Trollope should have made her one—so that the hedonistic reader might empathize with her. Pollard, *Anthony Trollope,* 148.

7. Kincaid disagrees, asserting that the lovers go to Australia at the end of the novel because "the old society can hardly be stretched far enough to tolerate the union of an earl's daughter with a tailor." Kincaid, *The Novels of Anthony Trollope,* 162. But Anna and Daniel do not intend to settle in Australia. After the honeymoon, they return to "the old society." I think that J. Hillis Miller is correct that the lovers are finally "reassimilated." Introduction to Anthony Trollope, *Lady Anna.*

8. Wall notes that the authorities who pressure Anna to marry Lord Lovel "go to unscrupulous lengths. . . . A number of those on the establishment rather than the egalitarian side of the question act sufficiently badly to suggest that *Lady Anna* is a work with levelling tendencies." Wall, *Trollope and Character,* 308.

9. Skilton rightly claims that in *Lady Anna* "the basic assumption is disruptive of the social order, and Trollope has carried his idea through to the end." Skilton, *Anthony Trollope and his Contemporaries,* 98. But I would argue that the book does not disrupt the *moral* order. Because Tracy believes that Trollope accepts the moral authority of Victorian mores, he cannot acknowledge that *Lady Anna* is at once socially radical and morally conservative. Tracy writes that "Trollope does not look upon [Daniel] as an interloper who threatens society by an attempt to force himself into a higher position than is his right. Daniel is proud of his own place in society, and unwilling to admit that that place makes him unworthy of marriage with Lady Anna." Tracy, *Trollope's Later Novels,* 148. It is true that Daniel claims to be morally worthy of Anna—but he never denies that a huge social gulf has opened up between them. And Trollope is on Daniel's side because Daniel is indeed a morally scrupulous man—though an "interloper" in purely social terms. *Lady Anna* does not support Tracy's equation of the social and the moral.

10. Miller argues that the community's final acceptance of Anna and Daniel "is based on a general . . . recognition that in fact Anna's obdurate keeping of her word" does "take precedence over the value of keeping the gulf fixed between

ranks." I think that Miller gives the community too much moral credit—and Anna too little. Its assault on her honesty was very determined, its concession as grudging as possible. J. Hillis Miller, Introduction to *Lady Anna*.

11. See Tracy, *Trollope's Later Novels,* 146. L.J. Swingle has a different view of what is at stake in this episode: "The Keswick poet disappoints Daniel, telling him that 'the love of which we poets sing' is not to be found in life itself. . . . Trollope knew that writers of the romantic period are hardly the best counselors for a lover to turn to, if that lover seeks mere endorsement of his dreams." L.J. Swingle, *Romanticism and Anthony Trollope: A Study in the Continuities of Nineteenth-Century Literary Thought* (Ann Arbor: University of Michigan Press, 1990), 63–64.

12. By and large, the critics agree. Edwards, for example, writes that "Trollope's own attitude, almost as a matter of course, is that [Anna's] duty to her lover supersedes her duty to her class." Edwards, *Anthony Trollope,* 129.

13. Of course, critics who argue that Trollope accepts *all* the mores of his society as morally authoritative, are reluctant to admit that his criticism of the Lovels is devastating. Thus Pollard, after acknowledging that Reverend Lovel is the voice of "prejudice" in the novel, adds that "Trollope could not rest easy in seeing such a man defeated, a man who was 'true to his instincts, genuinely English.'" Nor could Trollope, Pollard claims, "be altogether happy that [Anna] had proved untrue to her lineage" by marrying Daniel. Pollard, *Anthony Trollope,* 149. However, there is nothing in *Lady Anna* itself to support these assertions, which rest entirely upon Pollard's belief that *in general* Trollope equates morality and mores.

6 Moral Responsibility in *John Caldigate*

1. Quoted in N. John Hall, *Trollope: A Biography* (Oxford: Clarendon Press, 1991), 456.

2. Several critics note that Mrs. Bolton differs from Trollope's other Evangelicals. Pollard writes that Mrs. Bolton is "one of the most impressive characters Trollope ever created. . . . She belongs to a different order of creation from the rest [of his Evangelicals]." Pollard, *Anthony Trollope,* 159. Ruth apRoberts argues that "Trollope exacts some sympathy for pietistic Mrs. Bolton." ApRoberts, *The Moral Trollope* (Athens, Ohio: Ohio University Press, 1971), 117.

3. Jerome Schneewind, *Backgrounds of English Victorian Literature* (New York: Random House, 1970), 133

4. See John R. Reed, *Victorian Will* (Athens, Ohio: Ohio University Press, 1989), 40.

5. Bernard Semmel, *John Stuart Mill and the Pursuit of Virtue* (New Haven and London: Yale University Press, 1984), 23.

6. Ibid., 195.

7. Richard Norman, *The Moral Philosophers: An Introduction to Ethics* (Oxford: Clarendon Press, 1983), 147.

8. Anthony Trollope, *John Caldigate* (London: Zodiac Press, 1972), 21. Quotations from *John Caldigate* are cited in the text using the following abbreviation: *Caldigate*.

9. Edwards and Tracy both sense a disjunction between John's self-presentation upon his return to England and the facts about his conduct in Australia that are later revealed. They attribute this to a failure of art: Edwards claims that "the belated disclosure of Caldigate's affair with Mrs. Smith" is "hard to reconcile with the conception that we have previously formed of his character," while Tracy asserts that the novel is "perfunctory in . . . motivation." Edwards, *Anthony Trollope,* 219; Tracy, *Trollope's Later Novels,* 233. But the distortion is in John's self-image, not in Trollope's view of him, as the narrator's sour remarks about his self-deception demonstrate.

10. What, exactly, is John's "fault"? Edwards remarks that the novel endorses "Caldigate's own view that the most serious of his offenses was fornication." Finding this a "ridiculous" position, Edwards concludes that Trollope's "aversion to the Puritanical Boltons," who are John's antagonists, makes him reluctant to judge John as harshly as he should: "Even the fact that Caldigate had lied about . . . Mrs. Smith . . . is not held against him." Edwards, *Anthony Trollope,* 219. As several critics have noted, John's conduct in Australia was by no means unforgivable—if the differences between Australian and English sexual mores are taken into account. But if John had told the truth about his colonial activities, he would have had no chance of marrying Hester. He obtains her father's consent under false pretenses. His lies *are* the problem. Trollope may have felt that this point was so obvious that he did not need to stress it.

11. Semmel, *John Stuart Mill and the Pursuit of Virtue,* 139–40.

12. Tracy argues that Trollope is unfair to Mrs. Bolton. "Trollope does not distinguish between her valid objections to Caldigate and his conduct and her hysterical fanaticism," he writes. "Her justified doubts about Caldigate are never really given a hearing." Tracy, *Trollope's Later Novels,* 239, 242. But if Tracy thinks that Mrs. Bolton's doubts about Caldigate are partly justified, where could he have gotten that idea except from the way the issue is treated in the novel?

13. N. John Hall, *Trollope: A Biography,* 457.

14. According to Kincaid, Bagwax is a character of "Dickensian origins . . . 'all heart.'" Kincaid adds that Bagwax "is perhaps Trollope's one traditional hero: simple, noble, and with true romantic energy." Kincaid, *The Novels of Anthony Trollope,* 246. I agree that Bagwax is a moral hero, but he struggles against temptation to become one. His goodness is not the natural warmth that distinguishes Pickwick and Tom Pinch. Does a character of this sort appear in any of Trollope's novels? I think not.

7 *Cousin Henry* and the Role of Expediency in Moral Reasoning

1. N. John Hall, *Trollope: A Biography,* 456.

2. See Ruth apRoberts, "*Cousin Henry*: Trollope's Note from Antiquity," *Nineteenth- Century Fiction* 24 (1969):93–98.

3. Cicero, *On Duties,* 113.

4. Ibid., 120.

5. Cicero, *On Duties,* 118, 120. ApRoberts discusses these cases in "Trollope's Note from Antiquity," 94–95. In Book III of *On Duties,* Cicero also poses the case of a man who is able "as if with some magic potion, to displace true heirs and to usurp their position." Cicero, *On Duties,* 128. Among Cicero's cases, this one resembles Henry's most closely in terms of its facts, as apRoberts remarks. "Trollope's Note from Antiquity," 95. But because Cicero's magician takes active steps to displace the true heirs, his conduct raises different moral issues from Henry's. Like the merchant and auctioneer who conceal pertinent information, Henry merely withholds what he knows.

6. Cicero, *On Duties,* 119.

7. Ibid., 120.

8. Ibid., 121.

9. Anthony Trollope, *Cousin Henry* (New York: Oxford University Press, 1988), 8. Quotations from *Cousin Henry* are cited in the text using the following abbreviation: *Henry.*

10. These are Henry's moral antecedents, as the people of Carmarthenshire understand. Polhemus's assertion that "the animosity which everyone feels for [Henry], and his own guilt-ridden anxieties, are the absolute donnees of the book for which we can see no explicit cause" seems therefore to be mistaken. Polhemus, *The Changing World of Anthony Trollope,* 232.

11. Several critics remark that Indefer's vacillations resemble Henry's. Tracy argues that his "struggle between conscience and inclination is a parallel to Henry's subsequent dilemma," Tracy, *Trollope's Later Novels,* 257, while Edwards asserts that "*Cousin Henry* deals with . . . a landed proprietor's vacillation between affection and duty." Edwards, *Anthony Trollope,* 197. But Isabel and William are so self-assured in manner that critics fail to notice that they too vacillate. Tracy, for example, claims that Henry "is timid, Isabel imperious, he is vacillating, she decisive." Tracy, *Trollope's Later Novels,* 255.

12. Anthony Trollope, *The Duke's Children* (London, Oxford, and New York: Oxford University Press, 1973), II:398.

13. The critics also disagree on this point. Tracy argues that Indefer "sacrificed duty to affection" in willing the estate to Isabel, and that he did so through "weakness." Tracy, *Trollope's Later Novels,* 258. But Lansbury argues that it was Indefer's duty to leave the estate to Isabel: When Indefer "made over Llanfeare to Henry Jones . . . he was disregarding his duty to those who considered they had a contract with him that guaranteed them a good landlord." Lansbury, *The Reasonable Man,* 149.

14. Citing Apjohn's remarks, Richard Burke maintains that "primogeniture was clearly an article of faith for Trollope." But Burke also argues that Trollope acknowledges a "need to be flexible" about this "abstract principle." I would say that a custom about which one ought to be flexible is *not* an "article of faith" in the same

sense that an exceptionless moral principle is. Richard Burke, "Accommodation and Transcendence: Last Wills in Trollope's Novels," *Dickens Studies Annual,* 15 (1986):299.

15. A number of critics remark upon the gender inversions in *Cousin Henry.* Polhemus argues that the "feminization" of Henry reveals "the latent fear of Victorian men that they were losing their freedom of ethical choice in a constricting moral matriarchate." See Polhemus, "Trollope's Note from Underground," *Nineteenth-Century Fiction,* XX (March 1966):385–9. But it's hard to find warrant for such fear in *Cousin Henry,* where Isabel, though a powerful personality, remains socially powerless until Mr. Apjohn restores her rights. Lansbury writes that "the analogue for Henry, the weak, womanish craven, is the young gentleman, courageous, resourceful, popular, and sympathetic, who . . . happens to be a young woman, Isabel Brodrick." Lansbury, *The Reasonable Man,* 144. Lansbury seems uncertain about what the point of this gender inversion might be.

16. Another social conservative in Trollope's novels of the 1870s ultimately decides to disinherit the natural male heir. Roger Carbury, in *The Way We Live Now,* hates to disregard primogeniture, but there seems little doubt that he is right to do so. The natural heir, Sir Felix Carbury, is a moral monster by whose side Cousin Henry looks like Mother Teresa.

17. Cicero, *On Duties,* 27.

18. Ibid., 26.

19. Wall remarks that Isabel "almost likes being a martyr to principle." Wall, *Trollope and Character,* 285. I find this something of an understatement.

20. Wall argues that Isabel "accepts her uncle's social prejudice against Owen." Ibid., 285. But if Indefer's objection to Owen is based only on prejudice—and I agree that it is—then it seems odd that the principled Isabel should defer to it. This anomaly is resolved if we understand Isabel's penchant for whatever opposes her own interest.

21. Lansbury argues that Isabel rejects William at this point because she will not "endure a marriage of poverty"—for "her children would be the real victims of such a marriage." Lansbury, *The Reasonable Man,* 146. But with William's secure income of £250, dire poverty does not threaten the couple. Isabel never mentions (or thinks about) the sufferings of her prospective children. To prove Isabel an exemplary heroine, Lansbury distorts the facts that reveal her moral perversity.

22. Polhemus, *The Changing World of Anthony Trollope,* 233. For a sensible critique of Polhemus's reading, see Pollard, *Anthony Trollope,* 161–2.

8 *Dr. Wortle's School* and the Consistency of Common Morality

1. Anthony Trollope, *Dr. Wortle's School* (London: Oxford University Press, 1973), 42. Quotations from *Dr. Wortle's School* are cited in the text using the following abbreviation: *Wortle.*

2. In one of his essays, Trollope denies that the injunction to keep the sabbath day holy makes sense in modern Europe and concludes that it "is no Commandment for us." From this we can infer that he was not unwilling to question the moral authority of the commandments. "The Fourth Commandment," *The Fortnightly Review,* XVII (15 January, 1866):538.

3. Sadleir remarks upon Wortle's "bewilderment," as he considers the Peacockes' dilemma. Sadleir, *Trollope: A Commentary* (London: Oxford University Press, 1961), 396.

4. Anthony Trollope, *The West Indies and the Spanish Main,* 2nd edition (London: Chapman & Hall, 1860), 63.

5. Anthony Trollope, *An Eye for an Eye* (New York and London: Garland Publishing, 1979), II:102, emphasis added.

6. Tracy believes that Trollope's *primary* purpose in *Dr. Wortle's School* is to show that human interdependence makes it impossible to follow an idiosyncratic moral code: "Society and its laws must be placated." Tracy, *Trollope's Later Novels,* 262. Peacocke does underestimate the negative consequences of defying society—but the novel considers many other moral issues as well.

7. Where does Trollope stand? According to Cockshut, he sides with the community: "Only once . . . does Trollope ask himself how the Peacockes should have behaved, and then he answers the question unequivocally." They should have parted. "Trollope would not have thought it worth while to discuss at length a question which was capable of a certain and obvious answer." Cockshut, *Anthony Trollope: A Critical Study,* 220. Though he argues that "the question of justification is not finally answered," Tracy agrees with Cockshut that the community's view is superior to Wortle's: Wortle decides "for a subjective moral code. . . . Objective morality and objective truth are left to [the community]." Tracy, *Trollope's Later Novels,* 265, 269.

8. And so several critics argue that the novel endorses the Peacockes' decision to remain together. They cite Trollope's sympathy for the Peacockes as proof that he is a "moral relativist" or "situation ethicist" who believes that general moral principles must bend to the circumstances of the particular case. Sir Hugh Walpole is the first critic to suggest that in *Dr. Wortle's School* Trollope adopts "the modern view of greater consideration for the individual case." Quoted in Cockshut, *Anthony Trollope: A Critical Study,* 220. For other formulations of this idea, see Polhemus, *The Changing World of Anthony Trollope,* 238; Pollard, *Anthony Trollope,* 163; and Wall, *Trollope and Character,* 339. I think that *Dr. Wortle's School* examines a case in which the application of principles is conceptually difficult, rather than one which offers a simple choice between cruelly applying principles and charitably bending them (as these critics imply).

9. Letwin suggests that *Dr. Wortle's School* takes interpretation as its central subject. The novel, she argues, asks whether there can be legitimate disagreement about how to interpret rules. What is at issue "is how moral rules are to be understood." Are they "commands, ordering what ought to be done," or are they merely "a shorthand" guide to practice, which permits "a sensitive moral judgment"

to revise "the simple conclusions drawn from ordinary interpretations of rules?" Letwin, *The Gentleman in Trollope,* 228. I agree that the novel problematizes interpretation, but I believe the interpretive dispute it focuses upon is more highly structured than Letwin allows. It is not a question of applying the rules as simple "commands" versus interpreting them with sensitivity to the situation, but one of deciding *how* the facts of the situation relate to a complex set of rules. And this is a task in which perfect agreement cannot be achieved.

10. Several critics agree that the novel does not settle the moral issue it raises. Wall argues that although the book is resolved at the level of plot, "any reader requiring an equally positive resolution of the ethical problems raised by the narrative is likely to be disappointed." Wall, *Trollope and Character,* 338. See also Pollard, *Anthony Trollope,* 163.

9 Reason and Reform in *The Fixed Period* and *The American Senator*

1. Tracy rightly suggests that the novel focuses on the problems of "abstract reformers." Tracy, *Trollope's Later Novels,* 287. Other critics have argued that Trollope intended death to be the novel's subject, but failed to realize his intentions. Cockshut remarks that, "as a study of death [*The Fixed Period*] is very puzzling," because it does not reveal "a coherent attitude to death." Cockshut, *Anthony Trollope,* 91. Pollard argues that Trollope "sacrificed the possibilities that lay in [the first prospective victim] Crasweller's contemplation of his own death." Pollard, *Anthony Trollope,* 166. But if one does not assume that the novel is intended to be about death, these "flaws" disappear.

2. Quoted in William Whewell, *Lectures on the History of Moral Philosophy,* 39.

3. Trollope's implicit judgment of Neverbend's scheme has been the subject of critical dispute. Tracy, apRoberts, and Kincaid all argue that the novel judges the scheme favorably. Tracy argues that "the principle is theoretically correct." Tracy, *Trollope's Later Novels,* 294. ApRoberts thinks that Neverbend's idea is a "fine piece of social engineering." ApRoberts, *The Moral Trollope,* 46. Kincaid argues that euthanasia comes to seem less horrifying as Neverbend wins the reader's sympathy. Kincaid, *The Novels of Anthony Trollope,* 259–60. In response to apRoberts and Kincaid, Letwin remarks that the novel "has been acclaimed as an admirable proposal for euthanasia and also as a literary experiment, which ingeniously leads us into ridiculing the narrator, only to find that we have failed to see the moral of the story—that death is too important a matter to be left to God. But anyone who believes that can believe that Dean Swift dined on Irish babies." Letwin, *The Gentleman in Trollope,* 179. Obviously I'm on Letwin's side here.

4. Anthony Trollope, *The Fixed Period* (Ann Arbor: University of Michigan Press, 1990), 45. Quotations from *The Fixed Period* are cited in the text using the following abbreviation: *Fixed.*

5. Pollard proposes yet another unconvincing definition of the moral issue raised by euthanasia. "It is easy," he writes, "for Neverbend to argue that wars, armies, and capital punishment are all usages of death by organized society . . . what he ignores is the degree of necessity that must be evident before any argument for death . . . can be accepted." Pollard, *Anthony Trollope,* 166. According to Pollard's analysis, then, its order to kill a baby would be obeyed, if Parliament could prove that the baby's death was really important. But Crosstrees says that the order would be disobeyed even if the death could save Great Britain from destruction.

6. William Whewell, *Lectures on the History of Moral Philosophy,* 226–7.

7. Kincaid points out that Neverbend not only "anticipate[s] all the arguments against the system but actually holds these contrary views himself." Kincaid, *Anthony Trollope,* 249. Of course he does: the "contrary views" derive from common morality, which has formed Neverbend as a moral being. Kincaid thinks that Neverbend's residual allegiance to ordinary morality humanizes him. Up to a point it does, but his inconsistency also undermines his authority as a reformer.

8. William Whewell, *Lectures on the History of Moral Philosophy,* 197.

9. Ibid., 206.

10. Tracy also sees the issue in these terms: Neverbend's reform fails because he makes insufficient allowance for "the irrationality of human behavior." Tracy, *Trollope's Later Novels,* 289. But *The Fixed Period* never endorses Neverbend's claim that his plan is rational; instead, it vigorously undermines the concept of reason.

11. Michael Walzer, *Interpretation and Social Criticism,* 64.

12. Several critics accuse Trollope of evading the moral issues he has raised by bringing the British in to settle them. Tracy writes that "Trollope presents no final solution to the moral question. He simply sets it aside. The John Bright appears." Tracy, *Trollope's Later Novels,* 288. Harvey asserts that "Trollope evades the issue by bringing in the British navy as a *deus ex machina.*" Harvey, *The Art of Anthony Trollope,* 33. But the navy is *not* a *deus ex machina,* for it was summoned by the Britannulan people themselves. Its actions represent their wishes and hence are related to the moral issues raised by the novel. Further, as Walzer remarks, ambitious attempts at reform often lead to violent repression—which can be undertaken by either the progressive or the conservative side. The novel's resolution is thus implied by the logic of the situation.

13. G.E.M. Anscombe, *The Collected Philosophical Papers of G.E.M. Anscombe, III: Ethics, Religion, and Politics* (Minneapolis, Minnesota: University of Minnesota Press, 1981), 34.

14. Letwin makes a similar point: "Embedded in the humorous sketch is a brutal picture of how dreams of bringing heaven to earth can reduce real men and women to dust." Letwin, *The Gentleman in Trollope,* 183.

15. Some critics accept Gotobed's claim to speak from the perspective of reason. Kincaid argues that the Senator "defines the irrational from the elevated position of Pure Reason." Kincaid, *The Novels of Anthony Trollope,* 236. For apRoberts, as for Gotobed himself, America *is* a more sensible society than England: "America is the

child of the Age of Reason . . . and has in fact been able to establish things on a basis more rational than the old." To embrace its folkways, then, is to embrace reason itself. ApRoberts, *The Moral Trollope,* 177. But *would* Trollope say that America's uniform institutions are more rational than Britain's hodgepodge of traditional arrangements? Tracy points out that Gotobed "comes from the corrupt Washington of Grant's second term," where an "orgy of bribery and theft" suggests that American "reason" has not yet solved the problems of political life. Tracy, *Trollope's Later Novels,* 227.

16. Anthony Trollope, *The American Senator* (New York: Dover Publications, 1979), 71. Quotations from *The American Senator* are cited in the text using the following abbreviation: *Senator.*

17. According to Jackson Trotter, *The American Senator* weighs the "pleasures and pains" of hunting against one another. Trotter is right, I think, that when customs are not obviously immoral, Trollope is willing to discuss their desirability in expediential terms—and that he finds foxhunting a desirable custom by this measure. Jackson Trotter, "Foxhunting and the English Social Order in Trollope's *The American Senator,*" *Studies in the Novel,* XXIV:3 (Fall 1992):236.

18. That the Senator compares one set of mores with another may explain the much-discussed indeterminacy of the novel. Critics have noted that some of Gotobed's criticisms of England seem sensible, while others do not. John Hagan accuses the book of being a "mere confusion" in this regard. John Hagan, "The Divided Mind of Anthony Trollope," *Nineteenth-Century Fiction* 14 (1959):18. ApRoberts writes that "the device [of the foreign observer] enables [Trollope] to impose a large, relativistic view" on the novel. ApRoberts, *The Moral Trollope,* 188. The novel is indeed relativist in one sense: no common standard can be appealed to in comparing the customs of two nations, unless they violate common morality (which will not often be the case).

19. Kincaid notes that "there are victims [of English customs] even more serious than Goarly. Arabella Trefoil and her mother, Lady Augustus, are badly battered." Kincaid, *The Novels of Anthony Trollope,* 238. Other critics who see Arabella as the victim of an immoral society include Pollard, *Anthony Trollope,* 41–42 and apRoberts, *The Moral Trollope,* 183–5. But Letwin argues that "women who desperately pursue marriage as the only way to survive are portrayed . . . as mean-minded, ruthless exploiters. . . . Arabella . . . is treated with contempt," for only a "twisted view of the world" prevents her "from seeing any alternative to marrying." Letwin, *The Gentleman in Trollope,* 165. But what alternative *is* there for such a woman?

20. Several critics have noted that *The American Senator* offers an unusually thorough description of rural Britain, circa 1875. For example, Michael Sadleir writes that the novel places "before the reader . . . the whole geographical and social pattern of an English county." Michael Sadleir, *Trollope: A Commentary,* 397.

21. N. John Hall, ed., *The Letters of Anthony Trollope* (Stanford, Calif.: Stanford University Press, 1983), 731.

22. Ibid., 730.

23. Several critics have tried to resolve the apparent schism between the novel's subplots in a similar manner. See, for example, Kincaid, *The Novels of Anthony Trollope,* 236–9, and apRoberts, *The Moral Trollope,* 178–85.

24. Anthony Trollope, *He Knew He Was Right* (New York: Dover Publications, 1983), 2:33.

10 Morality without Rules in *Mr. Scarborough's Family*

1. Anthony Trollope, *Mr. Scarborough's Family* (London: Oxford University Press, 1973), 2. Quotations from *Mr. Scarborough's Family* are cited in the text using the following abbreviation: *Scarborough.*

2. The only explanation Scarborough gives for his hatred of entail is that it limits the freedom of the property owner. The novel offers no direct support for Edwards's hypothesis that Scarborough dislikes entail and primogeniture because "they take no account of either the moral deserts or the practical competence of possible heirs." Edwards, *Anthony Trollope,* 201. In fact, Scarborough's views are internally inconsistent: if private property is an unjust institution, why ought property owners be allowed to dispose of their assets as they please?

3. Maurice, *The Conscience,* 115.

4. Ibid., 89.

5. Ibid., 165.

6. Kincaid argues that the novel supports Scarborough on this point: because his society "has passed by such trifles as morality," Scarborough must "search for a new and adequate set of principles." Kincaid, *The Novels of Anthony Trollope,* 251. But Kincaid offers no evidence to bolster his assertion. "Pace . . . some modern critics," Wall rightly remarks, "society's standards" are not shown to be in "serious decline" in this novel. Wall, *Trollope and Character,* 332.

7. Many critics have noted that good nature is the central concept in Scarborough's invented morality. See, for example, McMaster, *Trollope and the Law,* 138–40; Overton, *The Unofficial Trollope,* 186; Edwards, *Anthony Trollope,* 203–6; Letwin, *The Gentleman in Trollope,* 93; and Roger Slakey, "Trollope's Case for Moral Imperative," *Nineteenth-Century Fiction* 28 (1973):312.

8. As Pollard puts it, Scarborough believes that a "sense of justice based on personal relationships transcends the law." Pollard, *Anthony Trollope,* 171.

9. But something peculiar is going on here. Scarborough becomes a beneficent property owner because he realizes that he has not earned his wealth and therefore feels guilty about using it selfishly. In a way, then, his example supports the time-honored English belief that possessing "a stake in the country" promotes responsible behavior in the landowning class.

10. This point seems to have escaped the notice of several critics, who see Scarborough's transgressive conduct in exclusively legal terms. Thus Wall writes that Scarborough "succeeds in saving the estate . . . by means that are in flagrant

breach of legal propriety." Wall, *Trollope and Character,* 326. McMaster calls Scarborough "a defier of law with a sense of justice." McMaster, *Trollope and the Law,* 140.

11. Whether the likeability of its hero proves *Mr. Scarborough's Family* to be a morally relativist work has been much discussed. Taking the affirmative side are apRoberts, *The Moral Trollope,* 155–7; Polhemus, *The Changing World of Anthony Trollope,* 241; Kincaid, *The Novels of Anthony Trollope,* 254; and Overton, *The Unofficial Trollope,* 177–93. Slakey takes the negative side in "Trollope's Case for Moral Imperative." Though Letwin does not generally see Trollope as a moral relativist, she argues that in this book good intentions take precedence over moral rules: "The story . . . shows how a gentleman may disregard formalities." I find Letwin's reading perverse. It contains several false assertions, such as the claim that Augustus Scarborough (who defames Harry Annesley) is "virtuous" by "conventional standards." Letwin, *The Gentleman in Trollope,* 91–92.

12. It is interesting that virtually every critic who has written about *Mr. Scarborough's Family* quotes this striking (and extremely ambiguous!) remark.

13. N. John Hall, ed., *The Letters of Anthony Trollope,* 871, 878, 903, 932.

14. It seems to me that critics who compare Prosper unfavorably to Scarborough miss this point. ApRoberts writes that Prosper's "unconscious selfishness is in some respects more reprehensible than Scarborough's fraud." ApRoberts, *The Moral Trollope,* 157. Letwin argues that "here as elsewhere, what matters for how moral quality is judged is the motive." Letwin, *The Gentleman in Trollope,* 93. Yes, Scarborough's motives are better than Prosper's—and yes, motive is important in judging the moral quality of an agent. But Scarborough's *conduct* is far worse than Prosper's.

15. As Herbert puts it, "the subplots of *Mr. Scarborough's Family* are . . . as comical as the main plot is the reverse." Herbert offers an interesting analysis of the "'daring' experimental devices" through which the main plot transposes "comedy into tragic realism." Herbert, *Trollope and Comic Pleasure,* 122–9 (the quotations are from 124 and 126).

16. Cicero, *On Duties,* 75.

17. Edwards remarks that the novel's "strongest message is the precariousness of natural human affections." Edwards, *Anthony Trollope,* 208.

18. Several critics judge Dolly by the very moral standards that she intelligently calls into question. Thus Overton argues that without benevolence, Dolly's rectitude is valueless, "virtually emptied of meaning." Overton, *The Unofficial Trollope,* 187.

19. Tracy notes that "in various bedroom scenes, in which Dolly and Mr. Grey come together in their night-clothes for long talks, the atmosphere is that of a marriage," but offers no explanation of what this might signify. Tracy, *Trollope's Later Novels,* 309. Kincaid *does* offer an explanation, which I find unconvincing: "Trollope's most open excursion into twisted sexuality marks an appropriate sym-

bol for a world that so distorts all the values which count." Kincaid, *The Novels of Anthony Trollope,* 256.

Conclusion: Three "Moral Trollopes"

1. *The New York Times,* 30 October, 1991.

2. I think it is no accident that Joseph Fletcher both invented situation ethics *and* argued the case for active euthanasia in *Morals and Medicine* (1954). Nor is it accidental that apRoberts judges Neverbend's scheme for euthanasia of the elderly to be "a fine piece of social engineering" (apRoberts, 46). If one is willing to disregard common morality in the pursuit of some greater good, one may well end up justifying murder—as Trollope was aware.

3. Herbert, *Trollope and Comic Pleasure,* 163.

4. Kincaid, *The Novels of Anthony Trollope,* 13.

5. For a similar discussion of apRoberts's treatment of Cicero, see Kincaid, *The Novels of Anthony Trollope,* 15.

6. Overton is annoyed by the way apRoberts's followers read *Orley Farm*. Such critics, he argues, represent Trollope as "justifying" Lady Mason's crime, despite the fact that he thought forgery "absolutely wrong whatever the circumstances." Overton, *The Unofficial Trollope,* 149. Roger Slakey makes a similar point in "Trollope's Case for Moral Imperative," 307–8.

7. But among these essays, only one took vigorous exception to apRoberts's conflation of Trollopian morality with situation ethics: Roger Slakey argued "Trollope's Case for Moral Imperative."

8. Harvey, for example, argues that "Trollope asserts the need for moral relativism, for the necessity to attend scrupulously to the situation of the individual," as if the term "moral relativism" *meant* "considering the circumstances before making a moral judgment." "Moral relativism" can mean many things, but not *that* surely? Harvey, *The Art of Anthony Trollope,* 9.

9. Overton, *The Unofficial Trollope,* 149.

10. Ibid., 175.

11. Kincaid, *The Novels of Anthony Trollope,* 15–16.

12. Letwin makes fun of critics who venerate Trollope "for his supposed unwillingness to distinguish between right and wrong." Letwin, *The Gentleman in Trollope,* 34.

13. Because she fails to see this, Letwin takes the transgressive John Scarborough to be the moral center of *Mr. Scarborough's Family*. Scarborough's conduct, she argues, respects a "distinction between a merely conventional honesty, which consists in observing established rules, and a more profound honesty." Letwin, *The Gentleman in Trollope,* 94.

14. Like Letwin's, Tracy's briefly sketched "moral Trollope" is very conservative. In Trollope's novels, Tracy claims, "social integration . . . is synonymous with

moral integration. . . . Morality consists in knowing one's proper place in the social order, and in conforming to society's demands." Tracy, *Trollope's Later Novels,* 73.

15. Booth, *Anthony Trollope: Aspects of His Life and Art,* 130.
16. Kincaid, *The Novels of Anthony Trollope,* 27.

Index

A Note about the Author

JANE NARDIN is a Professor of English at the University of Wisconsin-Milwaukee, where she teaches courses in British prose fiction and women's studies. Her publications include books on Jane Austen, Barbara Pym, and Anthony Trollope.